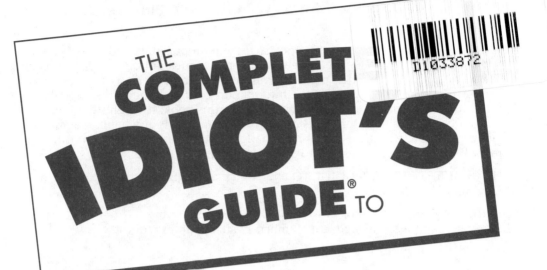

THE COMPLETE IDIOT'S GUIDE® TO

Leadership

Second Edition

by Andrew J. DuBrin

alpha books

Macmillan USA, Inc.
201 West 103rd Street
Indianapolis, IN 46290

A Pearson Education Company

International Standard Book Number: 0-02-863954-5
Library of Congress Catalog Card Number: Available upon request.

02   01   00   8   7   6   5   4   3   2   1

Interpretation of the printing code: The rightmost number of the first series of numbers is the year of the book's printing; the rightmost number of the second series of numbers is the number of the book's printing. For example, a printing code of 00-1 shows that the first printing occurred in 2000.

Printed in the United States of America

This is a *CWL Publishing Enterprises Book,* developed by John A. Woods for Alpha Books. For more information, contact CWL Publishing Enterprises, 3010 Irvington Way, Madison, WI 53713-3414, www.cwlpub.com.

Publisher
Marie Butler-Knight

Product Manager
Phil Kitchel

Managing Editor
Cari Luna

Senior Acquisitions Editor
Renee Wilmeth

Development Editor
Jennifer Williams

Senior Production Editor
Christy Wagner

Copy Editor
Brad Herriman

Illustrator
Jody Schaeffer

Cover Designers
Mike Freeland
Kevin Spear

Book Designers
Scott Cook and Amy Adams of DesignLab

Indexer
Lisa Wilson

Layout/Proofreading
Angela Calvert
Svetlana Dominguez
Nancy Wagner

Contents at a Glance

Contents

Foreword

Leadership—or more accurately, the lack of it—has been receiving a lot of attention recently. Much of that attention comes from the cynics, whose hero, "Cynic-in-Chief" Dilbert, keeps climbing the best-seller lists. As I write, *Dilbert* books occupy two slots on *The New York Times* hard-cover honor roll and one on the paperback.

If you check the data, Dilbert is in good company. Recent studies show that nearly half the population is cynical, less than 10 percent of citizens think members of Congress are honest, and two thirds of front-line employees say they have little trust in top management. This is pretty tough feedback, especially since my colleague, Barry Posner, and I have found, from over 15 years of research, that credibility is the foundation of leadership.

So when I received the manuscript for the first edition of *The Complete Idiot's Guide to Leadership,* I thought it might be some kind of cruel joke. After all, I've written three books on the topic, and I take it seriously. I could just hear the snide comments: "Finally someone has written an honest book about leadership." Or, "Isn't that re-dundant? Aren't leaders already idiots?" A perfect set-up for another *Dilbert* cartoon. That's all we need. More fuel to stoke the flames of cynicism.

But I was wrong. Andrew DuBrin's book is a very serious work about a very serious subject. Dr. DuBrin has given us a down-to-earth treatment of what can be a head-in-the-clouds exercise. He does an absolutely masterful job of surveying the vast leader-ship landscape and then focusing in on the most critical issues a leader faces.

Also, Dr. DuBrin definitely has a way with words. *The Complete Idiot's Guide to Leader-ship, Second Edition,* is a highly readable book, free of the jargon that so often pollutes the pages of business books these days. It's also chock-full of practical tips and assess-ments and rich with suggestions you can put to use immediately. Only a handful of books on any subject ever manage to attain that exalted goal, and the one you're holding in your hands right now certainly does.

One of Dr. DuBrin's most unique contributions is his honest treatment of power. He's not shy about admitting that leadership is a lot about influence. He's even got advice in here on "How to Manipulate Others and Still Like Yourself in the Morning." (My guess is that we'd all secretly like to know that, but we're afraid to admit it.) Mr. DuBrin is not at all shy about extolling the virtues of power and revealing ethical approaches to manipulation.

But don't get him wrong. Mr. DuBrin has not written a version of *Looking Out for Number One*. He's not saying we climb our way to the top over the backs of our col-leagues. In fact, he tells us just the opposite: "Studies have repeatedly demonstrated the commonsense belief that people want leaders they can trust. Similarly, they want leaders who trust them." He also says, "The number-one factor in gaining the trust of your group members is to show consistency between intentions and actions."

Now, I don't agree with Mr. DuBrin on everything—and neither should you—but on this score I most definitely do. Which gets me back to an earlier point: Credibility is the foundation of leadership. Without personal credibility, the bountiful treasure of techniques abundantly available in *The Complete Idiot's Guide to Leadership, Second Edition,* is fool's gold. You really would be an idiot to try them.

So this book comes with a warning: Proceed at your own risk! The kind of leadership espoused by Mr. DuBrin is not for the fainthearted. It requires great courage and discipline. It's only for those who are willing to reach outward to their constituents and inward to themselves.

In the end, leadership development is self-development. The mastery of the art of leadership is really about the mastery of the self. What Mr. DuBrin extends to us is a rich collection of principles and practices, which, when combined with personal credibility, enable leaders to get extraordinary things done.

Jim Kouzes

Chairman of TPG/Learning Systems, a company in The Tom Peters Group, and co-author of the best-selling books *The Leadership Challenge* and *Credibility.*

Introduction

Welcome aboard the leadership train! Leadership in politics, government, sports, and business has always been an exciting topic. During the past 14 years, interest in business leadership has surged. Without effective leadership at all levels in organizations, it is difficult to sustain profitability, productivity, quality, and good customer service. In dozens of ways, leadership does make a difference.

Effective leadership is certainly good for entire organizations and their units (such as departments or divisions). The person providing the leadership can also get some goodies, such as higher status, pay, visibility, and a feeling of being an insider. Being a leader may have its headaches, but it is also glamorous.

If you want good insights and skills into leadership to supplement the many platitudes and evangelical statements that abound, you have come to the right place. My intent in this book is to help readers enhance their leadership effectiveness whether or not they currently occupy a formal leadership position.

A major reason a second edition of this book has been written is that so many readers found the first book directly useful in their leadership work. As one reader told me by e-mail, "I was reading the leadership guide on Thursday night, and I applied some of the ideas Friday morning." For similar reasons, loads of leadership development programs incorporated the first edition of this book.

Now let's take a peek at what's in this book.

Part 1, "Think Like a Leader," gets you started on a systematic study of leadership. It covers such key material as the meaning of leadership, building your self-confidence and emotional intelligence, and the thinking patterns of leaders. You will also learn about acquiring charisma and communicating like a leader.

Part 2, "Act Like a Leader," emphasizes some of the major activities carried out by leaders in order to accomplish objectives. You will learn about influence tactics, including using flattery, acquiring power, and choosing an effective leadership style. In addition, you will find suggestions for becoming a multicultural leader, creating visions, transforming a hurting organization, and creating a learning organization.

Part 3, "You Can Become a Team Leader," focuses on exercising leadership to suit the rapidly growing trend toward accomplishing work in teams. The topics include motivating others on the team with rewards and recognition and managing conflict.

Part 4, "How to Help Groups Lead Themselves," deals heavily with unleashing the power within groups, such as group decision-making. However, there is also focus on the manager taking decisive action to help the group, such as turning around problem people.

Part 5, "Helping Others Develop Their Potential," emphasizes one of the most potentially rewarding aspects of being a leader, such as being a coach and facilitator and encouraging group members.

You are invited to frequently use the glossary. It puts in one place all the key words in the book, along with a few others that are important for leadership.

Special Features

In addition to the regular text, this book contains four extra features designed to help you learn about leadership.

Key Word

Key Word boxes define the technical terms in more depth than they are explained in the regular narrative of the chapter. Understanding the vocabulary of leadership is a great learning device. Knowing the precise meaning of terms can help you avoid the trap of using terms too loosely to really guide people.

Another Perspective

Another Perspective boxes keep you focused on the fact that expert opinion may vary on some leadership topics. Even if I disagree with the perspective being presented, I bring it to your attention for the sake of intellectual honesty.

Advisor

Advisor boxes give you additional suggestions that supplement information in the text. Sometimes the Advisor boxes will take the form of an inside tip about using a given tactic.

Watch Out!

Watch Out! boxes give you suggestions about how to avoid traps in using a particular leadership technique or when not to use the technique.

Acknowledgments

My primary thanks on this project goes to John Woods of CWL Publishing Enterprises, who invited me to write this book and worked with me during its development. John, along with the Alpha Books team, made many useful editorial suggestions with respect to the content and organization of the book.

Another group must be acknowledged. A financial advisor could not write a book about personal finance and ignore the work of hundreds of previous writers on the topic. Similarly many of the ideas in this book are based on the work of other leadership authors and researchers. Thanks also to the effective and ineffective leaders I have known. Many of the insights I have gained through knowing them have worked their way into this book.

Trademarks

All terms mentioned in this book that are known to be or are suspected of being trademarks or service marks have been appropriately capitalized. Alpha Books and Macmillan USA, Inc., cannot attest to the accuracy of this information. Use of a term in this book should not be regarded as affecting the validity of any trademark or service mark.

Part 1
Think Like a Leader

Gary, the vice president of operations, was walking in the company parking lot when he encountered Rachel, an industrial engineer who was one of the newly appointed production supervisors. The vice president and the supervisor then walked together toward the same building. While they were walking, the supervisor said, "Hmmm, we must have morale problems. Look at all the litter and soft-drink cans in the parking lot."

The vice president responded, "Rachel, you've confirmed my good judgment in promoting you to a leadership position."

"Thanks, Gary, but why?" asked Rachel.

"Because you think big," said Gary. "You search for the implications of ordinary events. Another person would have looked at the litter and simply concluded that the maintenance people were not doing their job. Instead, you looked at the possible message indicated by the litter."

Popular wisdom is that to be a leader, the starting point is to look like a leader: Have good posture, be well groomed, wear clothing similar to that worn by leaders in a particular field, and smile frequently. However, you are much more likely to become a leader, or further develop as a leader, if you think like one. In the six chapters in this part, you will learn dozens of ideas to help you develop the thinking patterns of a leader, including making effective use of emotional intelligence.

Chapter 1

What Is Leadership?

> ## In This Chapter
>
> ➤ The meaning of leadership
>
> ➤ The difference between leadership and management
>
> ➤ Effective leaders versus effective managers
>
> ➤ Leadership as a relationship and a partnership
>
> ➤ To lead is to inspire, persuade, influence, motivate, and create positive change
>
> ➤ Leading changes and transformations

Imagine it's the end of your professional career and you're about to retire. You've been lucky enough to work for a company long enough to collect at least a small pension and participate in a retirement party. Which of the following toasts do you want the emcee to propose?

A. "_____ was a wonderful worker here and in the other six companies he (or she) worked for. Nobody heard a peep out of _____, yet we all admired _____ for being a quiet, behind-the-scenes worker bee."

B. "What an inspiring leader _____ was during six years of employment with us. _____ was also an inspiring leader at other phases in his (or her) career. Long before _____ received the first of two promotions, we knew that _____ had the right stuff to be a leader."

To those of you who responded B, keep reading. This book will get you started on the road to leadership, or if you're already somewhere along the way, you'll improve your present leadership capabilities.

The first step in developing your leadership ability is understanding the nature of leadership. It is difficult to do justice to the complexity of leadership with a one-sentence definition. This chapter will explain what leadership is and how it differs from management. You will also learn about the most important leadership activities—inspiring, persuading, influencing, and motivating.

What Leadership Really Means

Leadership, like love, can be explained in many different ways. Here are several definitions to get you thinking like a leader:

➤ Leadership is interpersonal influence directed toward attaining goals and is achieved through communication. By communication we refer simply to sending and receiving messages. According to this definition, a leader might stop by a person's cubicle and give her a word of encouragement about increasing her number of visits to influential dealers. Communication is such an important part of leadership that it will be mentioned in various places in this book. See especially Chapter 5, "Communicate Like a Leader."

➤ Leadership is a way of influencing people beyond routine compliance with directions and orders. A leader, for example, might influence workers to want to work beyond 40 hours per week so they can share in the glory of the success of the department.

➤ Leadership is an act that causes others to act or respond in a shared direction and bring about positive changes. A leader, for example, might excite the group about trying to move in the same direction of converting the organization to a true Net company.

➤ Leadership is the key dynamic force that motivates and coordinates an organization to accomplish its objectives. Without being inspired by a leader, a total organization or a department might drift along with no careful focus on a key objective such as trying to improve worker safety.

➤ Leadership is the ability to inspire confidence and support among the people who are needed to

Another Perspective

Some skeptics say that leadership is unimportant, and that forces in the environment are responsible for the results achieved by individuals and organizations. Following this point of view, a company like Cisco Systems would have achieved greatness if it had been run by anybody. If you believe this, don't worry about management when investing in a company. There is no need to study leadership.

attain organizational goals. This is another way of stating the obvious—that the leader's job is to capture the cooperation of people who do the actual work in the organization.

Key Word

If people do not do anything differently from what they would have done without your presence, you have not exerted **leadership.**

A leader who can inspire, persuade, influence, and motivate can spearhead useful changes. Bringing about change is a critical leadership goal because most improvement requires a departure from the status quo. A leader creates a vision for others and then directs them toward achieving that vision. To be a leader, you must have followers who have confidence in you and who give you their support and commitment to a goal. This is what *leadership* really means.

So What's So Good About Being a Leader?

If being a leader didn't have loads of potential benefits, not so many people would want to become leaders. A key advantage of being a leader is that it gives you a feeling of power and prestige. The prestige comes from the fact that so many people admire leaders. Leaders are often in a wonderful position to help others, thereby finding their jobs satisfying. Part of helping others is making a contribution to society. A woman who started a soccer league for poor city children claims that many of these children have avoided wrongdoing as her leagues have spread to 40 cities. Imagine how good this woman feels.

Leadership positions pay well, with top corporate leaders earning about 170 times as much as entry-level workers, and also receive stock options that can create enormous personal wealth. Being placed in a leadership position is also valuable because it is a good vantage point for further promotions. Leaders also enjoy the feeling of being in on things. As a leader, you are often privy to information excluded from others. Consider, also, that leaders have the satisfaction of controlling money in the form of budgets.

The Difference Between Leaders and Managers

To understand leadership, you must understand the difference between leadership and management. Management includes planning, organizing, leading, and controlling. Although leadership is part of a manager's job, a manager must spend time on the planning, organizing, and controlling functions. Leadership strives to accomplish change, whereas management focuses on maintaining equilibrium. An effective leader inspires people to work hard to improve profits; an effective manager makes sure people are adequately paid for their effort. Here are some differences between leadership and management:

➤ Management is more formal and scientific than leadership. It relies on foundation skills such as planning, controlling, and making effective use of information technology.

➤ Management uses an explicit set of tools and techniques, based on reasoning and testing, that can apply to a variety of situations. Leadership has fewer explicit tools.

➤ Leadership requires eliciting teamwork and cooperation from a vast network of people and motivating a large number of people in that network.

➤ A leader frequently displays enthusiasm, passion, and inspiration to get others to attain high levels of performance. Managing involves less outward emotion and a more conservative demeanor to achieve goals once they are defined.

➤ A leader makes frequent use of his or her imagination and creative problem-solving techniques to bring about change. A manager tends to make frequent use of standard, well-established solutions to problems.

➤ The key contribution of the *leader* is creating a *vision* for the organization. The leader specifies a far-reaching goal as well as a strategy for reaching that goal. The key contribution of the *manager* is implementing the vision.

➤ In addition to creating visions and inspiring people, leaders engage in other productive activities, including working with customers. John Chambers, the CEO of Cisco Systems, spends about 30 hours per week listening to and interacting with customers.

Key Word

A **vision** is an idealized scenario of the future of an organization—a goal that entices people to work toward a rosy future. A **leader** creates the vision and a strategy to reach the vision; a **manager** uses a set of skills to work toward achieving the vision.

Watch Out!

Although it's important to appreciate the differences between leadership and management, don't go overboard. Taking the differences to the extreme, the leader becomes an inspirational figure up in the clouds and the manager becomes a plodding bureaucrat mired in the status quo.

Much of the rest of this book is about what leaders do. Do not be disappointed or surprised that many of the ideas also apply to managers. Despite the differences between leaders and managers noted here, their jobs overlap.

Avoid the trendy thinking that leadership is so important it turns management into an insignificant activity. Although people need to be inspired, persuaded, influenced, and motivated, they still need to be well managed. Leadership is an integral part of management but not a substitute for it. The world vitally needs both good leaders and good managers. Many exceptional leaders are also exceptional managers, such as Louis Gerstner, who spearheaded the resurgence of IBM and repositioned the company in a positive direction. Gerstner has found the right blend of leadership and management to achieve greatness.

Advisor

If you are committed to becoming a leader or improving your leadership stature, make every day count. Today, leadership could mean contributing a sparkling idea at a meeting. Tomorrow, it could mean giving a warm smile and a handshake to the new entry-level worker assigned to your team. Two days from now, your act of leadership might be to show a co-worker how she can improve her productivity without putting in more hours on the job. Leadership involves little acts of daily accomplishments as well as achieving breakthroughs.

A Leader Is a Manager

A disturbing implication of some of the current writing on leadership is that being a leader is *good* whereas being a manager is *bad*. I want you to appreciate the wonders of leadership, but I do not want to denigrate the importance of management. Remember that a leader is also a manager. Following a framework that has stood the test of time, a manager plans, organizes, controls, and *leads*. Especially in a business environment, a leader is also supposed to carry out the other functions of management.

An Example of a Leader and Manager

Take a look at a person who was, until his recent retirement, one of the business world's best leaders *and* managers, Larry Bossidy, CEO of Allied Signal (before its merger with a giant chemical company). Although not a household name, the company is a giant auto parts and aerospace conglomerate. Before being recruited into Allied Signal, Bossidy honed his leadership and management skills at General Electric, working as the number-two executive behind the legendary Jack Welch.

Bossidy inspired his managers with his charismatic presence and his insistence on growth. Growing a business is a definitive act of leadership. As a leader, he was brutally demanding and readily fired managers who could not meet his targets for growth or return on invested capital. Bossidy was at his best simplifying complex issues for people and giving them clear targets. For example, here are three of his strategies for growth:

1. **Cut the fat.** This is the first step in boosting productivity; only the lean grow profitably.
2. **Set killer goals.** Targets that make people stretch to reach them motivate people better than reasonable ones.
3. **Claw your way to victory.** Allow no excuses. Push managers relentlessly to meet your growth goals.

As a leader, Bossidy inspired people with his formidable presence and his extraordinary goals. As a manager, he carefully developed plans and, wherever feasible, pruned costs. The way he handled acquisitions illustrates his managerial aplomb. Bossidy avoided giant takeovers. Instead, he opted for small, readily digestible acquisitions that fit a niche in his product line, such as adding a windshield-wiper blade manufacturer to Allied Signal's auto parts group. This acclaimed leader successfully combined high-level leadership and management skills.

An Example of a Leader Who Is Not a Manager

When a leader neglects being a good manager, the results can be disastrous. Bob, a former vice president in an advertising agency, has many good leadership qualities, but he is a poor manager. As a result, his credibility diminished to the point where he lost his leadership effectiveness.

Advisor

You might be an inspiring, charismatic leader who consistently motivates others to peaks of performance. Even if you are, you still need to back up your leadership ability with planning, organizing, and controlling. An inspiring leader can sometimes squeeze by with an executive assistant or assistant manager who acts as a strong backup. However, keep in mind that a leader needs enough managerial skills to make effective use of the managerial skills of others.

Bob inspired people with his warmth, charm, and creativity. He could line up subcontractors for major projects, dazzling them with promises of riches and glory if they would undertake projects for his firm. Clients were mesmerized by his intellectual energy and creative suggestions—both important aspects of leadership.

As a manager, Bob was disorganized and had poor follow-through. Agreements with subcontractors were often broken. When he did keep a promise, the subcontractors (for example, a small advertising agency) often had to struggle to obtain their advances. Bob was too disorganized to effectively delegate the details. Even worse, he often forgot what he had told people.

Bob's problems had many causes: He did not seriously understand the capabilities of his firm; he did not ask for enough input from the people in his command; he did not find out what each person could contribute. Even when he did have an accurate idea of what his team could accomplish, he did not pay attention to *when* they could accomplish it. As a result, Bob frustrated both his team members and his clients. As complaints about his performance accumulated, Bob was eventually invited to leave the advertising agency.

A Leader Is Involved in a Partnership

Another way of understanding leadership is to think of it as both a relationship and a partnership between the leader and the group members. Forming a partnership depends on building a relationship. You, as the leader, relate to others in a similar way as you relate to family members and friends. Instead of being detached and distant, you have rapport with and good feelings about group members.

Think of the difference in how you interact with people while riding a shuttle bus in an airport versus riding in a car pool van. During your ride at the airport, you probably relate very little to the people around you, except for the exchange of a few pleasantries. If you are a member of a van pool, you probably develop a relationship with each person in the van.

The term partnership reflects the relatively equal power between the leader and all of his or her constituents. Leaders who are partners of group members welcome their partners' input. As a leader, you can still provide direction and inspiration while regarding partners as group members rather than employees or subordinates. For a valid partnership to exist, the following conditions must be met:

➤ The leader develops a vision only after receiving input from his or her partners.

➤ Group members have the right to disagree with the leader and are regarded as valuable contributors to the group effort.

➤ Both the leader and the group members are held accountable for results. If the group members want to be treated as partners, they have to risk being accountable for failures as well as accomplishments.

➤ The leader and the group members are honest with each other. Not telling the truth is a violation of the implied contract between the leader and the group members.

➤ The leader and the group members recognize that squabbles are inevitable, as they are in most partnerships. In an effective partnership, most of the squabbles are resolved in an equitable fashion instead of being left to fester.

Given that leadership is a partnership, the leader and the group members have serious responsibilities toward each other. Each member of the group, the leader included, feels a personal responsibility for achieving the group's mission. For the partnership to work, open communication must include good news *and* bad news. You can tell a leader has a good partnership with a group when a member can say to the leader without fear of retribution, "I just screwed up, and I need your help." Similarly, the leader should be able to say to a team member, "You've made what I consider to be a big mistake, and I want to help you fix the problem."

Advisor

A useful mental set for improving your leadership effectiveness is to think of yourself and your work group as partners in a small business. As the leader, you may be the partner with the biggest stake in the business, yet everyone is striving for success and is dependent upon everyone else. If you cannot trust your partners, and if they cannot trust you, your enterprise is in big trouble.

How Good Are You at Inspiring, Persuading, Influencing, and Motivating?

A leader is a person who inspires, persuades, influences, and motivates others. These are the basics of leadership. How do you accomplish these actions? Here are a few examples to illustrate what I mean by inspiration, persuasion, influence, and motivation.

Inspiration

The ability to inspire others represents the highest form of leadership. A leader must usually have a magnetic personality or set a wonderful example (or both) to inspire others. Consider these two scenarios:

1. Cheryl has been going about her job in a mundane manner for several years. She gets the job done but never works at her capacity or brings forth an exceptional idea. A new manager, Nick, is appointed to the unit. Nick's excitement about his work and the emotional support he gives group members create a change in Cheryl's attitude. Cheryl now strives to perform the best she can and contributes imaginative ideas for increasing productivity.

2. Max has been on a career plateau for several years. He hasn't received a promotion or a higher salary in three years. Max blames office politics for both conditions. A new supervisor, Jennifer, is appointed to Max's unit. Jennifer takes an interest in Max and listens carefully to his tale of woe. Jennifer also challenges Max to take more responsibility for his career stagnation. A light flashes in Max's mind. He is inspired to take several courses to earn a certificate in his field. This enhances his credentials for a promotion or salary upgrade. Jennifer also influences Max by her own positive approach to self-development. She reads career-related publications and attends professional seminars.

The two managers just described did an effective job of influencing group members to make positive changes. Keep this in mind as a guiding principle when leading others.

Persuasion

Persuasion is another key aspect of a leader's role. A leader must often get people to change their minds or take an action they had not considered.

Amy, a materials handling manager in an appliance manufacturing company, observes that two of her purchasing agents are not making good use of the information technology available to them. For example, when they want to purchase a particular part, they spend a lot of time interacting with sales people instead of relying heavily on purchasing over the Net. Amy wants to encourage them to make more effective use of e-commerce.

Amy sits down with the purchasing agents, individually and as a group, to present the arguments for using Net-based purchasing systems. Her logical persuasion works. The supervisors then ask for coaching on making more effective use of purchasing exchanges on the Net. Amy did not have to resort to threats or punishment. She *led* the supervisors by means of persuasion.

Watch Out!

When you are busy carrying out your everyday managerial responsibilities, it is easy to neglect actions that merit the term leadership. Avoid the trap of getting so caught up in conducting routine transactions with others that you neglect to inspire, persuade, influence, or motivate them. To be a leader, you have to modify the behavior of your target people in some way.

Influence

Influence is almost synonymous with leadership. Leadership is often defined as the process of influencing others to achieve objectives. A leader in a work setting influences group members to accomplish such things as …

➤ Taking on more responsibility for recruiting culturally diverse employees to the company.

➤ Shooting for higher quality standards when there are too many defects in the current product or service.

➤ Raising corporate ethical standards in dealing with customers, suppliers, and co-workers.

In all three instances, the leader influenced a team member to do something positive that helped the organization. Many leaders, unfortunately, influence group members to engage in negative, unethical acts that hurt the organization in the long term. An example would be lying about possible delivery dates or making false claims about the firm's capabilities.

Key Word

An objective can originate from your group. The group members might say, for example, "We want to be the most outstanding credit department in the entire organization." As the leader, you **influence** the group in achieving this objective.

Motivation

Motivation is also part of the nuts and bolts of a leader's job. To motivate another person is to somehow get that person to put added effort into the job. Motivation is a perennial challenge built into the leadership part of a manager's job. Motivation refers to actual behavior—not promises or fantasies! It is easy to be deceived by the glib-talking group member who describes in glowing terms how he or she wants to become a superior performer. This person might also share dreams of becoming a senior vice president. The first evidence that you have motivated that person is when he or she works harder than usual on today's tasks.

Leaders Accomplish Big Changes

I have one more defining characteristic of a leader for now: An effective leader brings about change and transformation. The major justification for paying top-level business leaders so much more than other workers is that the leaders spearhead constructive change. Bringing about such change often begins by pointing an organization or group in the right direction. Several heads of old-economy manufacturing firms have said in recent years, "Let's become less dependent on selling hardware and more dependent on selling services to other companies." Effective leaders typically feel uncomfortable with the status quo. They ask themselves such questions as …

➤ "What's broken that needs fixing?"

➤ "What is working okay but could stand some improvement?"

➤ "What is so sacred about our standard way of handling this?"

➤ "What changes would help us rise above the competition?"

➤ "Why doesn't our company have a better reputation?"

➤ "What changes would elevate us to a level of excellence?"

Leaders who can ask and find answers to the last question are classified as transformational leaders. They bring about sweeping, positive changes in organizations. As you read this book, keep in mind that becoming a transformational leader is the ideal you want to achieve.

The Least You Need to Know

➤ Leaders influence people to follow a course of action through persuasion or example.

➤ As a leader, you form constructive relationships and partnerships with people.

➤ Effective leaders inspire, persuade, influence, and motivate others and spearhead useful changes.

➤ Leaders transform mediocre organizations into excellent organizations, in part by pointing people in the right direction.

Chapter 2

Build Your Self-Confidence

In This Chapter

➤ Having self-confidence is important for leadership

➤ Thinking positive thoughts

➤ Taking an inventory of your assets

➤ Rewing up your need for power

➤ Obtaining a few easy victories first

➤ Bouncing back from setbacks

➤ Developing emotional intelligence as part of self-confidence

---

Assume you are a manager in a company rumored to be facing bankruptcy. At a company-wide meeting, the CEO sobs, "I'm sorry. I'm just no good in a crisis. I don't think I can get us out of this mess. Maybe one of you would like to try your hand at turning around a troubled company."

In a situation such as this, employees feel insecure. The people you manage would be so preoccupied with finding new employment that they wouldn't be able to concentrate on their work. You would want the president to behave in a confident, reassuring manner. On the other hand, if the president acted arrogantly, or if he or she treated the crisis lightly, you might not feel secure either.

In this chapter, I give you detailed advice about how you can build up the right amount of self-confidence to become an effective leader. Building self-confidence represents an excellent foundation for becoming an effective leader. Almost all successful leaders are self-confident. Almost all effective leaders also have high emotional intelligence which contributes to their self-confidence.

Why Self-Confidence Is Important

In most leadership situations, the leader who functions best is self-confident enough to appear in control and reassure others. However, if a leader is so self-confident that he or she does not admit errors, listen to criticism, or ask for advice, this situation creates a problem.

Developing or strengthening your self-confidence is a foundation for improving your leadership ability. Self-confidence and leadership feed upon one another. If people perceive you as self-confident, they are likely to accept you as a leader. As people accept you as a leader, your self-confidence increases. In turn, you meet with greater acceptance as a leader, followed by yet another small boost in self-confidence. Emotional intelligence fits in because if you can deal effectively with your own emotions and those of others, you will feel much more on top of situations involving people.

A large helping of self-confidence is also important because it contributes to your own belief in your capability to perform a task—referred to as *self-efficacy*. People with a heightened sense of self-efficacy tend to have good job performance. They also set lofty goals for themselves. Self-efficacy contributes to leadership effectiveness; a leader with high self-efficacy believes that a task is doable. As a result, this leader can inspire others to carry out a difficult mission—for example, correcting a serious customer problem.

Self-efficacy is also important for leaders because if you believe you can perform the task at hand, your level of motivation will increase. By being motivated yourself, you will serve as a positive role model on the task. Assume that you wanted to motivate your team members to speak Spanish so you could relate better to Latino customers and suppliers. If you believed you could learn Spanish, other team members would be more convinced they could, too. *Está bien.*

Key Word

Self-efficacy is akin to being self-confident about your ability to execute a task. For example, have you ever had a computer file apparently disappear into cyberspace? A person with high self-efficacy on retrieving lost files might move right into the temporary file bin and retrieve the file you thought was lost forever.

Use Positive Self-Talk

To appear self-confident and to project a strong leadership image, positive self-talk must replace negative self-talk. Positive self-talk means saying positive things about yourself to yourself. Positive self-talkers also make positive statements about themselves when speaking to others. If your manager asks you to take on a difficult assignment, use positive self-talk and say, "Let me give it a shot. My track record in dealing with the near-impossible has been good so far."

The biggest leadership dividends from positive self-talk come when positive self-talk takes place in front of others. Read the following steps to get started on using positive self-talk. Self-discipline is needed to implement these seven steps successfully. Choose an incident or a quality you want to strengthen and apply each step to that incident or quality. Repeat this exercise often throughout the week to get this new habit of positive self-talk established in your mind:

1. Objectively state the incident that is creating doubt about your capabilities. The key word here is "objectively." Chris, who is fearful of his ability to conduct a customer satisfaction survey for the company, might say, "I've been asked to conduct a customer satisfaction survey for the company, and I'm not good at conducting surveys."

2. Objectively interpret what the incident *does not* mean. Chris might say, "Not being skilled at conducting a survey doesn't mean that I can't figure out a way to do a useful survey or that I'm an ineffective employee."

3. Objectively state what the incident *does* mean. To implement this step, you should avoid put-down labels such as incompetent, stupid, dumb, jerk, or air-head. All these terms are forms of negative self-talk. At this point, Chris should state what the incident is really about: "I have a problem with one small aspect of this job—conducting a customer survey. This means I need to acquire skills in conducting a survey."

4. Objectively account for the cause of the incident. Chris might say, "I'm really worried about conducting an accurate survey because I have very little experience of this nature."

5. Identify some positive thoughts to prevent your fear of the incident from recurring. Chris could say, "I'll buy a book on conducting surveys and follow it carefully," or "I'll enroll in a seminar on conducting customer surveys."

6. Use positive self-talk in an interaction. Chris imagines his boss saying, "This survey is really good. I'm proud of my decision to select you to conduct this important survey." When the opportunity arises, Chris will respond to his boss, "I'm glad you asked me to conduct the survey. I'm eager to take on new challenges, and I've done well with them in the past." Or Chris might say, "Thanks for the opportunity for professional growth."

7. This final step is important in keeping the momentum going. It is a general application of positive self-talk rather than applying it to a specific incident: Start each day with positive thoughts. Positive self-talk is a complex habit that requires frequent reinforcement and reinvigoration. Invest at least five minutes each day in creating constructive energy. Just before launching the day's activities is a good time for this exercise. Find a quiet place free from interruptions,

get comfortable, breathe deeply, and think positive thoughts. Tell yourself that you can meet any professional or personal challenges that life has to offer. Think about your recent positive accomplishments and all the compliments you have received in the last 30 days.

Eliminate Negative Self-Talk

The flip side of developing positive self-talk is to avoid negative self-talk. To boost your self-confidence, minimize negative statements about yourself to others. You will appear more like a leader. The following statements reveal a lack of self-confidence:

> "I may be stupid, but …" or "Nobody asked my opinion," or "I know I'm usually wrong, but …" or "I know I don't have as much education as some people, but …"

Self-effacing statements such as these serve to reinforce low self-confidence. Instead, regard your weak points as areas for possible self-improvement. Negative self-labeling can do long-term damage to your self-confidence and leadership ability.

Advisor

Suppose you have mastered the art of self-talk, and you begin to get vibes that you are irritating others with your image of perfection. Throw in an occasional self-effacing comment just to humanize yourself. You might say, "My 13-year-old told me he would teach me how to use my digital camera any day now. I've learned how to click the shutter but he's going to show me how to hook it up to the computer." Remember that your goal is to increase the ratio of positive self-affirmations to negative ones, not to glow like an announcer on a home-shopping network!

You've Got More Going for You Than You Thought

Many people suffer from low self-confidence because they do not appreciate their own good points. A basic tactic for increasing your self-confidence is to take an inventory of personal assets and accomplishments. Create an asset list to help you recognize what you already have. Most people who do not feel confident about themselves overlook their many good points.

For this exercise, personal assets should be related to characteristics and behaviors, rather than tangible assets such as property and investments. Accomplishments can be anything significant where you played a key role in achieving the results. Don't be modest in preparing your list of assets and accomplishments. You are looking for any confidence-booster you can find.

Two asset lists prepared by two different people will give you an idea of the kinds of assets and accomplishments you can include.

Wanda's Asset List

Good listener

Good problem-solver

Better-than-average information technology skills

Assertive in work and social situations

Inquisitive mind

Patient with people who make mistakes

Good conflict-resolution skills

Good sense of humor

Better-than-average appearance

Excellent dancer

Organized successful fund drive that raised $50,000 for church

Graduated twentieth in college class of 350

Captain of league-winning volleyball team

Mother of two well-adjusted, happy children

Angelo's Asset List

Good analytical skills

Excellent computer skills

Good sales skills

Works well under pressure

Known for dependability and follow-through

Good dancer

Good cook

Excellent physical appearance

Humble when necessary

Made award-winning suggestion that saved company $100,000 in first year

Made winning run in ski meet that enabled my team to place first

Gave CPR that saved life of an auto accident victim

The value of these asset lists is that they add to your self-appreciation. Most people who write down their good points come away from the activity with at least a temporary boost in self-confidence. The temporary boost, combined with a few successful experiences, can lead to a long-term gain in self-confidence. Be sure to add to your list whenever you accomplish or learn something new.

An important supplement to listing your own assets is hearing the opinion of others about your good points. This tactic must be used sparingly, however, and mainly with people like you who are interested in personal growth. A good icebreaker is to tell someone you think will be receptive that you want to create a list of your assets for a leadership-development exercise. Choose a person who knows your work or capabilities and ask whether he or she can spare a few moments for this important experience.

Advisor

For many people, hearing positive feedback from others does more toward building self-confidence than recording feedback from yourself. The reason is that self-esteem depends, to a large extent, on what we think other people think about us. Consequently, if other people—whose judgment you trust—think highly of you, your self-image will be positive. Heightened self-esteem and self-image contribute mightily to your self-confidence.

Rev Up Your Need for Power

A thirst for *power* is a distinguishing characteristic of successful leaders in business and other fields. In other words, they crave to control resources—including people. Leaders with high power needs have four dominant characteristics:

➤ They act with vigor and determination to exercise their power.

➤ They invest time in thinking about ways to alter the behavior and thinking of others.

➤ They care about their status in comparison with the people around them.

➤ They regard power as one of life's most precious commodities.

These characteristics of the power-oriented person can be developed. It's a question of thinking through each item and saying to yourself, "Is this really true of my thinking?" Next, remind yourself of your new power attitude from time to time. As you watch a long private yacht sailing down river or bay, say to yourself, "Ahh yes. Power is good." Also, attempt to visualize how a very powerful person would react in this situation. For example, "If Donald Trump were asked the same question I am being asked, what would be his response?"

How is power linked to self-confidence? As a person becomes more powerful—acquires more power—he or she grows in self-confidence. It does wonders for your self-confidence when others extend themselves to do favors for you because they perceive you as powerful. The link between power and self-confidence runs in both directions. Power adds to self-confidence, and self-confidence helps you acquire power. If people perceive you as self-confident, they also perceive you as having a powerful personality. A powerful personality, of course, adds to your leadership stature.

Key Word

The ability or potential to influence decisions and control resources is a mark of **power.** Power is required to exercise influence over others as, for example, in getting others to part with resources such as money.

How Strong Is Your Need for Power?

To develop a tentative analysis of your need for power, see how many of the following statements you agree with. The more you agree with, the more likely it is that you already have a strong power need:

➤ I would like to have a high school or hospital named after me.

➤ Power is exciting and wonderful.

➤ If I could, I would like to include the rich and the famous as my friends.

➤ I wish I could have a huge, beautifully decorated office at the top floor of an office tower.

➤ It would thrill me to see my photo on the front page of *Time, Business Week, Fortune,* or any other national magazine.

➤ I would like to have a large staff ready to carry out my directions at a moment's notice.

➤ A fancy title is very important to me.

➤ It would thrill me if an Internet search engine came up with 75,000 listings under my name.

Watch Out!

Be aware that an extreme need for power can backfire. Craving power can lead to unethical, immoral, and illegal acts. A person obsessed with power may backstab rivals. Some power–obsessed people become paranoid, on guard against people they perceive as threats. Have you ever heard of a powerful person who maintained an "enemies list" of people to disparage and harm at the right moment?

➤ I think that power adds to a person's sex appeal.

➤ It would feel great if strangers greeted me by name in public places.

➤ I would get a thrill out of Web site named www.(insert your full name).com.

In Chapter 8, "Grabbing Power," I describe ways of gaining power. Right now, I want you to concentrate on something more fundamental—cultivating your *need* for power. My logic is that if you develop a strong need for power, you boost your self-confidence. An important contributing factor is that a person who craves power develops a power presence. Your craving for power, within ethical and legal limits, makes you appear self-confident.

Concentrate now on enhancing your desire for power. If you already have a strong power need, you can work through this section quickly. However, you might pick up a few ideas for further solidifying your power motive. Begin by imagining some of the potential benefits of being powerful.

People will attempt to curry favor with you. Think of all those people smiling at you when you enter the office. You are likely to earn a well-above-average income, thus alleviating or eliminating any financial problems you may have.

You will feel "in on things" as people feed you more inside information because they perceive you as powerful. You will be able to savor tidbits of information about such events as plans for expanding or downsizing.

You will be able to control money and other organizational resources. Even though you may not be able to spend the money personally, you will get satisfaction from knowing that your judgment on financial matters is trusted.

You will receive respect from a wide range of people who appreciate power. As a direct result, your prestige will increase. You will gain status both for your power and the leadership position that will most likely accompany your power.

You will have the opportunity to help others. Power gives a person the resources to help others. A powerful person, for example, might be able to find a job for someone in need of employment.

Watch Out!

Sometimes when people start thinking like this, they may develop the bad habit of actually believing they are better than others and expect others to defer to them. This is a big mistake. What you want is for people to respect you because they know you have their best interests in mind as well as your own and, therefore, want to defer to you rather than feeling they are required to do so.

Visualize a More Powerful You

Another step in revving up your need for power is to visualize what it would be like to be more powerful. Sit back, relax, and get your imagination going. Create a videotape in your mind of yourself becoming more powerful. Imagine enjoying some of the benefits you just read about.

Think of men and women wanting to open doors for you. See yourself walking into a meeting a few minutes late and the other participants stopping their chatter to greet you. Picture yourself choosing whatever clothing you want to wear without considering the price. Imagine decorating your office in almost any way you choose, including art from around the world.

Create a visual image of various people asking your opinion on different topics and listening carefully even if what you have to say is nothing more than common sense.

Think of crowds of people wanting to shake your hand or tap you on the arm because they are attracted by your powerful presence. Imagine the sights, sound, taste, and touch of power.

Grab a Few Easy Victories

Self-confidence accumulates with a variety of successes, so start with relatively easy tasks. Suppose you want to submit ideas to your company that will create substantial change and give you a surge in prestige and recognition. You realize that the probability of getting a breakthrough idea accepted is small. A good way to build self-confidence is to first make several small suggestions that are likely to be accepted. For example, a research analyst in a financial services firm suggested that data-entry people use a paper holder to reduce neck strain when entering data on their computers. This simple suggestion meant that workers would suffer less and worker compensation claims (and insurance premiums) might be reduced. After this suggestion was successfully implemented, the research analyst made bolder suggestions for ergonomic redesign in the office.

A variation of the easy-victory strategy is to place yourself in a less competitive environment, especially if you find that you are in over your head in your present environment. It's bad for your self-confidence to keep getting clobbered. A less competitive environment—such as working with more cooperative co-workers—might be just what you need to establish a satisfactory level of self-confidence.

After obtaining several easy victories, move on to bigger challenges. Small accomplishments are important because they pave the way to tackling more complex activities. A person who aspires to be a restaurant owner might work first as an assistant manager, and then as manager, of someone else's restaurant. If you achieve something that stretches your capability, that achievement serves

Advisor

The "win a few easy victories" tactic works well because it is based on the success cycle. Each little success builds your self-confidence, which leads to a bigger success, which leads to more self-confidence, and so on.

as objective evidence that you are a capable—and, therefore, confident—individual. As a result, you strengthen an important leadership characteristic.

Bounce Back from Setbacks and Embarrassments

One of the best self-confidence builders is to convince yourself that you can conquer adversity such as setbacks and embarrassments. The vast majority of successful leaders have dealt successfully with at least one significant setback in their career, such as being fired or demoted. In contrast, crumbling after a setback or series of setbacks usually lowers your self-confidence. The following are two major suggestions for bouncing back from setbacks and embarrassments.

Get Past the Emotional Turmoil

Adversity has enormous emotional consequences. The emotional impact of severe job adversity can rival the loss of a personal relationship. The stress from adversity leads to a cycle of adversity followed by stress, followed by more adversity. The following tactics can help you cope successfully with the emotional aspects of adversity:

➤ **Accept the reality of your problem.** Dealing constructively with the emotional aspects of a crisis does not mean denying the reality of your problem. Admit that your problems are real and that you are hurting inside.

➤ **Do not take the setback personally.** Remember that setbacks are inevitable as long as you are taking some risks in your career. Not personalizing setbacks helps reduce some of the emotional sting.

➤ **Don't panic.** Recognize that you are in a difficult circumstance under which many others would panic. Convince yourself to remain calm enough to deal with the problem or crisis, no matter how severe.

➤ **Get help from your support network.** After interviewing hundreds of people about how they bounced back from career and personal setbacks, I reached an important conclusion: Getting emotional support from family members and friends helps people overcome the emotional turmoil associated with adversity. No other technique was even a close second to talking out your problems with a trusted listener.

Learning how to bounce back from adversity can be a major step forward in your quest to build your career as a leader, or any other type of work. Not being able to shake loose from adversity is debilitating.

Find a Creative Solution to Your Problem

An inescapable part of planning a comeback is to solve your problem. Typically, an off-the-shelf solution is not available. Instead, you need to search for creative alternatives. Here is a widely used problem-solving method:

1. **Diagnose and clarify the problem.** What is the real problem created by your adversity? Are you suffering losses in income, self-esteem, job satisfaction, personal relationships, and well-being (or any combination of the preceding)?

2. **Search for creative alternatives.** What options are open? To be resilient, you may have to find a creative solution to your problem.

3. **Make a choice.** If your career crisis is to be resolved, you must make a tough decision at some point.

4. **Develop an action plan and implement it.** What steps must you take to get out of this mess?

5. **Evaluate outcomes.** Did your recovery plan work or will you have to try another alternative? Within six months, you usually know whether you made a workable choice.

Being able to work through tough problems is a powerful elixir for low self-confidence. If your self-confidence is already high, it will continue to strengthen as you solve more problems successfully.

Another Perspective

Finding creative solutions to the problems you face lies at the heart of being resilient. The owner of a printing company was losing customers to desktop publishing. He needed time to regroup and cash to tide the business over for the intermediate range. His creative solution was to sell the company building and lease it back. Proceeds from the sale gave the business the cash it needed to survive.

Develop Your Emotional Intelligence

How well a person manages his or her emotions and those of others makes an impact on leadership effectiveness. For example, recognizing anger in yourself and others and being able to empathize with people can help you influence others more effectively. In recent years, a grab bag of different aspects of emotions, motives, and personality that help determine interpersonal effectiveness and leadership skill have been placed under one label, *emotional intelligence*. This type of intelligence has to do with the ability to manage ourselves and our relationships effectively. Many of the topics in this book would be considered part of emotional intelligence, including being trustworthy, exercising visionary leadership, and promoting teamwork.

Psychologist Daniel Goleman's extensive research indicates that the most effective leaders are alike in one essential way: They all have a high degree of emotional intelligence. General intelligence (or IQ) and technical skills are essential, basic requirements for success in executive positions. Yet without a high degree of emotional intelligence, a person will not make an effective leader. Leaders who are star performers have higher emotional intelligence than average-performing leaders.

Emotional intelligence is linked to self-confidence in two important ways. First, a strong and positive sense of self-worth is part of emotional intelligence. Second, if you are comfortable with your own feelings and can relate effectively to others, you will be more self-confident.

Having very low emotional intelligence (including emotional control) can damage a leader's reputation. A factor contributing to the intense dislike of Chainsaw Al Dunlap, the slash-and-burn executive, was the intensity of his outbursts toward his managers. While at Sunbeam Corporation, Dunlap would throw papers or furniture, thump his hands on his desk, and shout so ferociously that a manager's hair would be blown back by the torrent of air rushing from Dunlap's mouth. "Hair spray day" became a code expression among top managers, signifying that Dunlap was throwing tantrums that day.

Key Word

When you have qualities such as understanding your own feelings, empathy for others, and knowing how to regulate your emotions in order to enhance living, you have **emotional intelligence.**

So How Do I Develop a High Emotional IQ?

Many organizations now sponsor emotional intelligence training programs, so you might be able to attend one. However, you would still need to practice what you learned. A realistic starting point in improving your emotional intelligence is to work with one of its key components, empathy.

1. Obtain as much feedback as you can from people you know. Ask them if they think you understand their emotional reactions and how well you understand them. Get the opinion of someone from another culture because a higher level of empathy is required to communicate with somebody much different than yourself.

2. If you find any area of deficiency, work on the deficiency steadily. Perhaps you are not perceived as someone who takes the time to understand a point of view that is quite different from your own. Work intensely at understanding other points of view.

3. A few months later obtain more feedback about your ability to empathize. If you are making progress, continue to practice.

4. Repeat the first three steps for another facet of emotional intelligence such as keeping your anger under control.

Advisor

A problematic aspect of attempting to become more emotionally intelligent is that the term covers so much territory. It is better to peck away at specific aspects of emotional intelligence such as empathy, creating visions, and enhancing collaboration among people. Many of the ideas in this book will contribute to your emotional intelligence.

The Least You Need to Know

➤ Think positive thoughts about yourself.

➤ Write down your good points to boost your self-confidence.

➤ Visualize a more powerful you.

➤ Follow a few easy victories with bigger challenges.

➤ Deal creatively with the emotional turmoil associated with adversity.

➤ Hone your emotional intelligence so you can deal more confidently with your emotions and those of others.

MY TEAM + MOTIVATION = ENDLESS POSSIBILITIES

THE PLAN

Chapter 3

How Do Leaders Think?

In This Chapter

➤ Making good use of your intuition

➤ Looking at the big picture

➤ Asking tough questions: how and when

➤ Learning to be more creative and innovative

➤ Becoming a more penetrating thinker

➤ Reading people better

Rob had four years of experience as a marketing analyst when he decided to apply for a job as a sales promotion manager at another company. At the end of his first interview, the hiring manager asked, "Rob, do you have any other questions?"

Rob responded, "Oh yes, I do. What is your policy about surfing the Web during working hours? I like to check up on sports scores and the stock market every hour or so. It helps me relax."

After Rob left, the hiring manager wrote down on his yellow pad: "Generally, good candidate, but I question his ability to think like a leader. He focuses on trivial details and doesn't see the big picture."

In this chapter, you will learn the value of thinking big and how to adopt the thinking pattern of leaders. This information is extremely important. The mental side of leadership can contribute as much to leadership effectiveness as personality.

Trust Your Gut Feelings

A major part of a leader's job is to make decisions, both big and small. Intuition is a key personal trait many leaders rely on to make good decisions. *Intuition* is an experience-based way of knowing or reasoning in which weighing and balancing the evidence are done automatically. Effective leaders do not rely on analytical and data-driven techniques alone. They also rely heavily on hunches and intuition. Using this method, the decision-maker arrives at a conclusion without using the step-by-step logical process.

Key Word

Trusting your **intuition,** you might arrive at a sudden insight or solution to a problem without having to evaluate the facts. You will not have to systematically weigh the pros and cons of the possibilities you are facing.

Watch Out!

I have been touting the importance of intuition for effective leadership. Do not think, however, that all leadership decision-making is "shoot from the hip." In many instances, especially when dealing with unfamiliar territory, you will still want to sift through the evidence bit by bit before making a decision.

Being intuitive generally means that you rely heavily on the right half of the brain. The left half of the brain controls analytical thinking, whereas the right half controls creative and intuitive thinking. Effective decision-makers achieve a balance between analytical and intuitive, or left-brain and right-brain, thinking. Rather than operate independently of each other, the analytical and intuitive approaches should be complementary aspects of decision-making.

A strong leader knows when to rely on intuition and when to be more analytical. You could say that a strong leader intuitively knows when to use intuition and when to use careful analysis!

Intuition can be developed and sharpened, although it won't happen overnight. Enhancing your intuition is like sharpening your common sense. In fact, intuition incorporates common sense. If you are willing to make the effort to become a more intuitive thinker, keep the following suggestions in mind:

➤ **Immerse yourself.** Get plenty of experience in the area where you want to become more intuitive and exercise leadership. An experienced leader, for example, might have good intuition about just how far to stretch group members with demanding goals. One of the reasons he or she knows the limits is because he or she faced a similar situation 50 or more times.

➤ **Get tuned in.** Stay carefully attuned to those little sensations inside your body when you make a decision. In fact, the term "gut feeling" means that you are carefully attuned to the physiological signs of emotion within your body. You know that your gut (intestine) is telling you something because you have a curious internal rumbling or flutter. This little sign is a signal that your thoughts are creating an emotional response. Your gut reaction often suggests to you "Go forward" or "Watch out."

➤ **Lend an ear.** Listen carefully when that little voice inside your brain says, "This is the right move!" or "This is the wrong move!" If you don't listen now, you may be plagued later with the thought, "I should have listened to my instincts."

➤ **Focus.** Concentrate on the task at hand so that you can be more aware of your intuition. The challenge is to put aside distracting problems before you enter an important decision-making situation. For example, clear out your e-mail inbox before tackling a demanding situation such as negotiating with a vendor or conducting a performance appraisal.

➤ **Log your successes.** Maintain a log of the accuracy of your intuitive decisions. When you trust your hunches, record the nature of the hunch and, later on, whether it proved to be accurate. For example, "On July 1, I predicted, without benefit of market research, that our two-headed ice scraper would be a big hit. I was right on target." Getting feedback on the accuracy of your forecasts enables you to fine-tune your intuition.

Intuition comes about from a combination of judgment and experience. Keep practicing making decisions, and your intuition will sharpen.

Another Perspective

Intuition, of course, can be wrong. If the information packed in your brain is flawed, so will be your intuition. As a check on your intuition, from time to time attempt to trace the reasons behind your decision. Ask yourself, "Now what evidence do I have that my plan of action will work?"

Start Seeing the Big Picture

As the anecdote at the beginning of this chapter implied, thinking big is part of being a leader. Leaders are supposed to see the broad implications of almost every action they or their group members take.

Strategic Thinking

Seeing the big picture is part of thinking strategically—a requirement for executive leadership. *Strategic thinking* is the ability to think in terms of how your actions help the organization adapt to the outside world. It also involves understanding the long-range implications of your thinking.

Key Word

Hiring a highly competent supervisor to help strengthen the organization is a mark of **strategic thinking.**

Monro Muffler and Brake, a fast-growing automotive service company, illustrates an effective adaptation to the outside world. Originally, their main line of business was to install brakes and exhaust systems for individual consumers. However, company leaders began to realize that many of their customers were too busy to bother making separate trips for muffler and brake repair at Monro, and routine auto servicing (such as an oil change) elsewhere. Monro, therefore, added routine service to capture more business. Adapting to the outside world meant catering to the needs of busy customers.

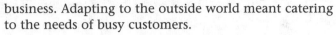

Key Word

A **systems thinker** understands how any change implemented at one place in the firm creates changes in the rest of the firm as well, immediately and in the future.

Systems Thinking

Another way of understanding what it means to perceive the overall picture is to become a *systems thinker*. The systems thinker attempts to grasp how a change introduced in one part of the system (or organization) creates changes in the other parts of the system as well. The systems thinker also attempts to forecast how a change today will affect the company in the future.

Assume that the director of marketing pushes for total customer satisfaction. One change initiated in the organization triggers another change, resulting in the type of chain reaction.

Chain of consequences in an organizational system.

Big Thinking

A person who is a little thinker must work diligently to become a big thinker. That's about as easy as a pessimist becoming an optimist! Yet it can be accomplished. Start with an *awareness* of the need for thinking big. Combine your new awareness with diligent *practice*. Here are a few suggestions to help you develop your new habit:

➤ Attempt to stop thinking little, especially with respect to giving high priority to your own self-interest. Imagine a person working in an office supply store 35 years ago. He hears that a company will start selling a newfangled machine that makes photocopies. Instead of imagining the positive implications for his company, he says, "That new Xerox machine will hurt my sales of carbon paper. I'll write a letter to the CEO telling him that almost nobody will choose photocopies over carbon paper." A big thinker would have said, "A revolution in office supplies might be on the horizon. What can I do to join this revolution? What supplies will people need to make photocopies?"

➤ Spend some of your discretionary time with big thinkers rather than little thinkers. Big thinkers will help you develop a positive, broad outlook because they rise above petty problems to look at the long-range goal. Little thinking can be contagious; it's easy to get channeled into a mode of little thinking. (Furthermore, if you don't agree with me, it's because you are not thinking big.)

➤ Study company vision statements and read the work of futurists. Even if futurists are not always right, reading about their forecasts will help elevate the level of your thinking. Glance through the *Harvard Business Review* for articles about business strategy. Get in touch with the World Future Society (Bethesda, Maryland). The best source of information about the future might be a newsletter published by Jossey-Bass, Inc., *The Future at Work: Managing Forces That Are Reshaping Organizations and Our Work Lives*. Also, check out "futurists" on the Web.

➤ See if you can be assigned to a cross-functional team within your firm. A cross-functional team is a small group of employees from different units who work together on specific problems and projects such as product development. Working with these people will help you appreciate how your work affects them. (You will learn about teamwork in Part 3, "You Can Become a Team Leader.")

Watch Out!

In your quest to be a big thinker, do not neglect the important details that enable your company to run smoothly. Remember that a good leader is also a good manager. An effective big thinker combines systems thinking with a daily concern for running a tight ship.

➤ Imagine yourself wearing different company hats. If you are concerned about the quality of your product, imagine yourself wearing a "manufacturing hat." Tomorrow you may notice that your department is spending money too freely, so don your "finance hat." Next Monday, you might observe that several of your group members are struggling to balance family and work demands. Off the shelf comes your "human resources hat."

Why and When to Ask Tough Questions

Strong leaders might not always have the right answers, but they usually have the right questions. A hard-hitting part of a leader's job is to ask tough questions. A *tough question* is one that makes a person or group stop and think about why they are doing or not doing something. In this way, group members are forced to think about the effectiveness of their activities.

Why Should I Ask a Tough Question?

The purpose of a tough question is not to intimidate, cajole, or belittle another person, but to help that person think through whether the status quo is good enough. A tough question often sets the stage for creative thinking because it questions whether an accepted practice could be radically changed. The beauty of a tough question is that it encourages people to ask themselves, "Why didn't I think of that? It seems so obvious."

Watch Out!

Ask your tough questions after the warm-up phase of a meeting has been completed. People respond better to tough questions after they are already moving toward serious thinking. You might lose the potential good effect of a tough question if it is asked before people are mentally ready to think in depth.

Here's an example of asking a tough question. One of the leading companies in the garbage disposal field embarked on a program that lets customers pay their bills with a direct transfer of funds from their banks to the bank of the waste removal company. Consumers receive a statement every two months. The statement notes that the person is not required to send a payment but that the amount owed will be deducted from the customer's bank account.

A top manager at the waste disposal company had a neighbor who used the system. Out of curiosity, the manager asked to see the billing statement. She noted that it included a payment envelope and discovered that an envelope was included with each statement. Checking within the company, the manager learned that including the envelope was standard practice on all customer statements—whether they were to be paid by mail or by bank transfer.

The manager then asked a tough question: "Why are we sending payment envelopes to customers who do not use them? Are we trying to help the envelope company?" This prompted the manager of information systems to develop a routine that prevents including wasted envelopes with customer statements.

A tough question can also ask another person or group why they have *not* thought of something. Here are a few more examples of tough questions:

➤ A team leader remarks to another member of the group: "The one-day promotion assumes it will not rain on June 5. What will you do if it rains?"

➤ The division general manager says to the manufacturing manager: "The delivery date you promised assumes that the one supplier you have for the main components will deliver as promised. Suppose they don't? Why do you depend so heavily on one supplier?"

➤ The vice president sends a memo to the sales manager: "I share your pride in the fact that sales are up 10 percent, but how does that compare to the sales increase of our three biggest competitors?"

To prepare yourself for answering tough questions, challenge your plan of action. Ask yourself "What have I missed? What else should I have thought about? What could possibly go wrong with my plan?"

Advisor

Asking tough questions is cool. It adds immensely to your stature as a leader because many people expect a leader to ask provocative questions. Leaders are sometimes regarded not as people with the right answers, but as those with the right questions. Nevertheless, at times you may want to go beyond just asking tough questions. You may want to have some alternatives in mind that might have escaped the group members. However, do not jump right in and present your alternatives. Wait until people have responded to the tough questions. You then say, "Great, but have you also considered ...?"

When Should I Ask Tough Questions?

Being good at asking tough questions requires developing the right mental habits. When reviewing the work or proposals of others, ask yourself these five questions:

1. Where's the hidden flaw in this?
2. How could this be better?
3. What didn't he, she, or they think of?
4. Where are the backup plans in case something goes wrong?
5. Nothing is this good; what would the CEO think of it?

Tough questions can be asked during group meetings, individual meetings, and while traveling with a work associate. But time the question for a moment when you think the other person would be receptive to heavy thinking. Avoid something like, "Please pass the ketchup. And by the way, do you think you should abolish the human resources department?"

Put Some Creative Punch Into Your Thinking

Creativity gives you a tremendous edge as a leader. Developing a great idea or two enhances your credibility with your constituents. If you forage through the career path of top executives, you find that many key people launched their careers with a good idea. An outstanding example is Jeff Bezos, the founder of Amazon.com. You most likely already know something about Bezos, who generally is considered to have started the e-commerce and e-tailing revolutions. What could be new to you, however, is how he applied the creative thinking process to initiate the idea of selling books over the Internet (as reported in *Time* magazine).

Back in May 1994, 30-year-old Bezos was sitting in his Manhattan office exploring the fledgling Internet. He was astonished to learn that the Internet was growing at a rate of 2,300 percent annually. "It was a wake-up call," he says. "I started thinking, 'Okay, what kind of business opportunity might there be here?'" Thinking up business opportunities was Bezos's job at D. E. Shaw, a firm that prides itself on hiring some of the smartest people available and then figuring out what kind of work they might profitably do.

The federal government decided to get out of the Internet business and allow private companies to step in and develop it, Bezos recalls. "I'm sitting there thinking we can be a complete, first mover in e-commerce." He researched mail-order companies, figuring that things that sold well by mail would do well online. He made a list of the top 20 mail-order products and looked for where he could create the most value for customers. "Unless you could create something with a huge value proposition for the customer, it would be easier for them to do it the old way," he reasoned. And the best way to do that was to "do something that simply cannot be done any other way."

Bezos's reasoning ultimately led to books. There weren't any huge mail-order book catalogues simply because a good catalog would contain thousands, if not millions of listings. The catalogue would need to be as big as a phone book—too expensive to mail. That, of course, made it perfect for the Internet, which is the ideal container for limitless information.

By the middle of 2000, some analysts were saying Bezos has overplayed his hand and that Amazon is in financial trouble. Time will tell, but Bezos is a visionary and an inspiring leader for the people in his company.

Leaders think as Bezos does. They see possibilities and opportunities others overlook. Instead of being locked into traditional ways of looking at objects and ideas, they think imaginatively. Here are seven key steps you can take to sharpen your creative problem-solving ability:

Another Perspective

Creativity can also be regarded as lateral thinking—a mental process that spreads out to find many different alternative solutions to a problem. For example, a human resources manager might ask, "How many different positions in this company can be performed by people whose welfare support will be discontinued?" Vertical thinking on the same topic would be, "What position do we have that could be filled by somebody coming off welfare?"

1. Keep track of your original ideas by maintaining an idea notebook or computer file. Few people have such uncluttered minds that they can recall all their past flashes of insight, especially when they need them.

2. Stay current in your field and hunt for ideas. Having current facts at hand gives you the raw material to link information creatively. Creativity often takes the form of associating ideas that were previously unassociated. An example is linking the idea of selling movie tickets with the idea of selling tickets through vending machines.

3. Participate in creative hobbies, such as doing puzzles or pursuing arts and crafts. Learning another language well (or not so well) also fosters innovation because you are forced to think in new and different ways.

4. Adopt a risk-taking attitude when you find creative solutions. You will inevitably fail a few times—not to worry. One or two innovative ideas per year is sufficient to develop a reputation as a creative problem-solver.

5. Develop a creative mental set. Allow your foolish side to emerge. Creativity requires a degree of intellectual playfulness and immaturity. Many creative people are accomplished practical jokers.

6. Be curious about your environment. The person who routinely questions how things work, or why they do not work, is often likely to have an idea for improvement.

7. Identify the time when you are most creative. Attempt to accomplish your creative work during that period. Many people are at their peak of creative productivity after ample rest, so work on your most vexing problem at the beginning of the workday.

8. Engage in creativity-building exercises such as the one presented in the following Advisor sidebar. The purpose of these exercises is to help you develop the mental flexibility required to be a creative problem-solver on the job.

Keep in mind an important point about creative problem-solving. The more ideas you generate, the more likely you are to find a great idea. Creative problem-solving is a numbers game.

Advisor

To become a creative problem-solver, you may have to overcome your belief in two myths. One myth is that people are either creative or not creative. In reality, creativity is like height and intelligence; everybody has it but in varying degrees. A second myth is that creativity applies only to the arts and technical fields. In truth, creativity is just as important in business as anywhere else.

www.GetRich.com for Creativity Improvement

Assume that you are intent on starting a new Internet company. Develop an appropriate domain name for your company such as www.antiquecarparts.com for a company that sells antique car parts over the Net. Explain the nature of the business, not necessarily restricting yourself to the same business model as others have used. Also explain how your firm would generate revenue. Think in terms of a business that might be successful enough to eventually sell stock to the public—an initial public offering (IPO). This is why the exercise is called "www.GetRich.com."

A recommended approach to this exercise is to give yourself a strict time limit, such as 10, 30, or 60 minutes. After the time expires you have to declare whatever business opportunity you have thought of. Such forced problem-solving is a proven method of developing creativity.

If your business starts to take off, please allow your author to purchase stock usually reserved for "friends and family."

Develop Your Insight

A distinguishing intellectual strength of leaders is that they can size up situations and people and arrive at an in-depth understanding that others might miss. This is the same ability that enables leaders to ask tough questions. A major advantage of a penetrating insight is that it helps another person understand a situation more clearly, spotting the illogic in their thinking. (The term *penetrating insight* is redundant because an insight penetrates.) The other person you help often appreciates your efforts and is drawn to you because of your contribution.

Andrew Grove, the CEO of Intel, has been a well-known business leader for many years. Grove has an affinity for offering insight about business. His favorite motto (insight) is "Only the paranoid survive."

When you first hear this statement, you might think that Grove is paranoid. When you think about his motto, however, you realize that in a highly competitive industry such as computer chips, suspicion is a success strategy. For example, Grove has spent millions of dollars in legal fees to sue companies for alleged copyright and patent violations.

Developing powers of penetrating thinking requires intense listening and concentration. Search for incongruities and underlying meanings. Here are two examples to help you appreciate the nature of offering another person a breakthrough insight:

> **Alan's breakthrough insight:** One of the people in Alan's group, who is 37 years old, says that he is too old to work on an MBA. He protests, "It would take me four years at night to earn an MBA. By then I will be 41 years old." Alan responds, "How old will you be in four years if you do not get an MBA?" The group member then suddenly realizes that time will pass regardless of whether or not he fills it with an important personal and professional accomplishment.

> **Julie's breakthrough insight:** One of Julie's peers says that she is terribly frustrated in her career because her previous three managers were too stupid to understand her contribution. She, therefore, has not been able to advance in responsibility. Julie responds, "Three stupid managers in a row seems implausible. Could it be that you are not packaging your ideas in a way that management can see the relevance of your work?" A lightbulb flashes, and Julie's co-worker begins to assess what she could possibly do better.

Offering penetrating insights to others enhances your leadership effectiveness because such insights sometimes help people overcome behavior that is blocking their progress. The right insight might help another person exit the path of self-defeating behavior.

Another Perspective

Penetrating insights can enhance your leadership effectiveness in another way. You might discover aspects about yourself that could profit from improvement. A manager might ask himself, "Hmm, I've been downsized three times. Is there something I'm doing wrong that has put me on the hit list three times?"

How Do I Develop a Leader's Ability to Read People?

Another distinguishing characteristic of successful leaders is the ability to size up or read other people. They make rapid judgments about the capabilities and foibles of others. Many business leaders I have known have sharper insights into others than do specialists in human behavior.

Many leaders believe that their most important skill is their ability to read people. The ability shows up not only in hiring people but also in choosing the right people to handle an assignment and in choosing the right supplier.

Sharpening your ability to size up people follows many of the same suggestions provided earlier in the chapter for developing your intuition. You needs loads of study, practice, and feedback. Here are a few starter suggestions:

➤ Sigmund Freud believed that almost no behavior is random. Whatever a person says or does has meaning, and your job is to figure out what it means. For example, if a person is late twice for an appointment with you, it might indicate a lack of commitment to your cause or purpose.

➤ Make a few predictions about people you meet for the first time, record those predictions, and then see whether they prove to be true. For example, you might observe that a new vice president talks a lot during his first visit to your office. You jot down "compulsive talker, mild listening disorder." As time goes by, verify your hunch by speaking to others and making additional observations.

Watch Out!

In the process of interpreting the behavior of other people, do not start to think that you are always right. For example, a cough during a meeting could mean that a person *is* bored or anxious. It could also mean the person has a sore throat.

➤ While dining with people, check out the process they use to select from the menu. If a person asks a lot of questions and even encourages the server to make the choice, it could mean he or she is indecisive. Follow up your hunch about indecisiveness by seeing how that person handles decision-making in other situations. Make additional observations and attempt to verify them by noting the person's behavior in different surroundings.

➤ Observe how another person treats restaurant staff or store associates. Again, verify your observations by comparing the person's treatment of these people with how he or she treats people in other situations.

➤ Attempt to make predictions about people's behavior in general by the way they dress, maintain the interior of their cars, or organize their desks. Verify your hunch by comparing it to observed behavior in other situations. One hunch might be, "This person is too neat and structured to be creative."

The general point of these suggestions is that you can sharpen your insights into people by making guesses about their character or behavior. You then look for corroborating evidence in other circumstances. Bit by bit, your judgments will sharpen, and you will have honed another important leadership skill.

The Least You Need to Know

➤ Pay attention to your intuition.

➤ Becoming a big thinker is important for effective leadership.

➤ Ask tough questions.

➤ Use creative thinking to solve problems.

➤ Enhance your ability to read people.

Chapter 4

How About a More Charismatic You?

In This Chapter

➤ Explanation of what charisma really means

➤ Ways to express your feelings assertively to contribute to your charisma

➤ Suggestions for being enthusiastic, optimistic, and energetic

➤ Ways to use candor as part of your charisma

➤ Ways to become an effective flatterer

➤ Suggestions for using animated facial expressions to enhance your charisma

➤ Suggestions for looking powerful and acting powerful

Sue and Dan were being considered for the general manager position at a division of a large clothing manufacturer. The company search committee submitted its final recommendations to the CEO. The committee said that both candidates were well qualified but that Dan had slightly stronger qualifications. "Why?" asked the CEO.

The head of the search committee indicated that Dan had a stronger technical background in textiles and was more experienced with finances. In addition, he had a good track record of working with labor unions. The search committee also reported that Sue was well qualified, but she was not quite as strong as Dan in those three critical areas.

After pausing for a few seconds, the CEO said, "Thank you; I've made up my mind. Let's hire Sue. The slight edge Dan has in relevant business experience does not counterbalance Sue's charisma. Our big problem at this division is that the work force is uninspired. Dan is a strong candidate, but Sue's leadership qualities make her my first choice."

As this example indicates, being charismatic can often give you the edge in boosting your career. In this chapter, you will learn what charisma really means and how you can develop a sensible plan for developing your own charismatic qualities.

What in the World Is It? And How Can I Get It?

You have probably heard the word *charisma* hundreds of times in recent years. To be called charismatic is a strong compliment, and to be called noncharismatic is a mild insult. Many people who do not believe they are charismatic want to become charismatic. Yet they are discouraged because they do not believe that charisma is a quality that can be developed. In their minds, charisma is much like height. They think it is a good quality that cannot be learned!

Before I move on to the good news about charisma (that maybe you can learn it), first take a careful look at what it means. Although the term has at least 12 slightly different meanings, for our purposes, charisma is personal charm and magnetism that is used to lead others.

Despite the fact that charisma appears to be a deep-rooted personality characteristic, much of it can be learned. For example, being emotionally expressive is a major contributor to charisma—and you can learn to become more emotionally expressive. Keep in mind also that if you are already perceived by many people as charismatic, you can further develop your charismatic qualities.

Recognize one more important fact before you dig into how to recognize and acquire charisma. As I just hinted, charisma is a perception. Although you want people to perceive you as charismatic, you can never hit 100 percent. Even the most charismatic leaders are regarded as bland or even detestable by some. For example, when people are asked to name a charismatic business leader, the name Lee Iacocca still surfaces. People remember how Iacocca charmed the public, the federal government, and company employees into helping Chrysler Corporation rebound from near disaster. You also might be familiar with Iacocca's recent venture as the founder of a motor scooter company—so people won't be so dependent on automobiles!

Key Word

Here is another meaning to ponder: **Charisma** is a special quality of leaders whose purposes, powers, and extraordinary determination differentiate them from others.

Despite Iacocca's many fans, admirers, and followers, he turned off many people. He was accused of being racist (anti-Japanese), sexist, vulgar, crude, and manipulative. Furthermore, at least one biographer accused Iacocca of taking too much credit for the ideas of others.

With this proviso in mind, that charisma is a subjective perception, check out the following examples of charismatic leaders from the world of business ...

➤ **Steve Jobs, co-founder of Apple Computer, Inc., and now CEO of both Apple and Pixar Animation Studios.** Jobs projects great visions that inspire people to work 80 hours per week and gets wealthy investors, including Bill Gates, to pour millions into his ventures. He is a folk hero among thousands of information technology fans.

➤ **Oprah Winfrey, the CEO of Harpo Entertainment.** One of the world's best-known public figures, Winfrey charms millions of television viewers with her presence. The mention of a novel on her show turns it into a best-seller. Winfrey is also a warm, compassionate boss whose charisma and power create loyal disciples.

➤ **Herb Kelleher, the CEO of Southwest Airlines.** A combination of a stand-up comic, marketing genius, and inspiring business leader, Kelleher captivates customers and employees. His successful company is one of the most widely studied in business schools. Somehow his outrageous behavior (such as kissing male and female employees on the mouth and chain smoking) is tolerated and adored.

➤ **Michael Milken, now the head of his own investment firm and volunteer math teacher to underprivileged children.** In his former glory days, Milken was paid $500 million in one year. As the self-anointed king of junk bonds, he mesmerized thousands of finance professionals into believing he was the savior of small businesses. Even while serving time in jail for violating security laws, his loyal band of followers attested to his greatness. (Milken illustrates that charisma can be used to accomplish evil as well as good deeds.)

Working for a charismatic leader is somewhat like being married to or living with someone you find attractive and stimulating. He or she is fun to be around. Perhaps not every day is outrageously exciting, but the charismatic leader gives you an extra reason to come to work. You think the guy or gal is wonderful to be around, and you are willing to extend yourself to please him or her.

Learn to Express Your Feelings

The best recognized way to develop charisma is to learn to express your feelings more openly and freely. A starting point in learning to be more emotionally expressive is to gauge your present status on this key aspect of behavior. Take the following quiz to help you analyze your current level of emotional expressiveness.

The Emotional Expressiveness Scale

Indicate how well each of the following statements describes you by circling the best answer: very inaccurately (VI); inaccurately (I); neutral (N); accurately (A); very accurately (VA).

	VI	I	N	A	VA
1. While watching a movie there are times when I will shout out in laughter or approval.	1	2	3	4	5
2. During a group meeting, I have occasionally shouted my approval with a statement such as "Yes" or "Fantastic."	1	2	3	4	5
3. During a group meeting, I have occasionally expressed disapproval by shouting an expression such as "absolutely not" or "horrible."	1	2	3	4	5
4. Several times, while attending a meeting, someone has said to me, "You look bored."	5	4	3	2	1
5. Several times while attending a social gathering, someone has said to me, "You look bored."	5	4	3	2	1
6. Many times while at social gatherings or business meetings, people have asked me, "Are you falling asleep?"	5	4	3	2	1
7. I thank people profusely when they do me a favor.	1	2	3	4	5
8. It's not unusual for me to cry at an event such as a wedding, graduation ceremony, or engagement party.	1	2	3	4	5
9. Reading about or watching sad news events, such as an airplane crash, brings tears to my eyes.	1	2	3	4	5
10. When I was younger, I got into more than my share of physical fights or shouting matches.	1	2	3	4	5
11. I dread having to express anger toward a coworker.	5	4	3	2	1
12. I have cried among friends more than once.	1	2	3	4	5
13. Other people have told me that I am affectionate.	1	2	3	4	5
14. Other people have told me that I am cold and distant.	5	4	3	2	1
15. I get so excited watching a sporting event that my voice is hoarse the next day.	1	2	3	4	5
16. It is difficult for me to express love toward another person.	5	4	3	2	1
17. Even when alone, I will sometimes shout in joy or anguish.	1	2	3	4	5
18. Many people have complimented me on my smile.	1	2	3	4	5
19. People who know me well can easily tell what I am feeling by the expression on my face.	1	2	3	4	5
20. More than once, people have said to me, "I don't know how to read you."	5	4	3	2	1

TOTAL

Discover your emotional expressiveness.

Scoring and interpretation: Add the numbers you circled, and use the following as a guide to your level of emotionality with respect to being charismatic and dynamic:

90 to 100: Your level of emotionality could be interfering with your charisma. Many others interpret your behavior as out of control.

70 to 89: Your level of emotionality is about right for a charismatic individual. You are emotionally expressive, yet your level of emotional expression is not so intense as to be bothersome.

10 to 69: Your level of emotionality is probably too low to enhance your charisma. To become more charismatic and dynamic, you must work hard at expressing your feelings.

Now that you have given careful thought to your level of emotionality, you are in a position to judge how much development you need to become more emotionally expressive. People who want to improve their leadership effectiveness often need to enhance their emotional expressiveness. Of course, some people give free rein to their emotions. These folks might need to learn how to express feelings in a more constructive way to be truly charismatic. My suggestion that emotional expressiveness contributes to charisma may only work about 90 percent of the time. (Note: The principles of leadership are not as accurate as those for chemistry or physics.)

Connect Feelings with Facts

So you know you need to express your emotions more effectively. But do you know how you feel?

In general, people do not have much trouble making facts known to other people. How you communicate those facts (your feelings and attitudes) may be creating a problem. For example, it is easier to say to a work associate, "You promised me your input by today," than to say, "I'm disappointed that you did not follow through on your commitment to give me your input by today." Maybe you shouldn't be disappointed, but these are your honest feelings. Effective leaders show their feelings.

Here is the hard part. To supplement your statements of fact, you must identify your feelings associated with the fact. The feeling points to an internal reaction you have to an object or person. Suppose you are applying new software to a work problem. After one hour of trying, the software does what you want it to do. The facts surrounding the event include ideas like these:

➤ "It took one hour for me to get the software to run right."

➤ "I stuck with the job, and I was finally successful."

➤ "I worked my way through the task without asking a computer expert to help me."

➤ "I fell behind in my work because I spent so much time playing with the software."

47

➤ "I learned a new skill that will help me when I face a similar problem in the future."

Advisor

To supplement your statements of fact, you must identify your feelings associated with the fact. Doing so will help you appear more emotionally expressive and charismatic. In spare moments, write down or think about events that have happened to you recently. Identify the facts, then specify the feeling associated with the facts. As you look through the rear view mirror of your car, you might note factually that a police officer on a motorcycle is approaching you rapidly and the motorcycle siren is screeching. Your associated feelings might be, "I'm humiliated, ticked off, and angry. If I get a speeding ticket, I'll be disgusted with myself."

All of the preceding factual statements reflect your intelligence and good problem-solving ability. However, they do not express your *feelings* surrounding the event. If you can identify your feelings in everyday events, you take a giant step toward becoming more emotionally expressive. Here are some of the feelings most likely associated with the preceding facts:

➤ "I'm so frustrated that it took me an hour to get the software to run right."

➤ "I'm elated. My persistence paid off. After sticking with the job, I was finally successful."

➤ "I'm so proud. I worked my way through the task without asking a computer expert to help me."

➤ "I'm so upset. I fell behind in my work because I spent so much time with the new software."

➤ "I'm excited. I learned a new skill that will help me when I face a similar problem in the future."

After developing skills in identifying your feelings, the next step is to practice expressing them to others. A general strategy is to reinforce many of the factual statements you make with the feelings behind them. To be perceived as dynamic, you must express your feelings to others as well as yourself. Here are a few examples of how charismatic people reinforce facts with feelings in speaking to others:

Editor to Editorial Assistant: "You put in 10 hours of personal time to complete the project. It excites me that you care so much about the company."

Restaurateur to Executive Chef: "We cut our expenses without laying off people or sacrificing quality. I want to share my delight with you."

Where Do You Get Enthusiasm, Optimism, and Energy?

A remarkable quality of charismatic people is that they maintain high enthusiasm, optimism, and energy throughout their entire workday and beyond. An executive search consultant (a.k.a. headhunter) based in New York City made this comment about the strongest prospects he targets: "I've had meetings as late as 10 at night with the executives I'm pursuing. They are as fresh as if it were 8:30 in the morning. You'll never hear one of them complain about how late it is or that he or she is exhausted. When these managers talk about their jobs or careers, they have a gleam in their eyes."

Becoming more energetic isn't as simple as tapping a toggle button. Elevating your energy—the main ingredient of charisma—takes considerable work. The following suggestions will get you started:

➤ Get ample rest at night and sneak in a 15-minute nap during the day when possible. If you have a dinner meeting where you want to shine, take a nap and a shower before the meeting.

➤ Switch to a healthy, energy-enhancing diet.

➤ Keep chopping away at your To Do list so you do not have unfinished tasks on your mind, draining your energy.

➤ Attempt to get your personal problems under control so they do not drain your productive energy from work. Similarly, get your work problems under control so they do not drain energy from your personal life.

Another aspect of being enthusiastic, optimistic, and energetic is maintaining an *action orientation*. "Let's do it!" is the battle cry of the charismatic person.

An action orientation also means that you prefer not to agonize over dozens of facts and nuances before making a decision. After enough information is collected to reinforce intuition, the charismatic person takes action and encourages other people to do the same.

Key Word

A person who has an **action orientation** is a person who wants to get things accomplished and decisions implemented.

Be Candid

The truth hurts, but this doesn't seem to deter charismatic leaders. They are remarkably candid and open with people. Although not overly insensitive, the charismatic leader is typically explicit in giving his or her assessment of a situation. A charismatic sales manager told one of her sales reps, "I know you want to become a sales manager, but I could not honestly recommend you for such a position now. You are too disorganized and impulsive." The sales rep was shocked and disappointed at first but learned an important lesson. He was jolted into realizing that how he performs today influences his opportunities for the future.

Charismatic people are candid on the positive as well as the negative side. They size up people and situations quickly and accurately and are willing to share those perceptions. Charismatic people speak directly rather than indirectly. As a result, other people know where they stand.

Expressing thoughts directly parallels expressing feelings directly. Instead of asking a group member, "Are you terribly busy this afternoon?" the charismatic leader asks, "I need your help this afternoon. Are you available?"

Advisor

Candor—on both the negative and positive side—is part of a charismatic person's tool kit. As long as you are not insensitive to the feelings of others, an open expression of your feelings and opinions has a magnetic pull. One reason candor is so effective is that it is distinctive. Only a minority of people are candid.

Becoming candid is not easy if you have a deep-rooted habit of talking in circles and softening your ideas. An important goal in expressing your candid thoughts and feelings is that the people with whom you interact should have no doubt about your true opinion.

Just before expressing your opinion about a person, idea, or object, prepare a 10-word statement in your mind. This activity will build your skill in expressing thoughts candidly. Practice it often. Here are six examples of candid expressions that you can use on the job:

➤ You are definitely promotable.

➤ Your job will be terminated in 30 days.

➤ You are an outstanding performer.

➤ One reason I want you on our team is because of your honesty.

➤ One reason I don't want you on our team is that you have a reputation for being devious.

➤ Sorry, I will not be placing another order with your firm. We have chosen another supplier who has higher-quality products.

If you are just learning to be candid, the initial results are likely to be a pleasant surprise. Quite often the recipient of the candid expression will say something to this effect, "Thanks for being honest. I'm glad I know where I stand."

A charismatic leader's success with being candid is partially attributable to the way in which the message is delivered. A negative message is most likely to be accepted when it is delivered in a matter-of-fact, nonjudgmental manner. The message should also be nonhostile and nonretaliatory.

Another important part of a charismatic leader's candor is that he or she formulates a believable vision. For example, an automotive plant manager might state, "We will become the plant with the highest quality and lowest accident rate in North America." Creating visions is such an important part of leadership that it receives separate attention in Chapter 12, "You Can Become a Motivational Force."

Flatter Sensibly

Charismatic leaders are candid, but they are also flatterers. They tend to look for actions and characteristics of others that are worthy of a compliment. *Flattery*—of the honest variety—makes others feel good, and part of the charm of charismatic leaders is that they make others feel good. Not everybody is talented at flattering others, so a short course in effective flattery is presented next. To build your skills in flattering others, practice these suggestions as the opportunity presents itself. Rehearse your flattery approaches until they feel natural. If your first attempt at flattery does not work well, analyze what went wrong the best you can.

Key Word

Flattery in the sense used here refers to pleasing by complimentary remarks or attention. We are not referring to flattery in the sense of giving insincere or excessive compliments.

➤ **Use sensible flattery.** Effective flattery has at least a spoonful of credibility, implying that you say something positive about the target person that is quite plausible. Credibility is also increased when you point to a person's tangible accomplishment. Technical people in particular expect flattery to be specific and aimed at genuine accomplishment.

➤ **Individualize your compliments.** Avoid using the same old compliment on everybody to avoid appearing insincere. Everyday compliments such as "nice tie" or "nice dress" are sometimes referred to as *throwaway* compliments. An assist toward individualizing compliments is to carefully research what others have done to merit flattery.

➤ **Compliment what is of major importance to the flattery target.** You might find out what is important to the person by observing what he or she talks about with the most enthusiasm. Somebody you are trying to inspire might be more interested in his community garden than his job so reach him by praising him for his do-it-yourself rhubarb.

➤ **Flatter others by listening intently.** Listening intently to another person is a powerful form of flattery. Use active listening (see Chapter 24, "Your Role as Coach and Facilitator") for best results.

➤ **Flatter by referring to or quoting the other person.** By referring to or quoting (including paraphrasing) another person, you are paying that person a substantial compliment.

➤ **Use confirmation behaviors.** Use behaviors that have a positive or therapeutic effect on other people, such as praise and courtesy. Because confirmation behaviors have such a positive effect on others, they are likely to be perceived as a form of flattery.

➤ **Give positive feedback.** A mild form of flattering others is to give them positive feedback about their statements, actions, and results. The type of feedback referred to here is a straightforward and specific declaration of what the person did right.

➤ **Remember names.** Remembering the names of people with whom you have infrequent contact makes them feel important. To help remember the person's name, study the name carefully when you first hear it, and repeat it immediately.

➤ **Avoid flattery that has a built-in insult or barb.** The positive effect of flattery is eradicated when it is accompanied by a hurtful comment, such as "You have good people skills for an engineer" or "You look good. I bet your were really beautiful when you were younger."

Use Animated Facial Expressions

A person who resembles a statue is rarely described as charismatic. To exhibit personal dynamism, it is essential to frequently use animated facial expressions. Use big smiles, little smiles, expressions of delight, frowns, scowls, looks of puzzlement, surprise, and reassuring nods. Visualize any leader whom you regard as charismatic. My guess is that this man or woman uses a variety of facial expressions in the presence of others.

To develop your skill at using animated facial expressions, follow these suggestions:

➤ Pay attention to leaders you admire and note their facial expressions. Practice modeling their behavior.

➤ Practice in front of a mirror or camcorder. Videotaping is better than using a mirror because many people find it difficult to modify their facial expressions when looking into a mirror.

➤ While looking into the mirror or recording on tape, think of various moods you want to project. Then do your best to match your facial expression to the mood.

➤ If you need some guidelines for matching facial expressions to your moods, emulate television actors, newscasters, newsmakers, and especially comedians.

Another Perspective

Experts don't agree on why some people are perceived as charismatic. The generally accepted idea is that an individual's personal characteristics create the impression of charisma. Another viewpoint is that if a leader accomplishes great results (such as Louis Gerstner's triumphs at IBM), he or she is perceived as charismatic. In other words, results lead to charisma rather than charisma leading to results.

Remember that animated facial expressions project leadership characteristics. They reflect the fact that you are listening and involved in the activities of the moment.

Do You Look Powerful? Do You Act Powerful?

An indispensable part of projecting charisma is to look and act powerful. Looking powerful is more subtle than it appears on the surface. If you take literally the advice of wardrobe consultants, you will look like a sales associate in a retail store or a young professional in most metropolitan offices.

On the other hand, if you ignore conventional wisdom about looking powerful, you risk looking unimportant and lacking in charisma. Here are some specific ways to increase your power look:

➤ Dress with taste and style. Suits for men and women should be conservative but not overly conservative. Your shirts may have initialed cuffs. Consider using an expensive fountain pen and watch. Women may consider adding a scarf to their outfits. If casual clothing is the norm, wear carefully pressed pants or slacks, starched, open-collar, button-down shirts, and a sport coat.

➤ Decorate your office or cubicle tastefully, perhaps with stainless steel, leather, and polished glass. Use family photos and other mementos sparingly.

➤ On occasion, when standing, place your hands on your hips and place your feet shoulder-width apart. (Try it; it projects self-confidence.)

➤ For emphasis when speaking, point the index finger parallel to the ground and the thumb at a right angle—similar to aiming a water pistol. (Do this only if you feel comfortable with this gesture.)

Do You Move and Act Purposefully?

People who stride though the workplace as if they have an urgent intent project charisma and personal dynamism. Top-level managers move and act purposefully even when they are passing through a lobby. Keep these examples in mind:

At meetings. You arrive early for a meeting. Don't stand outside the room waiting for others—it makes you look as if you're wasting time. Instead, take a seat in the meeting room and either read your memos or work on your To Do list.

In the hallway. You are walking down the hallway to attend a meeting. Stop to chat only if it meets some business purpose. Otherwise, walk in a straight line at a brisk pace. Charismatic people are not rudderless.

The Least You Need to Know

➤ Charisma is almost universally recognized as a major leadership quality.

➤ Although some successful leaders are not *universally* perceived as charismatic by many people, attempting to lead others without charisma puts you at a disadvantage.

➤ Although popular opinion suggests that charisma is a mysterious inner quality possessed by a small number of captivating people, you can develop many of the qualities associated with charisma.

➤ The most effective and feasible methods of developing or enhancing your charisma include learning to express your feelings more assertively and becoming more enthusiastic, optimistic, and energetic. Also, flatter generously.

Chapter 5

Communicate Like a Leader

In This Chapter

➤ Embellishing what you say to add impact

➤ Using metaphors and analogies to inspire others

➤ Telling a story

➤ Sending the message by your body language

➤ Projecting power with your linguistic style

➤ Using junk words, clichés, and other detractors

➤ Being a credible communicator

The CEO of a company that makes interiors for corporate jets was touring its manufacturing site. Stopping by the department that installs seating, he asked the supervisor, Herb, how well his department was meeting its goals. Herb replied:

"Like, I'm not sure. We have lots of goals, you know. Like it's tough figuring out what you guys really want. You know, it's crazy down here. You know where I'm coming from?"

The CEO wasn't exactly sure where Herb was coming from—but he was sure where Herb wasn't going. The CEO told the plant manager that Herb was not to be promoted. In addition, the CEO requested that the plant manager carefully review Herb's performance to make sure he was an effective leader.

Maybe you feel sorry for Herb and believe that the CEO judged him too harshly based on a brief interaction. Yet an inescapable fact is that to be credible as a leader, you must communicate as a leader does. In this chapter, you will learn about the major distinguishing feature of the communication styles of leaders. Obviously, not all effective leaders communicate in the same manner, but important similarities are worth your careful study.

You are invited to get started by taking the accompanying self-quiz. The questions will help you think through where you are strong as a communicator and where you need improvement.

A Self-Portrait of My Communication Effectiveness

The following statements relate to various aspects of communication effectiveness. Indicate whether each of the statements is mostly true or mostly false, even if the most accurate answer would depend somewhat on the situation. Asking another person who is familiar with your communication behavior to help you answer the questions may enhance the accuracy of your answers.

		True	False
1.	When I begin to speak in a group, most people stop talking, turn toward me, and listen.	_____	_____
2.	I receive compliments on the quality of my writing.	_____	_____
3.	The reaction to the outgoing message on my answering machine has been favorable.	_____	_____
4.	I welcome the opportunity to speak in front of a group.	_____	_____
5.	I have published something, including a letter to the editor, an article for the school newspaper, or a comment in a company newsletter.	_____	_____
6.	I have my own Web site.	_____	_____
7.	The vast majority of my written projects in school received a grade of B or A.	_____	_____
8.	People generally laugh when I tell a joke or make what I is a witty comment.	_____	_____
9.	I stay informed by reading newspapers, watching news on television, or logging on to news information Web sites.	_____	_____
10.	I have heard such terms as "enthusiastic," "animated," "colorful," or "dynamic" applied to me.	_____	_____
	Total:	_____	_____

Interpretation: If eight or more of the preceding statements are true in relation to you, it is most likely that you are an effective communicator. If three or less statements are true, you may need substantial improvement in your communication skills. Keep in mind also, that scores on the quiz you just took are probably highly correlated with charisma.

Impress Them with Heavy-Impact Language

Certain words used in the proper context give power and force to your speech. Used naturally and sincerely, these words can strengthen your leadership stature and your ability to inspire others. Current buzzwords usually have a positive impact. Note the emphasis on *current*. Yesterday's buzzwords have low impact. Here is a sampling of heavy-impact, embellishing language:

➤ Tell group members that you want them to "unleash their creative potential" instead of simply asking for a few suggestions.

➤ Explain that your group has a "well-articulated vision of where we are headed," instead of simply saying that you prepared a list of goals.

➤ Talk about having attended a "prestigious" trade show rather than simply a trade show.

➤ Use the expression "on the verge" of accomplishing something as long as a project is underway.

➤ Mention that you want to "bond" with customers instead of simply stating that you want to establish a good working relationship.

➤ Ask the team to "vaporize a distributor" instead of simply selling direct to customers.

➤ When your group picks up some useful feedback from a customer satisfaction survey, proclaim that your unit "demonstrated the capabilities of a learning organization."

➤ When your department wins an interdepartmental skirmish or wins a bid over a competitor, say that you "nuked" them.

Watch Out!

Using heavy-impact, embellishing language is an important addition to your leadership tool kit. If embellishment is taken too far, too often, the embellisher might appear deceptive and devious.

Dazzle with Analogies and Metaphors

A well-chosen analogy or metaphor appeals to your intellect and imagination. Effective leaders, therefore, make frequent use of analogies and metaphors. An analogy draws attention to the similarity between the features of two things so people can make a comparison. "Our company is much like Microsoft in its early days," is an analogy many founders of small high-tech companies make when attempting to inspire workers.

A metaphor is also a comparison, but it is less obvious than an analogy. The comparison is between two objects not ordinarily associated with each other. Comparing a small high-tech company to a cougar cub is a metaphor. Whether your comparison is a metaphor or analogy is not important. What really counts is whether the comparison grabs people. Workers are inspired by analogies and metaphors that are relevant to the challenges they face. Here is a sampling of analogies and metaphors leaders have used in their interactions with group members:

➤ Up to now, our group has been playing roller derby. It's time we started acting as a football team.

➤ We are a young company, competing against the established giants, much like Dell Computer in its early days.

➤ Let's hang in there and pull together. I envision a great success for our delivery service. Don't forget that Federal Express started from scratch in 1975 and now has 110,000 employees worldwide.

➤ Don't be discouraged by placing second in our bid to receive that contract. Michael Jordan didn't make his high-school basketball team on the first try.

➤ I like to think of our team as a group of wallabies, those lovable kangaroo-like animals from Australia. Most people like us, but we would be better off if we weren't hopping in so many directions.

➤ Don't let those comments about our new model being mundane discourage you. Look at the bum rap people give donkeys, yet donkey-owners love their hard-working, faithful animals. A donkey can be counted on for years of good performance. Besides that, a donkey-owner forms an emotional attachment to his or her unglamorous sidekick.

Watch Out!

Analogies and metaphors can be potent motivational tools. However, they can also fall flat and annoy people. Before using your metaphor or analogy on the job, first try it out with a friend or family member. Carefully watch the expression on his or her face to see if it works. Also get the other person's opinion in words.

Are you looking for a useful analogy or metaphor? A good starting point is to make comparisons with sports, successful companies, the military, and animals. Sexual analogies can inspire some people, but others perceive them as a form of sexual harassment.

Inspire with Storytelling

Another aspect of the communication style of effective leaders is that they make extensive use of memorable anecdotes to get messages across. They inspire and instruct team members by telling fascinating stories, thus managing by anecdote. Using anecdotes is a powerful leadership technique for several reasons:

➤ People like to hear anecdotes.

➤ Anecdotes help build the corporate culture.

➤ Workers can remember a principle or policy better if it is accompanied by an anecdote.

Message-sending anecdotes might relate to such subjects as a company president who goes out of his or her way to help an individual customer or a lower-ranking employee who defied authority to meet his or her responsibilities. For example, a receptionist at IBM denied admission to the company chairman, Tom Watson, because Watson was not wearing a security badge. Instead of firing the young woman, Watson praised her devotion to duty.

An inspiring anecdote supports an important company value such as customer satisfaction, quality, or employee safety. At Saks Fifth Avenue, for example, many employees have heard the story of how far management will go to satisfy a customer. The scenario occurred at the original Saks on Fifth Avenue in Manhattan. According to the legend, an elderly customer insisted that the only dress she wanted in the store was the one in the window. A store manager overheard the conversation between the store associate and the customer. The store manager removed the dress from the mannequin to satisfy the customer and placed another dress on the mannequin. The customer was delighted, and the store associate was shocked because window displays were considered sacrosanct.

Advisor

Telling anecdotes is such a useful management and leadership technique that it merits special attention. Create a useful anecdote file of your own. Collect anecdotes you observe personally, those you hear from others, and those you read in books, magazines, and newsletters. You might even find a useful anecdote on the Internet. As part of developing your anecdotal skills, observe how people being interviewed on talk shows present anecdotes. Another potential model is a professional storyteller. Perhaps you will have a chance to observe one. Also, observe comedians at comedy clubs and on TV. They often use anecdotes as a form of humor.

Watch Out!

Forms of nonverbal behavior can have different meanings in different cultures. In the United States and Canada, "perfect" is symbolized by joining your thumb and forefinger to make a circle. According to Letitia Baldrige, in Japan this gesture means you are expecting a kickback. In France it means "zero," and in many other countries the same symbol is an outright vulgarity.

Key Word

Congruence is a way of synchronizing the ways in which you attempt to deliver a message. If you want people to clean up their work areas, send the information in a neat form—not a messy-looking e-mail message or written note. And when you express sympathy, make a conscious effort to look sad, and have a sorry-sounding tone.

Does Your Nonverbal Language Project Leadership?

You're probably familiar with the different ways of communicating nonverbally, through gestures, posture, and eye movements. Nonverbal communication is the transmission of messages through means other than words. It includes body language as well as such diverse behavior as appearance, tone of voice, and the surroundings in which you deliver a message.

Certain gestures signal others that you are self-confident and a leader. Not everybody interprets body language and other nonverbal signals uniformly. Using the types of nonverbal communication described here will impress many, although not all, of the people you want to influence and inspire.

Get Your Verbal and Nonverbal Behavior in Synch

This section delves into specific aspects of nonverbal behavior that will strengthen your leadership ability. However, I first want you to be aware of the principle of *congruence*. Suppose you say to a group member, "I'm sorry to hear that your data file crashed. Tell me about it." At the same time, you have a concerned, saddened look on your face, and you squint intently. You sit in your chair as if you want to be there until the person finishes his or her story. You achieve congruence, and you come across as sympathetic—an important leadership characteristic.

Replay the same scenario. You make the statement, "I'm so sorry to hear that your data file crashed. Tell me about it." At the same time, you have a bored, disinterested look on your face. You shift your gaze in several directions. You fidget in your chair, and your posture appears aimed at leaving the scene quickly. You are displaying incongruence, and you leave the other person feeling flat and disappointed. Furthermore, you do not strengthen the relationship between you and the group member.

The important general principle is that you can strengthen your verbal message by ensuring that your words and nonverbal language are in synch. When your verbal and nonverbal messages match, you convey the impression that you are trustworthy and honest. If your nonverbal message reinforces your statement of concern, group members believe that you are interested in their plight.

Recognizing the importance of congruence in your communication is an important first step in becoming more congruent. Your aim is to integrate the various ways you send messages so that you appear more credible and influence others more effectively. Following are several actions that will help you become more congruent. Assuming this behavior will multiply the effectiveness of your communication:

> ➤ When you tell others you feel relaxed and happy or describe another positive state, consciously relax your muscles and facial expression.

> ➤ When you say to another person, "Tell me about your day (or vacation, new project, child, grandchild, spouse, significant other, or motorcycle)," gaze intently at the person and widen your eyes. Leaning toward the person also supports your request, as does a quizzical, inquiring look.

> ➤ When you deliver an affirmation to another person such as "We must have lunch" or "I'll call you," elevate or modulate your voice tone. Also, give at least a small smile and avoid a deadpan expression.

The focus now shifts to how various types of specific nonverbal communication can contribute to your effectiveness as a leader.

The Eyes Have It

When used congruently, the head, face, and eyes provide the clearest indication of attitude toward others. If you are addressing Carl, a group member, turn your head toward him, look at his face, and make eye contact. Your full attention suggests self-confidence and respect for Carl.

When you have good eye contact with the person you are addressing, that individual interprets what you have to say more favorably than if you avoid eye contact. If you make eye contact with group members in turn, they pay more attention to your message and perceive you as more confident.

Stand Up Straight!

Posture is perhaps the most obvious nonverbal signal of self-confidence and belief in yourself. Standing up straight generally reflects high self-confidence, whereas stooping and slouching indicate a poor self-image and weak leadership capability. Leaning toward other individuals suggests that you are favorably disposed toward them and what they have to say.

Personal Space

How far away do you stand from people you are attempting to influence? The distance can shape their perceptions of your effectiveness as a leader. If you are in actual physical contact with another person or up to 18 inches away, your message might be interpreted as a confidence or you might appear brash. However, you might also be perceived as intimidating or harassing.

Standing from one and a half to four feet from the person you're addressing is best for projecting face-to-face leadership. If you move from four to eight feet away from the person you're addressing, you might appear to be shying away from others.

Watch Your Hands!

Hand gestures provide an opportunity to project confidence and an in-charge attitude. Consider these possibilities:

Another Perspective

To strengthen your perception of the importance of good posture in creating a leadership image, visualize one or two of the political figures you admire the most. What is his or her posture like, even while seated? Or think of an outstanding sports leader (such as a coach). Carefully observe that individual's posture.

➤ Punch a fist into the air to mean "Let's do it!"

➤ Use a finger as a pointing rod to emphasize a point or to direct others.

➤ Use open-palm slapping of another person's hand to signify strong agreement or to offer congratulations.

➤ Extending both palms in the same motion required for pushing a heavy object communicates forcefully the message, "I don't want to hear any more of this."

➤ Extend a thumb upward indicating strong approval.

➤ The politician-like two arms raised in a V shape with the first two fingers of each hand also in a V shape is a high-power leadership gesture of unity and victory.

How Do You Sound?

People often attach more significance to the way you say something than to what you say. A forceful voice, which includes a consistent tone without vocalized pauses, suggests power, control, and confidence. A whispery, wimpy voice detracts from a confident and take-charge image. A voice coach surveyed 1,000 men and women and asked, "Which irritating or unpleasant voice annoys you the most?" The answer was a whining, complaining, or nagging tone. To improve your voice quality, try these techniques:

➤ Listen to your recorded voice. Keep repeating the same message until you are satisfied that you sound like a confident person.

➤ Several times per week, visualize yourself speaking to group members. Practice using the voice quality you think conveys confident leadership.

Your Time Is Important

A subtle form of nonverbal communication in the workplace is how you use your time. Guarding time as a precious resource helps you project self-confidence and leadership. A statement such as, "I can give 15 minutes to your problem this Thursday at 3:45 P.M." says to another that you are in control of yourself. Too many of these statements, however, might make you appear unapproachable and lacking consideration.

Be prompt for meetings and, if you are the leader, start and stop meetings on time. Jot down appointments in your day planner or electronic device in front of others. Make references to dates one year into the future and beyond, such as "By 2005, we should have a 40 percent market share."

Advisor

Suppose you've tried several specific nonverbal communication signals on one or two people, and you don't get the response you wanted. Keep trying. Recognize that a given nonverbal signal (such as punching your fist into the air) influences some people but not others. Combine a few nonverbal signals, such as moving toward the person and using effective hand gestures.

Sometimes observing what nonverbal signals the other person uses will help you influence that person. For example, if your influence target likes to gently punch the arm of another person for emphasis, maybe you can get through to that person by tapping his or her arm.

Do You Appear Confident, Friendly, and Approachable?

Another important use of body language is presenting a confident but friendly image in the workplace. Such behavior is typical of the team, or participative, style of leader.

Consider these nonverbal actions to indicate you are confident, friendly, and approachable:

➤ A loosened tie *and* slightly exposed throat can portray openness and informality (for men).

➤ Dominant people tend to stand with their toes pointing outward, whereas less dominant people point their toes slightly inward.

Key Word

Mirroring is copying the behavior of another person. For example, if the person you're talking with folds her arms, you fold yours as well. If the person crosses her legs, then you do it, too. Mirroring subtly tells others that you want to have rapport with them.

➤ Shrugged or rounded shoulders make you appear less threatening. Taking off a jacket with padded shoulders can make you appear less distant.

➤ Placing your forearms on the table, palms up, makes your words seem more sincere.

➤ Matching your body movements to those of the person you are communicating with (called *mirroring*) without being too obvious, creates a sense of solidarity that conveys a feeling of agreement with the other person.

The quickest way to improve your nonverbal communication is to relax. Take a deep breath and consciously allow your muscles to loosen. A relaxed person makes it easier for other people to relax, and you appear more confident and calm.

Hit 'Em with Your Power-Oriented Language Style

A major part of persuading others and communicating as a leader involves choosing the right language style. I've already mentioned several aspects of language, or *linguistic style*. Although what makes a person persuasive is not entirely certain, several components of language style generally give power and authority to the message sender. Many of the following suggestions are based on the long-term research of linguist Deborah Tannen:

➤ Downplay uncertainty. If you are not confident of your opinion or prediction, make a positive statement anyway, such as, "I know this new system will cure our inventory problems."

➤ Use the pronoun "I" to receive more credit for your ideas. (Of course, this could backfire in a team-based organization.)

➤ Apologize infrequently, and particularly minimize saying "I'm sorry."

➤ Offer negative feedback directly, rather than soften the feedback by first giving praise and then moving to the areas of criticism.

➤ Emphasize direct rather than indirect talk, such as saying, "I need your report by noon tomorrow" rather than "I'm wondering if your report will be available by noon tomorrow."

Using colorful, powerful words and a power-oriented communication style enhances the perception by others that you are a leader.

Key Word

A **linguistic style** is a person's characteristic speaking pattern. It involves such aspects of speech as amount of directness, pacing and pausing, word choice, and the use of communication devices such as jokes, figures of speech, anecdotes, questions, and apologies.

Junk Words and Pauses

Do you use any of these junk words or vocalized pauses?

➤ Like (used invariably before almost any expression)

➤ You know (to start almost any sentence and as a break within a sentence)

➤ You know what I'm saying?

➤ He goes (to mean he says)

➤ Uhhhhh

➤ Tatatatatatata (a low, breathy whistle used continuously while searching for information, especially over the telephone)

➤ Frequent clearing of the throat for no physical reason

An effective way to decrease the use of these extraneous words and nonwords is to tape your side of a phone conversation and then play it back. Once you hear how these junk words and vocalized pauses detract from your speech effectiveness, you begin to monitor your own speech patterns.

Hackneyed Clichés and Recycled Anecdotes

Clichés and familiar anecdotes can be helpful communication tools because they signify shared knowledge. Nevertheless, effective leaders use them sparingly. Here are a few overused expressions and anecdotes (if you've heard them once you've heard them a hundred times; okay, don't use that expression, either):

➤ Making an illogical, amusing statement (such as "Let's carefully plan what we did wrong last year") and then attributing it to Yogi Berra.

➤ "It's not over until the fat lady sings."

➤ "You can't make an omelet without breaking eggs."

➤ Telling people that Babe Ruth broke the record for home runs but that he also broke the record for strikeouts.

➤ To illustrate cross-cultural sensitivity, telling people the story about how Chevrolet ran into trouble marketing the Nova in Mexico because *nova* is a Spanish expression for "does not go."

➤ To illustrate serendipity, telling people the story about how Post-it notes were invented at 3M.

➤ To say "This isn't rocket science" about something not particularly difficult to understand. (Come to think of it, "This isn't rocket science" is a synonym for *"The Complete Idiot's Guide to …"*)

The problem with using threadbare clichés and anecdotes is that it makes you appear unimaginative, uninspired, and boring if the listener has heard the same thing several times before.

Does Every Noun Want to Be a Verb?

A while back in the business and government arenas, people started converting everyday nouns into verbs. The practice made sense. The pencil led people to say, "I'll pencil my comments directly on your memo," and the telephone became the basis for expressions such as "I'll telephone you tomorrow." Soon people were *photocopying, faxing,* and *e-mailing* each other. By 1996, in honor of the turnaround manager Al Dunlap, a company that was dramatically shrunk in size to reduce costs was said to have been *Dunlapped.*

Key Word

Although **nouning** is a common practice, these new verbs cannot be found in any dictionary. For example, does your dictionary have this verb—"anecdote your speeches"?

As a leader, you want to appear current, so it makes sense to go along somewhat with the movement toward *nouning.* However, too much nouning makes you sound bureaucratic, immature, and verbally challenged. Top executives convert far fewer nouns into verbs than do workers at lower levels. Perhaps you've gone too far when you regularly incorporate phrases such as the following into your language:

➤ Cell-phone me your response by noon.

➤ Red-mark anything you don't like in my report.

➤ Network the best people you know.

➤ We had better dot.com our company.

➤ Be careful not to Dilbert your employees.

Be Credible

No matter how dazzling you are as a communicator, you still need to be credible to be a truly effective communicator. Attempts at persuasion, including inspirational speaking and writing, begin with the credibility of the messenger. If the speaker is perceived as highly credible, the attempt at persuasive communication is more likely to be successful.

Being trustworthy heavily influences being perceived as credible. A leader with a reputation for lying will have a difficult time convincing people about the merits of a new initiative such as downsizing. Being perceived as intelligent and knowledgeable is another major factor contributing to credibility. The reputation of Bill Joy of Sun Microsystems as a genius contributes to his ability to inspire others. (Joy has been referred to as the Thomas Edison of the Internet.)

The Least You Need to Know

➤ To influence others, use heavy-impact, embellishing language.

➤ Metaphors, analogies, and anecdotes can be powerful tools for inspiring group members.

➤ The skillful use of nonverbal communication is a key part of communicating.

➤ A comprehensive approach to communicating like a leader is to use a power-oriented language style.

➤ To help project a leadership image, avoid detractors such as junk words, vocalized pauses, insipid clichés, threadbare anecdotes, and turning too many nouns into verbs.

➤ Be credible to enhance your communication effectiveness.

Chapter 6

How to Develop Credibility

In This Chapter

➤ Acting credible in an incredible world

➤ Developing your own ethical code

➤ A six-step guide to making ethical decisions

➤ Developing consistency between words and deeds

➤ Developing ways to look trustworthy

Jason is the owner of a rapidly growing cleaning service for offices, stores, and malls in north Florida. One Saturday morning, Jason was reviewing the company books. He noticed that one customer, a professional and medical building in Jacksonville, appeared to have double-paid one month's invoice. Monday morning, Jason stopped by the cubicle of company bookkeeper Nancy to discuss the situation.

Jason asked Nancy to investigate the apparent overpayment as soon as possible. Nancy followed through within an hour. She reported back to Jason at noon: "According to the customer's records, they did not pay double. Let's just keep the money as a little bonus. I bet we've underbilled many other customers."

"Absolutely not," said Jason. "Let's get to the bottom of the problem. I don't want to fight with a good customer about overpayment, but we must straighten out the account."

"Why all the fuss?" asked Nancy. "This is an overpayment, not an underpayment." Nancy finally straightened out the situation in the customer's favor. She thought about the incident for a few days, and then told her boss:

"Jason, that little incident with the customer who overpaid us helped me understand something important about you. I now know why the business is growing rapidly and our turnover is so low. Everybody trusts you."

Even if you are already honest and trustworthy, reading this chapter will help you enhance your leadership effectiveness. You will learn more about how trust enters into leadership and how to communicate trust to others. You will learn that projecting trust requires more than saying to group members, "I am not a crook."

Act Credible in an Incredible World

A few years ago, the American Management Association asked a panel of academics and other experts to describe the perfect leader for the modern business world. Integrity and trustworthiness were the two qualities at the top of the list that were considered essential for leadership.

Integrity centers around values. Leaders with integrity are strongly dedicated to doing what they know is right. A small example is Jason, who took the initiative to credit a customer for an overpayment. A bigger example is the reputation for *integrity* that Hewlett-Packard leadership has developed. Top management insists on never releasing a product with known deficiencies. This does not mean every Hewlett-Packard product is perfect. It does mean, however, that company leaders do not intentionally look the other way when defective products are shipped to customers.

Key Word

Integrity is an unswerving adherence to moral and ethical principles. A person with high integrity is seen as honorable.

Studies have repeatedly demonstrated the common-sense belief that people want leaders they can trust. Similarly, they want leaders who trust them. Integrity feeds trustworthiness because a leader with high integrity is trusted. Trust of business leaders has declined in recent years for several reasons:

➤ The disparity between compensation for top managers and compensation for workers has been increasing steadily. The average compensation of the business executives is 200 times that of a production worker.

➤ Many companies have continued to elevate executive pay while downsizing and cutting costs in other ways.

➤ Many employee pension funds have been depleted or eliminated despite legislation designed to protect pension funds. Large numbers of employees have been forced to retire without the benefit of a company pension to which they contributed for many years.

➤ Several well-known companies have been accused of exploiting child labor at overseas affiliates. Executives at these same companies are among the most elaborately paid and most celebrated as outstanding leaders.

➤ Top leaders at a few well-known companies have been accused of elaborate schemes of sexual harassment.

➤ Several telephone companies have been convicted of "slamming," or involuntarily switching many people's long-distance phone service to their company. Several of the firms involved forged written consents to make the switch.

As you can see, trustworthiness and honesty is a theme that runs through our analysis of leadership. Take the accompanying quiz for an analytical look at your trustworthiness.

Behaviors and Attitudes of a Trustworthy Leader

The following are behaviors and attitudes of leaders who are generally trusted by their group members and other constituents. After you read each characteristic check whether this is a behavior or attitude that you appear to have developed already or does not fit you at present.

	Fits Me	Does Not Fit Me
1. Tells people he or she is going to do something, and then always follows through and gets it done	❏	❏
2. Described by others as being reliable	❏	❏
3. Good at keeping secrets and confidences	❏	❏
4. Tells the truth consistently	❏	❏
5. Minimizes telling people what they want to hear	❏	❏
6. Described by others as "walking the talk"	❏	❏
7. Delivers consistent messages to others in terms of matching words and deeds	❏	❏
8. Does what he or she expects others to do	❏	❏
9. Minimizes hypocrisy by not engaging in activities he or she tells others are wrong	❏	❏
10. Readily accepts feedback on behavior from others	❏	❏
11. Maintains eye contact with people when talking to them	❏	❏
12. Appears relaxed and confident when explaining his or her side of a story	❏	❏

continues

continued

	Fits Me	Does Not Fit Me
13. Individualizes compliments to others rather than saying something like "You look great" to a large number of people	❑	❑
14. Doesn't expect lavish perks for himself or herself while expecting others to go on an austerity diet	❑	❑
15. Does not tell others a crisis is pending (when it isn't) just to gain their cooperation	❑	❑
16. Collaborates with others to make creative decisions	❑	❑
17. Communicates information to people at all organizational levels	❑	❑
18. Readily shares financial information with others	❑	❑
19. Listens to people and then acts on many of their suggestions	❑	❑
20. Generally engages in predictable behavior	❑	❑

Scoring: These statements are mostly for self-reflection, so no specific scoring key exists. However, the more of the preceding statements that fit you, the more trustworthy you are—assuming you are answering truthfully. The usefulness of this self-quiz increases if somebody who knows you well answers it for you to supplement your self-perceptions.

Advisor

Developing your sense of ethics helps you become more credible. A display of good ethics demonstrates that you are credible and honest. Given that ethical behavior is expected in almost all daily activities, it is necessary to behave ethically in a situation in which many others would act unethically. The study about Jason who returned an overpayment illustrates a display of good ethics. Another example would be to return a set of Super Bowl or major concert tickets to a vendor because you did not want your objectivity to be clouded.

Write Down What You Stand For

Given that most people want their leaders to be ethical, it is important to take constructive steps to be thoroughly ethical. Even if you have not been accused of being unethical, it still pays to ensure that you appear highly ethical to others. If others think you have a problem with ethical behavior, it could prevent you from obtaining a leadership position you desire or from being fully effective as a leader. A dynamic first step in elevating the ethical aura you create is to develop a *personal ethical code.* Write down what you consider to be right and wrong, good and bad, and ethical and unethical in the conduct of your job and career.

An ethical code determines what is right or wrong (or good or bad) based on values. You can find some hints for writing your ethical code by researching ethical codes developed for your company, industry, or profession. You might find a code of conduct in the company policy manual. Ask the receptionist in the office of your lawyer, physician, insurance representative, or investment broker for a copy of that field's ethical code. Yes, all of the preceding professions have written ethical codes. Company codes of ethics typically include entries such as the following:

Key Word

Your **personal ethical code** should not be filed and forgotten. Refer to it periodically to make sure you are following your moral compass.

➤ Comply with safety, health, and security regulations.

➤ Demonstrate courtesy, respect, honesty, and fairness.

➤ Exhibit good attendance and punctuality.

➤ Do not use abusive language.

➤ Do not offer bribes.

➤ Maintain confidentiality of records.

➤ Comply with accounting rules and controls.

➤ Do not use company property for personal benefit.

➤ Do not propagate false or misleading information.

➤ Do not sexually harass subordinates, co-workers, superiors, suppliers, or customers.

➤ Make decisions without regard for personal gain.

➤ Provide products and services of highest quality.

After you study a professional or company code of conduct, you might incorporate some of the ideas into your personal code of professional ethics. Also include in your personal code how far you will bend your rules in order to get ahead. Specify what is off-limits to you. Are you willing to take credit for the ideas of others? Back-stab? Laugh at jokes that you do not think are funny to please a key person?

Most people with a sense of common decency already know that such acts as accepting bribes, lying, and sexually harassing others are wrong. A code of ethics helps solidify your thinking and enables you to become a solid corporate citizen. As a result, your leadership stature will increase.

Advisor

Update your code as new workplace issues surface that involve ethics. For example, what about the ethics of putting stolen ideas or misleading information on your Web site? A new entry to your personal code might state, "I will not slam the competition on our Web site." Remember that your personal ethical code reflects your beliefs and values and is not necessarily based on the code of conduct used by your profession (such as accountants, purchasing agents, or engineers).

Jiffy Guide for Making Decisions in the Gray Zone

Many decisions are easy to evaluate with respect to ethics because they are obviously ethical or unethical. Tops Friendly Market, a large chain of supermarkets, decided to allocate one space in each store parking lot for expectant mothers. The sign is adorned with a stork. No need to ponder over the ethics of this decision. (Of course, women who are one or two month's pregnant face the ethical challenge of whether to hog the parking place.) At the unethical end of the continuum, there's also no need to ponder whether promoting friends of a family-owned business over more qualified candidates is ethical.

Ethical tests have been developed to help workers make choices about decisions in the gray zone—neither clearly right or wrong. Of course, what is in the gray zone depends on your values. Assume as a leader/manager you have decided that your exempt (from over-time regulations) employees should work Saturday mornings. A challenge you face is that the company has been downsized and it is deliberately understaffed.

You are contemplating using an interesting "motivator." You plan to casually mention to your staff that a large number of people in the labor market want their jobs. In other words, "If you don't like working Saturday mornings without extra pay, you can easily be replaced." You can run the contemplated decision through an ethical screen developed by the Center for Business Ethics at Bentley College. Ask yourself the following questions:

➤ **Is it right?** The question is based on the theory of ethics that there are certain universally accepted guiding principles of right and wrong, such as "Thou shall not take false credit for the ideas of others," or "Thou shall not play video games during working hours." Some people think that the implied threat of firing violates the guiding principle of "Thou shall not manipulate people with too much force."

➤ **Is it fair?** This question is based on the theory of justice implying that certain actions are just and other actions are unjust. Maybe it isn't fair to expect professionals to work every Saturday morning under the thinly veiled threat of being fired if they don't like it. Maybe, because the practice is not infrequent, it is fair. Remember, it's your call.

➤ **Who gets hurt?** This question is based on the notion of attempting to do the greatest good for the greatest number of people. Some people might say, "A lot of families will be hurt if a key family member has to work most Saturday mornings." Others might say, "If the exempt staff pulls together to increase company productivity, the company will be able to protect a lot of jobs."

➤ **Would you be comfortable if the details of your decision were reported on the front page of your local newspaper or through your company's e-mail system?** Would you mind seeing the headline "_____ Orders Professional Staff to Work Saturdays, Under Hint of Being Replaced"? Think it through.

➤ **Would you tell your child (or a young relative) to do it?** Visualize telling a six-year-old child, "I've got a great way of getting people to work on Saturday morning for no extra money. Let me tell you about it so you can do it in case you're the boss someday."

➤ **How does it smell?** This question is based on a person's intuition and common sense. Some people might say, "My plan smells rotten. What a way to treat people." Others might say, "It smells fine. A professional person does what it takes to get the job done."

That's enough lecturing about morality and ethics for now. The following self-quiz gives you something concrete for assessing your ethical beliefs.

The Ethical Reasoning Inventory

Describe how well you agree with each of the following statements. Use the following scale: Disagree strongly (DS); Disagree (D); Neutral (N); Agree (A); Agree strongly (AS).

	DS	D	N	A	AS
1. When applying for a job, I would cover up the fact that I had been fired from my most recent job.	5	4	3	2	1
2. Cheating just a few dollars in one's favor on an expense account is OK if a person needs the money.	5	4	3	2	1
3. Employees should inform on each other for wrongdoing.	1	2	3	4	5
4. It is acceptable to give approximate figures for expense account items when one does not have all the receipts.	5	4	3	2	1
5. I see no problem with conducting a little personal business on company time.	5	4	3	2	1
6. Just to make a sale, I would stretch the truth about a delivery date.	5	4	3	2	1
7. I would fix up a purchase order with a date just to close a sale.	5	4	3	2	1
8. I would flirt with my boss just to get a bigger salary increase.	5	4	3	2	1
9. If I received $500 for a one-time consulting job, I would report it on my income tax return.	1	2	3	4	5
10. I see no harm in taking home a few office supplies.	5	4	3	2	1
11. It is acceptable to read the e-mail messages and faxes of other workers, even when not invited to do so.	5	4	3	2	1
12. It is unacceptable to call in sick in order to take a day off, even if only done once or twice a year.	1	2	3	4	5
13. I would accept a permanent, full-time job even if I knew I wanted the job for only six months.	5	4	3	2	1
14. I would first check company policy before accepting an expensive gift from a supplier.	1	2	3	4	5
15. To be successful in business, a person usually has to ignore ethics.	5	4	3	2	1
16. If I felt physically attracted toward a job candidate I would hire that person over a more qualified candidate.	5	4	3	2	1
17. On the job, I tell the truth all the time.	1	2	3	4	5
18. Software should never be copied, except as authorized by the publisher.	1	2	3	4	5
19. I would authorize accepting an office machine on a 30-day trial period, even if I knew we had no intention of buying it.	5	4	3	2	1
20. I would never accept credit for a coworker's ideas.	1	2	3	4	5
TOTAL					

Scoring and interpretation: Add the numbers you circled to obtain your total score.

90 to 100: You are a strongly ethical person who may take a little ribbing from co-workers for being too straitlaced.

60 to 89: You show an average degree of ethical awareness and, therefore, should become more sensitive to ethical issues.

41 to 59: Your ethics are underdeveloped, but you at least have some awareness about ethical issues.

20 to 40: Your ethics are far below contemporary standards in business. Begin a serious study of business ethics.

Excuse My Cliché, but Walk the Talk

A major workplace issue today is whether employees trust their leaders and managers. In the long run, group members who trust their leaders are likely to be more satisfied and perform better. The number-one factor in gaining the trust of group members is to show consistency between intentions and actions. Consistency is, therefore, similar to congruence in communication, described in Chapter 5, "Communicate Like a Leader."

"Walking the talk" means consistency between words and deeds. Suppose a CEO says, "Don't worry; this merger won't result in any job loss." If layoffs are forthcoming, the leader will not be trusted in the future. Layoffs themselves may not erode trust, but false promises do.

Leaders can gain trust through being consistent in words and deeds in a variety of ways that group members will recognize. A sampling of these behaviors follow:

➤ Tell employees you trust them and then follow it up with open-book management in which employees are privy to financial information about the company. Educating employees about how a company makes money, what its profits are, and other financial information is important. It reduces suspicion and ignorance about company finances, elevates trust, and improves morale.

➤ Avoid *mixed messages*. Leaders who deliver a consistent message are trusted the most.

➤ Ask for feedback on how well your intentions are lining up with your behavior. Ask riveting questions such as, "What commitments have I made that I didn't follow through?"

Key Word

A **mixed message** is a communication that has a built-in inconsistency or discrepancy, such as saying to the sales staff, "Complete honesty is our policy, but remember to charge whatever the traffic will bear."

➤ Keep careful track of what you promise group members, and verify for yourself whether words and deeds correspond.

➤ Conduct yourself in the way you ask others to conduct themselves. If you preach that others should practice good human relations, practice good human relations yourself.

➤ Minimize hypocrisy. For example, if you condemn others for wasting corporate resources, don't take elaborate business trips for yourself or ornately decorate your office. During Michael Ovitz's brief stay as the president of Disney Corporation, he hired six secretaries for himself while preaching frugality. As a result, some Disney employees distrusted him.

➤ Tell the truth. It is much easier to be consistent when you do not have to keep patching up your story to conform to an earlier lie.

➤ When your organization or organizational unit encounters a problem, move into the problem-solving mode instead of looking to blame others for what went wrong.

Advisor

It takes a leader a long time to build trust, yet one brief incident of untrustworthy behavior can permanently destroy trust. Leaders are usually allowed a fair share of honest mistakes. In contrast, dishonest mistakes erode leadership effectiveness quickly. You may recall the general who was charged with sexually harassing another general (the highest ranking woman in the military). Reporting to the first general was the military unit that investigated sexual harassment. His credibility plummeted faster than the stock market after the Federal Reserve hikes interest rates.

Stop Wearing Your Sunglasses Indoors

Developing the trust of others generally involves your inner core and your actions. If you communicate your ethical beliefs and if your actions match your words, group members will trust you. However, it is also important to *look* trustworthy.

Certain aspects of appearance and other facets of nonverbal behavior communicate the message that a person can be trusted. Some nonverbal indicators suggest a person of questionable trustworthiness. You can consciously control whether you show some of these indicators of trust or distrust. Other indicator behaviors are based on your genes and are, therefore, tough to modify.

Give careful consideration to the following aspects of nonverbal behavior that influence whether others will readily perceive you to be trustworthy or untrustworthy:

➤ Smiling frequently suggests authenticity as opposed to smiling constantly, which suggests a cover-up for real feelings.

➤ Smiling symmetrically suggests authenticity. In contrast, a crooked smile suggests duplicity.

➤ Flashing brief smiles and other facial expressions such as frowning suggests authenticity. In contrast, prolonged facial expressions suggest a lack of authenticity.

➤ Maintaining eye contact without staring sends a signal of trustworthiness.

➤ Being well dressed sends a signal of trustworthiness. However, don't be so well dressed that it appears you are hiding behind your clothing.

➤ Being well coifed helps create an impression of trustworthiness. However, your hair shouldn't be so gorgeous that it commands more attention than you do.

➤ Maintaining a relaxed, easy manner in front of others instead of fidgeting projects trust.

➤ Using a friendly, warm gaze instead of a beady-eyed look helps you appear trustworthy.

➤ Generally looking ahead and sideways contributes to a trustworthy image. Suddenly and frequently turning your head around makes others think you are paranoid and, therefore, difficult to trust.

➤ Keeping your eyes generally at least two-thirds open suggests trustworthiness, but squinting looks dishonest.

➤ Frequent nose rubbing usually suggests dishonesty or at least severe unease.

➤ Wearing sunglasses indoors (unless you are a celebrity, sports figure, or other entertainer) connotes deception and perhaps criminal activity.

Watch Out!

In addition to nonverbal indicators of trustworthiness, avoid projecting suspicion by constantly using phrases such as, "To be candid," "Let me be honest with you," "To tell the truth," and "Trust me on this one." All of these expressions send the gentle hint that on other occasions, you are not so truthful.

The Least You Need to Know

➤ Achieve credibility by showing integrity.

➤ Develop your own personal code to guide your daily decision-making.

➤ Test the ethics of a contemplated decision by running the decision through a six-point test.

➤ Develop a consistency between words and deeds by "walking the talk."

➤ Project an image of trustworthiness by an honest appearance.

Part 2

Act Like a Leader

Have you ever wondered why professional photographers and serious amateurs never produce photos in which their subjects look as though they are wearing raccoon masks? The reason is that the expert photographer adjusts lighting properly. In contrast, the low-skilled photographer shoots first and regrets mistakes later. It might take wonderful intuition and talent to be a competent photographer, but there are still procedures to follow if you want great photos.

Leadership, like photography, is more art than science, but this does not mean that leadership is an entirely intuitive process with no prescribed actions. In this part of the book, you will learn about many of the specific actions leaders take to accomplish their intended results. Effective leaders are aware of influence tactics such as thumping the table for effect and linking up with powerful people. Another action they take is maintaining cultural sensitivity. You won't see a multicultural leader using North American nonverbal signs overseas that alienate customers and work associates. You'll also learn how to formulate visions that get workers all fired up to help the company create a great future. (Well, at least some of the time!)

Your Tool Kit of Influence Tactics

Plant manager Max was discussing his performance for the previous year with Derek, his boss, the vice president of manufacturing. Max began the evaluation session by answering Derek's question about his key accomplishments:

"It's been a wonderful year in terms of stability. Our plant achieved the same high level of performance it did in the year before I took over. You'll notice that the plant was, again, one of the best in the company in terms of quality. Safety was pretty good, also. We only had four more lost-time accidents than in the previous year. I'm pretty proud of what I was able to achieve in my first year as plant manager."

While scratching his right cheekbone with his index finger and looking at Max, Derek said, "Max, you're right. You maintained the status quo. I can't fault you on that. But where was your leadership? What did you influence your staff to do differently than they did in the past?"

Another Perspective

Influence tactics are important in all leadership situations. After a retired nurse joined a bike club, she found that the outings left her with just an agenda and a road map. During the next two meetings of the club, she convinced the group that new club members wanted the companionship of other bikers. Now, the experienced club members make sure that nobody is left to bike alone.

Key Word

Leading by example is influencing others by acting as a positive role model. To reinforce the message that cultural diversity is important in the organization, several business executives have hired male assistants. Also, the hearing president of a college with a large deaf student population delivers major speeches in words and sign language simultaneously.

"When we put you in this position, Max, we expected you to accomplish something unusual. You just grabbed on to momentum that was already in place."

Derek has a point. The essence of leadership is to produce an influential increment over what would exist if the leader were not present. In this chapter, you will learn about a handful of highly effective tactics for influencing others in the workplace. As a consequence, you will exercise leadership.

You Are a Role Model

A simple but effective way of influencing group members is to lead by example. You should act as a positive role model so others can learn from your actions and attitudes. The ideal approach to *leading by example* is to be a "do as I say and do" leader.

Be sure your actions and words are consistent. Your actions and words should confirm, support, and clarify each other. Without such consistency, you lose credibility and people stop respecting you as a leader. Develop a reputation for being the type of person you tell others to be. Treat people in the same gracious and refined manner with which you want them to treat others.

You will obtain a better perspective on leading by example by becoming familiar with several different areas where the technique is especially relevant.

Get the Corporate Culture Across to People

A major job for any top leader is to build, strengthen, or reinforce the corporate culture. As you probably already know, the corporate culture is the values and beliefs of an organization that guide the actions of workers. As a leader, you can communicate values and expectations by your actions. Particularly well-suited to leading by example are actions showing loyalty, self-sacrifice, and service to the company beyond the call of duty. An example of service beyond the call of duty is the supermarket store manager who jumps in to open a new check-out lane during a period of peak activity.

Demonstrate What Good Customer Service Means

Good customer service is the watchword of business success. If your work involves customer contact, dedicate yourself to following through on commitments. Answer inquiries and complaints cheerfully. Avoid the temptation to mock the thorniest customers. Your high regard for the welfare of customers will be noticed by group members.

Anecdotes are often used to communicate the meaning of good customer service. Fred Smith, the founder of FedEx, used to tell the following story to managers to influence them about the importance of customer service (as reported in *Managers Edge*).

A blizzard shut down a radio relay located on top of a mountain, cutting phone service to several FedEx offices. The phone company said it would take five days to repair the problem. On his own, a FedEx telecommunications expert named Hal chartered a helicopter to get to the site. The pilot was unable to land, but he got close enough to the ground for Hal to jump and land safely. Hal slogged through the deep snow and fixed the problem.

The same anecdote brings us back to the importance of trust. According to Smith, Hal went to such great lengths to keep the organization serving customers properly because there was mutual trust between employer and employee. Hal knew he would not be reprimanded for going to such expense to fix the telephone problem.

Treat Company Policy with Respect

Most organizations have policies covering various aspects of employee behavior, such as absenteeism, tardiness, and honesty. Communicating these policies clearly and abiding by them yourself is effective leadership. Managers who grumble about policies and procedures encourage rule-bending by others. Avoid ignoring certain rules that you find inconvenient, such as prohibitions against hiring relatives into your department. If you disagree with certain policies, combat them by discussing your concerns with top management. It's shabby leadership to use group members as a sounding board for your dissatisfactions.

Watch Out!

Many people confuse superior work habits with being a workaholic. The opposite is true. People with superior work habits are so well organized that they have a reasonable amount of time for family life and recreation. So strive to have excellent work habits without sliding into workaholism.

Demonstrate Sparkling Work Habits

Group members will often look to you to set the pace in terms of intensity, hours on the job, and number of rest breaks. If you, as the leader, treat time as a precious resource, the workers in your area will likely intensify the pace of their work. Hours on the job also have an impact. A leader who appears to be out of the office too frequently for nonwork reasons may soon find that staffers are shortening their work weeks.

Do Your Share of Dirty Work

Leading by example is an excellent vehicle for demonstrating that certain undesirable, or even dangerous, tasks are of utmost importance. Managers at Florida-based Sunshine Cleaning Systems sometimes clean toilets and urinals for two reasons. The managers want to demonstrate the right way to clean bathrooms. At the same time, they communicate the fact that cleaning toilets and urinals is not degrading (especially when it's your core business!).

Another example of being a role model when it comes to executing tough tasks occurred at Xerox Corporation. A payroll manager from the Webster, New York, facility drove a snowmobile through a blizzard just to make sure that paychecks were delivered on time.

Show People What It Means to Act Professionally

What constitutes "professional behavior" varies widely from company to company. If you want to teach others the meaning of professional behavior, you must first define it for yourself. A useful interpretation of acting professionally is to behave with dignity, emotional maturity, and in such a way that people trust your judgment. At an open meeting between top management and plant employees, one of the employees shouted out, "I think the new management sucks. We work harder than ever and get peanuts for a raise." The plant manager responded to the unprofessional behavior quite professionally by saying, "You are entitled to your dissatisfaction. Remember though, we are trying to stay competitive so we can keep the plant open."

Next, strive to act professionally. If you expect group members to act professionally around customers and visitors, you should act professionally around the same groups. Equally important, you should also act professionally around the people who work for you.

Create a good impression by expressing positive attitudes about the company, your job, customers, and the company's goods and services. If you are pessimistic, your negative attitudes are soon reflected by members of the work group.

Be a Paragon of Health, Safety, and Appearance

Organizations are quite health-conscious, so it is important for you to talk about physical fitness and to appear fit yourself. One example of health-consciousness is the fact that most large organizations have wellness and physical fitness programs. Furthermore, companies are working assiduously to reduce premiums for health care by having fewer claims. This means encouraging employees to maintain good health and prevent illness (the state of wellness).

It is also important to talk about and demonstrate safety. How to demonstrate safety varies with the work site. Wearing a hard hat even in areas where not required symbolizes safety. Avoiding the reputation of a speeder is important. Keeping your own work area so cluttered that people can trip over boxes and computer peripherals on the floor would be an example of demonstrating poor safety.

The type of clothing you wear to work often influences others. An accolade often given to well-respected managers and leaders is they dress professionally. Professionalism in dress generally refers to appearing stylish without overdoing it and wearing clean, freshly pressed clothing. The same applies for casual day. Wearing a T-shirt imprinted with a vulgarity would be considered unprofessional by many.

Advisor

Suppose you are leading by example by maintaining a positive outlook about the company and top management. However, you still find too much griping and sniping among your group members. Reinforce your leading by example with specific comments about why you behave the way you do. You might say, "I could groan and moan with the rest of you, but instead, I try to appreciate the strengths of our employer. It's good for morale and productivity to be positive."

Evangelists Make Good Leaders

To be a leader, one must inspire others to accomplish worthwhile goals. A natural method is the *inspirational appeal,* or influencing another person to act in a particular way by triggering a strong emotional response. The information presented in Chapter 4, "How About a More Charismatic You?" will help you inspire others. The techniques for high-impact communications presented in Chapter 5, "Communicate Like a Leader," will also go a long way toward helping you be inspirational. Here, I present additional techniques a leader can use to inspire others in the workplace.

What Do You Want People to Do or Feel?

The starting point in making an inspirational appeal is to identify what you want people to do or feel. Then you choose the words, phrases, and ideas that fit your goal. For example, as a manager you might be discouraged with the lax attitude people have toward their workplace's cleanliness and tidiness. Your goal is for the workers to maintain a near-spotless work area, so your inspirational appeal to fit the situation might include comments such as …

➤ "How would you like to start looking like winners?"

➤ "A neighbor of mine visited our Japanese competitor last week. He couldn't help noticing that the factory looked as clean as a dealer showroom."

➤ "If we want others to think we are professionals, we have to start looking like professionals."

➤ "Do you think our office looks good enough to entertain young visitors on Take Your Daughter to Work Day?"

Key Word

An **inspirational appeal** is influencing another person by appealing to a strong emotion, such as patriotism, dislike for the competition, or family values. A plant manager might say, "If we can't raise our productivity 15 percent, the competition will snuff us out. When we have no jobs, how are we going to take care of our children?"

Appeal to Key Values

A basic tactic for inspiring others is to trigger thoughts related to strongly held (or key) values. Appealing to strong values is important because it leads to a commitment to the task from group members. These key values in the workplace include being the best, outperforming the competition, maintaining loyalty to the company, enhancing one's status, and being a good corporate citizen. A marketing manager in a company that makes sunglasses made the following pitch that revved up the sales group that works with dealers: "Aren't you guys tired of losing market share? Three years ago we had 35 percent of the market for upscale sport sunglasses. The newcomers into the field have beaten our share down to 20 percent. When are we going to retaliate?"

Another Perspective

Visions have to be carefully crafted to do their job of inspiring workers. It is important to periodically remind others of the vision to use it as an inspirational force. The vision created by leaders at CNN is a good example: "To create the first truly global information company, the global network of record, seen in every nation on the planet, and broadcast in most major languages."

Formulate an Awesome Vision

The vision a leader formulates should inspire others. For example, the vision that inspires employees at a Pepsi-Cola bottling plant in Springfield, Missouri, emphasizes their wish to be one of the highest-quality Pepsi bottling plants in the world. Your vision should not be the same as every other company's vision. Each company should develop a unique vision. A superlative example is IBM's current vision: "To lead big companies into the brave, new networked world."

Use High-Impact Words and Phrases

Each time you attempt an inspirational appeal, sprinkle your talk with high-impact words and phrases. Consult a thesaurus to enlarge your repertoire of high-impact words. You want workers in your unit to be more safety-conscious. In addition to stating that safety regulations must be observed, you might mention …

➤ "I don't want to see or hear about another crushed body in our factory."

➤ "Each month a few more computer users are crippling their wrists for life—all because of negligence on our part."

➤ "We need a safe, secure, and people-friendly environment."

Ask the Right Questions

An effective inspirational technique is to ask people questions that result in emotion-provoking answers. Your question prompts group members to give answers that stir their emotions and lead them to action. The question asked earlier in this chapter, "How would you like to start looking like winners?" is a good example. Asking a question is often better than simply making a statement such as, "I want you to start looking like winners." Answering a question results in more mental activity and commitment than simply listening to a message.

Advisor

Asking the right questions is a high-level leadership skill to develop, as described in the discussion about tough questions in Chapter 3, "How Do Leaders Think?" Here are a few more "right" questions for influencing others:

➤ "How would you like our department to get the recognition it deserves?"

➤ "Can you give me a good reason why we can't all double our commissions next year?"

➤ "How would you like our group to be labeled 'world class'?"

➤ "What fun is there in producing less profit than any other division in the corporation?"

Inspire People with Success Stories

Sharing success stories is a natural way of inspiring others to extend themselves. Browse through media sources and books for stories about ordinary people who rose to great heights of achievement. People are often inspired by stories of people similar to themselves who began a business in their kitchen or garage and built it into a national or world leader. For example, Mrs. Field's cookies had their humble origins in a homemaker's kitchen.

Can You See, Feel, Touch, and Taste It?

Another tactic for making an inspirational appeal is to appeal to more than one sense. You want people to hear your message, but you also want them to see it, feel it, touch it, and taste it. As in using visual imagery, encourage people to imagine the total experience of achieving the goal you believe is important. The manager facing an extraordinarily difficult deadline might inspire the group to achieve the goal with such statements as:

Watch Out!

To achieve rapid results with your inspirational appeals, follow up with a concrete plan of action. Without a plan of action, your inspirational statements may fizzle quickly. If you have *inspired* workers about the importance of elevating quality, involve them in actively developing an a plan to do this.

➤ "Can you imagine what it will *look* like to see 200,000 of these units packaged and loaded into trucks?"

➤ "Just think of how your family members will *squeal* with delight when you tell them you have earned a bonus of 50 percent of your annual salary."

➤ "Imagine how *relaxed* your body will feel after we achieve this momentous accomplishment."

➤ "We are on the way to our most profitable year in a decade. Can you just *taste* the great wine and food that will be served at our victory banquet?"

Be Personally Magnetic

Another way of influencing people is closely tied in with charisma and inspirational appeal. A personally magnetic individual literally draws other people to him or her with charm and charismatic-like qualities. The people who are drawn to the magnetic individual are likely to be influenced by him or her.

Personal magnetism also refers to a collection of personality traits that can be developed along the same lines as charisma. Many of the leaders mentioned in this book have high personal magnetism. Carly Fiorina, the top executive at Hewlett-Packard, is an outstanding example. People who know her describe her as glamorous, radiant, and warm. Fiorina's warmth makes her approachable. As a consequence, employees are not hesitant to bring problems to her attention.

Release Your Emotions at the Right Time

Part of inspiring people is making tactical use of emotional displays. By showing your emotions and feelings for effect, you are using them in a tactical, planned manner.

The emotions a leader displays for effect can be negative or positive. Table-thumping works because it shows people you are serious and triggers an emotional response in them. Outbursts of positive emotion are also helpful in triggering an emotional response from group members. Cheering wildly, laughing suddenly, or crying with joy can all boost leadership effectiveness.

The following suggestions will help you make good use of displays of emotion and feeling:

➤ **Be selective.** Save emotional displays for rare occasions. Otherwise, you appear to be emotionally volatile and perhaps unfit for your leadership role.

➤ **Be explicit.** Explain your feelings. Make statements such as, "I'm so disappointed that we missed our target again," or "I feel incredibly good that we produced 30 percent beyond what anybody imagined we could."

➤ **Be real.** Concentrate so that your nervous system matches your emotion. For example, if your eyes widen and blood rushes to your skin when you are screaming, you are more effective than if you don't experience anger inside.

➤ **Be ready.** Practice showing positive and negative emotion even when you don't feel that way inside. An inspirational leader can flip the toggle switch for emotional displays as needed.

Keep clearly in mind that making effective use of emotion is necessary to function as an inspiring leader. This is true because inspiration does not take place without emotion.

Key Word

Personal magnetism refers to a captivating, inspiring personality with charm and charismatic-like qualities. As such, magnetism encompasses more than charisma. Like high quality, good art, and elegant design, you know personal magnetism when you see it.

Watch Out!

Inspirational appeals and emotional displays are an important part of charismatic leadership. However, if you are constantly emotional, you detract from your image of being a reflective, strategic thinker. Also, being a drum beater all the time can be cloying. Inspirational appeals and emotional displays should be executed selectively.

"Hey, I'd Like Your Input"

Consulting with others before making a decision is a simple but effective influence tactic. The *influence target* becomes more motivated to follow your request because he or she is involved in the decision-making process. Consultation is most effective as an influence tactic when the objectives of the person being influenced match those of the leader. Keep these suggestions in mind when using consultation:

➤ When you consult another person, avoid making it appear that you (the *influence agent*) have already made up your mind. Otherwise, you appear patronizing.

➤ Tactfully rebut unusable suggestions. A marketing manager at the Cadillac division of General Motors asked a dealer who should be included on a direct mailing list to introduce the Catera (a new model at the time). The dealer replied, "Everybody in the country making more than $50,000 per year." The manager replied tactfully, "Sounds like a hefty investment, but I like your suggestion to be comprehensive."

Nothing Like Being the Resident Genius

Becoming a *subject matter expert* (*SME*) on a topic of importance to the organization is an effective strategy for gaining influence. Being an SME is a subset of influencing others through persuading them rationally. Being the "go-to guy or gal" with respect to an important topic or skill makes you more credible—even outside your area of expertise.

The area of expertise for an SME is wide open. You could gain specialized knowledge in information technology, understanding of a particular market, or high-level skill in a foreign language. At present, knowing enterprise software, such as SAP, is hot, hot, hot. An advertising agency in New York state received a big contract to advertise Air France in the United States. The agency needed somebody on staff to speak French to the client representative in France. A French-Canadian on the staff came to the rescue. Her ability to build rapport with the client hastened her promotion to Account Supervisor, enabling her to exercise more leadership.

Set Up a Favor Bank

Offering to exchange favors if another person helps you is another standard influence tactic. By making an exchange, you strike a bargain with the other party. The exchange often translates into willingness to reciprocate at a later date. The exchange might also include promising a share of the benefits if the other person helps you accomplish a task. For example, you might promise to place a person's name on a report to top management if that person analyzes the data and prepares the tables.

Exchanging and bargaining can also be considered building a favor bank. In other words, you do favors for people today with the expectation that you can make a withdrawal from the favor bank when needed. A human resources manager took the initiative to help a colleague in another company recruit a physically disabled compensation analyst. Several months later, the same human resources professional called on the colleague to nominate her for office in their professional society.

Here are three suggestions for making the tricky act of asking for favors more likely to succeed:

➤ When asking for a favor, give the other person as much time as possible to accomplish the task, by saying, for example: "Could you find 10 minutes between now and the end of the month to help me?" Not pressing for immediate assistance will also tend to lower resistance to the request.

➤ Giving a menu of options for different levels of assistance also helps lower resistance. As a manager, you might ask another manager to borrow a technician for a one-month assignment. A second option might be to request that the technician work 10 hours per week on the project.

➤ To ensure that any request is perceived as an exchange, specify the kind of reciprocity you have in mind, such as mentioning a co-worker's helpfulness to his or her manager.

Manipulate Others and Still Like Yourself in the Morning

Many people cringe when they hear or read the term "manipulation," especially in relation to leadership. If leaders are supposed to be models of ethics and trustworthiness, how can they be manipulative at the same time? The answer depends on how you define *manipulation*.

Suppose you perceive manipulation to be a devious influence tactic in which you trick the unsuspecting

Key Word

Manipulation, as described here, is an indirect, subtle, and covert method of influencing others that may or may not involve some deception. Deception involves straying from the truth, but not in a big way, and being tricky. If you are super-ethical, you probably will avoid deception.

target into doing something he or she never wanted to do. Furthermore, what you get the person to do is against that individual's best interests. There is no question that an effective leader should not engage in that type of manipulation.

Suppose, instead, that you perceive manipulation as a subtle or indirect influence tactic that may be necessary to help people achieve ends that will benefit both themselves and the organization.

Manipulation is sometimes necessary because more direct influence tactics might not be effective in a given circumstance. Manipulation, therefore, has an important place in leadership, given that a leader's major job is to influence others. Used unethically, however, manipulative tactics will backfire, undermining the leader's credibility and ability to influence others.

A challenge in applying manipulation is that specific techniques are rarely spelled out. People often say, "I'm being manipulated," but they fail to describe exactly what is happening to them. The following sections describe three manipulation techniques that leaders find useful.

The Bandwagon Technique

Everyone who has been exposed to advertising has experienced the bandwagon technique. This technique influences another person by pointing out that others are engaging in the prescribed activities. Here's how it works:

Sherri is the manager of information systems. Sherri's boss is dragging his heels on investing money in a Web site with links to other sites. To overcome her boss's resistance, Sherri informs her boss, "I've done some research on Web sites. We're the only company our size lacking one. Furthermore, we're losing out on some luscious commissions by not having links to the major players. What should we do next?" Her boss replies, "If that's the case, let's set one up right away."

To make effective use of the bandwagon technique, consider the following in your approach:

➤ Point to a specific reference group (such as other companies similar in size to yours) rather than the vague statement "Everybody is doing it."

➤ Avoid using the technique with people who pride themselves on being nonconformists. These people prefer to resist doing what everybody else is doing.

➤ Be specific about what you want your influence target to do. Tell him or her what you expect, but not necessarily how to do it.

➤ Make your influence target feel good about having moved in the desired direction. State that he or she has made a wise decision.

One reason the bandwagon technique often works is that many people have a strong need to affiliate with others. They feel good when doing what others are doing.

Joking and Kidding

Good-natured kidding is especially effective whenever a straightforward statement might be interpreted as harsh criticism. Joking or kidding can get the message across and lower the risk that the person you want to influence will be angry. Here is an example of using joking and kidding to influence a procrastinating team member to be more prompt:

> **Team Leader:** It looks as though I made an error when I gave you the date for completing your input to the project.
>
> **Team Member:** I didn't know you made an error. You told me June 30.
>
> **Team Leader:** Yes, but because it's now July 15, I assume I must have told you June 30 of next year.
>
> **Team Member:** (Laughs) I feel terrible. Give me two or three more days, and my portion will be done.

The leader was criticizing the team member in such a gentle way that this person got the point without becoming defensive.

Advisor

Joking and kidding is a particularly useful technique when you want to influence someone over whom you have little or no formal authority. If you need to get a higher authority to back you up to get somebody to act, you appear weak. In this case, an indirect (or manipulative) influence tactic may be useful. The joking and kidding should get your point across, but watch out for moving into the zone of hostile humor. It might be okay to say to a co-worker, "I know you have been so busy networking that you haven't had time to get me the information I need." However, don't say, "I know you've been so busy kissing up to people."

Hint at an Implied Benefit

Using the implied benefit technique, the influence agent alludes to certain advantages that may be forthcoming from complying with his or her demands. For example, some workers might resist a six-month assignment to a task force that they believe will be boring and unproductive. The influence agent states, "This task force could be a great opportunity. Performing on a task force is a wonderful way to get noticed by higher management."

The reluctant group members accept the task force assignment. If any one of them benefits professionally, the leader will have manipulated the individual into an activity that not only helped the organization but was also personally rewarding.

Do I Use Influence Tactics Alone or in Combination?

To get the most out of influence tactics, it might be necessary to use them in combination. One tactic alone might not get the job done. You must choose tactics carefully on the basis of the influence target and your objectives. Here are a few key points to consider:

➤ Begin with a gentle approach and then proceed to a stronger approach if necessary. For example, you might begin by leading by example, and then if the person does not comply, shift to manipulation.

➤ The joking and kidding technique is likely to work better with subordinates and co-workers than with superiors. A higher-ranking person often resents being kidded by a person of lower rank.

➤ Research by industrial psychologists shows that the most effective tactics include using rational arguments, inspirational appeal, and consultation. You might try a combination of all three tactics for heavy-duty influence attempts.

The Least You Need to Know

➤ Influence others by leading by example and displaying emotion.

➤ Being personally magnetic is a general way of influencing people.

➤ Reciprocity remains one of the most effective influence tactics.

➤ Consulting with others is an effective way to get them to see your way of thinking.

➤ Become a subject matter expert to enhance your ability to influence others.

➤ Manipulating others must always be done ethically.

Chapter 8

Grabbing Power

In This Chapter

➤ Developing a network of power contacts

➤ Acquiring power by working on critical problems

➤ Getting people on your side by forming coalitions

➤ Developing the right image for your group

➤ Bringing in an outside expert

Angelica is an industrial engineer who works for a manufacturer of industrial pumps. One day she notices that her colleague Jerry has a book about office politics on his desk. Angelica asks Jerry about his interest. Jerry responds that you have to understand office politics to succeed. With a quizzical expression, Angelica replies:

"Oh no, Jerry, you have it wrong. Now the emphasis is on teamwork. People throughout organizations are working together in harmony to achieve mutual goals. They all know that only through teamwork and total cooperation can the company capture a competitive advantage."

"Today managers even work cooperatively with competitors to form strategic alliances. Besides that, they know that competitive advantage can only be achieved by working with—not against—people. The era of backbiting, back-stabbing, and power-grabbing is over."

Angelica has an angelic and purist view of the workplace, as do many popular management gurus. She is partially right. The emphasis on teamwork and cooperation has at least slowed down competition for power, much in the same way the slogan "Speed kills" reduced some instances of highway speeding. However, as organizations continue to tighten their belts even in prosperous times, scrambling for power remains critical for leaders. World-wide competition is another factor driving down prices and, therefore, placing pressure on managers and other workers to reduce costs. Because resources, such as budgets and personnel, are scarcer, competition for them is more intense. Without power, a leader cannot achieve his or her objectives.

In this chapter, I describe a handful of basic tactics for acquiring power for yourself and your group. Previous discussions of how to become more charismatic and how to exert influence should also be considered ways of enhancing power.

Key Word

The ability or potential to influence decisions and control resources means you have **power.** Simply put, a powerful person can get things done and make things happen.

The Right Internal and External Networks Can Bring You Power

Networking is widely recognized as the number-one method for finding a job and keeping in touch professionally. Making systematic use of internal (within your company) and external (outside your company) contacts can pay big dividends in acquiring more *power* for yourself. As you, yourself, acquire more power, so does your group.

The people in your network can be a useful source of information about potential customers and reliable suppliers and can help you solve difficult problems. The link to power is that information is a major source of power. External contacts also provide power.

How Your Network Members Can Enhance Your Power

I just mentioned a few of the standard benefits of having a good network. Here are some additional ways you can benefit from your internal and external networking, all of which can give you a power edge:

➤ **Exchange of information.** What is top management thinking? What personnel changes are forthcoming, and what implications do these changes have for your group? Are there any merger rumors circulating? Answers to these questions give you some gossip power.

➤ **Quick answers.** How reliable is a given vendor? Where can you locate reliable, temporary workers for telemarketing in a hurry? Obtaining quick answers helps you solve problems rapidly—enhancing your leadership stature.

➤ **Support for your ideas.** You have an idea that you want to try, but you're uncertain of how your boss will react. Support from others might be just what you need to sway your boss. For example, one manager felt the time was right for the company to establish an overseas affiliate in India. He arranged a three-way luncheon with himself, his boss, and a network member whose firm had achieved recent success in the Indian market. The positive comments of the luncheon guest helped sway the boss's thinking toward doing business in India.

➤ **Emergency assistance.** Well-placed people in your network can help you resolve unanticipated, urgent problems. For example, you could borrow talent or supplies from another team or department to tide you over a problem.

How to Assemble a World-Class Network

To acquire power through a strong network, you have to go through the rigors of establishing and maintaining one. Almost any person of power, influence, competence, charm, or wealth is worth incorporating into your network.

The starting point in establishing a network is obtaining an ample supply of business cards that include standard information along with your phone and fax numbers and e-mail address. You then give that card to any person you meet who appears to fit your criteria for your network.

Recognize, of course, that most of your cards will be discarded—mentally, physically, or both. You are doing well if 10 percent of your initiatives result in cooperative network members.

Advisor

A key point to remember in building a network of strong people is that many others are also approaching these same individuals. Many powerful people, for example, are highly selective about whose network they join. Tread lightly in asking a powerful person to join you for lunch. If you want a person to be part of your network, stand ready to explain how you can help that person. What are the benefits of being part of your network? For example, are you willing to be a customer of your contact's company? Are you willing to get that person some valuable publicity?

In addition to passing out business cards, follow these specific suggestions for building your network:

➤ **Connect.** Get connected through friends and acquaintances you already have, especially the well-connected ones. Being a friend of a friend is a quick way to establish mutual trust and cooperation.

➤ **Join.** Befriend competent and successful people. Winners can do more for you so they are your most valuable network members. The same strategy can be used to impress people in your network. Other people are more eager to enter your network if they think they are joining a select group.

➤ **Branch out.** Diversify your luncheon companions, but as noted previously, recognize that some people regard luncheon appointments as an inconvenience. Arrange group luncheons of up to five people if possible. Each new member of your network may make your name known to a few more people, thus multiplying your number of direct and indirect contacts.

➤ **Volunteer.** Extend yourself to create a good impression at trade shows, seminars, and professional meetings. A potent tactic is to take a leadership role of any kind. Take your turn at a booth, be a panelist or discussant, or arrange to make even a brief presentation. If your organization will pay for it, schedule a happy hour in your room. Potential network members will be impressed with your generosity.

➤ **Socialize.** Stop to chat briefly with anybody you think is a worthwhile inclusion in your network.

➤ **Share.** Share credit with people outside your work group for accomplishments that involved the outsiders in any way. When other people offer congratulations, mention anyone else who deserves to share credit. The outsiders who receive credit may become part of your network or allies at a minimum.

Another Perspective

Another way to build your network of useful contacts is to arrange an informal event that is intellectually stimulating, fun, and arranged at a time and place that minimizes inconvenience. Anna, a project manager, arranged a coffee-and-dessert hour at a local coffee bar. The discussion topic was "How Outsourcing Is Affecting the Manager's Job." Each of the five stimulating people Anna invited was asked to bring an interested friend. The coffee hour was held on a Thursday night at 8:00 and proved to be a time of great conversation and networking.

Notice that the preceding power-enhancing tactics are economical with respect to time, money, and energy. I also recommend them because they have a nice professional touch.

Keep Your Network Alive

Building a network requires a heavy investment of time and energy and some money. As a valuable resource for enhancing your leadership, your network must be maintained and nurtured. Many leaders put considerable energy into establishing a network but fail to take action to keep it breathing. Here are a few suggestions to keep vibrant the network you've worked so hard to build:

Key Word

We all know that **networking** refers to establishing useful personal contacts. What needs to be emphasized, however, is that networking is based on effective communication with people you consider important.

➤ **Stay honest and trustworthy.** Effective *networking* is based on trust. If you have a reputation for discretion, your network will continue to expand. One small indiscretion, in contrast, can wipe out an entire network of relationships.

➤ **Keep in touch.** Stay in touch with your network contacts through such means as e-mail, handwritten notes, greeting cards, postal cards, athletic activities, and social events. Lunches are okay if the network member welcomes a work interruption during the day.

➤ **Display a positive attitude.** A positive attitude is especially important for impressing network members because their help is voluntary. A highly professional way of expressing a positive attitude is to communicate to network members that you take pride in your work and that you thrill at meeting your daily challenges. Your network members will be impressed and will be more likely to extend help than if earning money were your only motivation for working.

➤ **Acknowledge favors.** Whenever a network member does a favor for you of any size, acknowledge the good deed. A successful real estate broker, Elaine Rafferty, has memo pads printed with her name, company, and a headline, "You really helped me out." Elaine prepares for her network a handwritten note that acknowledges the specific type of help received and includes an expression of appreciation.

➤ **Be a do-gooder.** Reach out and provide assistance to network members who are experiencing adversity. Your kindness will be remembered when you have a favor to ask.

➤ **Give gifts of affection and warmth.** Gifts are especially well-suited for impressing members of your network when they are unanticipated. Especially recommended are small surprise gifts that suit your network members' interests.

➤ **Distribute pertinent articles.** If you want to impress network members at a more professional level than dispensing gifts, send them useful articles from newspapers, magazines, journals, and the Internet.

Advisor

If you cannot readily get situated to work on hot problems or cannot get into the hub, develop a contingency plan. Demonstrate how important your activities are to the organization. As a human resources manager, for example, present hard data to top management indicating that your family-friendly programs are increasing productivity and decreasing turnover. A family-friendly program, such as flexible working hours, makes it easier for people to manage the demands of work and family.

Key Word

Centrality is the extent to which a unit's activities are linked into the mainstream of the rest of the organization. A leader working in the hub of a company, therefore, acquires more power than a leader working at the periphery.

Grab On to Hot Problems

In the majority of business firms, the people who occupy the most powerful positions are those who are identified as having the solutions to pressing organizational problems. Similarly, people associated with breakthrough developments in the company tend to become the most powerful executives. The breakthrough development does not necessarily need the glamour of a flat-screen television receiver or a sports car. For example, if top management in your company projects that most of its profits will soon come from overseas operations, see if you can get assigned to the international group.

Closely related to grabbing on to hot problems is that a unit within the organization acquires power because of its *centrality*. A unit has high centrality when it is an important and integral part of the work done by another unit. The second unit is, therefore, dependent on the first unit. A sales department has high centrality, whereas an employee credit unit has low centrality. In short, if you want to increase your power as a leader, you are better off moving to the hub of activities.

Come Storming Out of the Gate

A display of quick, dramatic results can be useful in gaining acceptance for the efforts of you or your group.

Using this tactic, you quickly grab on to a modest amount of power and lay the foundation for acquiring more power. Once you impress top management with your ability to work on the first problem, you can look forward to working on the problems that will bring you greater power. An information systems manager provided this example of making a quick showing:

"Our group agreed to set up a database of credit ratings on customers. This was a bread-and-butter item, but we were willing to take on any assignment to show our skills. The database was a winner. We then suggested a program for tutoring executives on finding work-relevant information on the Internet."

"Based on our past success, our ideas were accepted. Our acceptance in the firm has gone way up now that we are working closely with key executives throughout the organization. My team's work is now considered so important that we are allocated two new positions for next year."

To successfully implement the gate-storming tactic, keep these points in mind:

➤ Others measure your value in terms of the useful results you can obtain for them—not in the sophistication of your techniques.

➤ The number-one reason for calling somebody back to work on another problem is the quality of the results the person achieved with the first problem. A plumber who does a good job fixing a small leak is likely to get invited back to install new bathroom fixtures. The plumber who messes up on the small leak will disappear from the customer's Rolodex.

➤ No problem is too humble to handle if you want to get your foot in the door.

➤ An individual contributor or manager who jumps in and tackles a small problem successfully is perceived to have leadership qualities.

In Union There Is Strength

The advanced political player in government and in business must form *coalitions*. The more people you get on your side, the better—such as getting managers and other key people throughout the organization to agree with your proposal or support your program. Forming a coalition is an extension of networking. The people with whom you form a coalition are typically well-established members of your network. Assume that a manager wants his company to embark upon a campaign of reducing the number of suppliers to better monitor their quality and delivery capability. The manager then calls on key people in his network to support the merits of the plan for weeding out suppliers.

Key Word

A **coalition** is joining forces with another individual or group so all of you wind up having more power. Recently large numbers of independent hardware store owners combined their purchasing power so they could compete more favorably on price with national hardware chains. By forming a coalition, the small stores are able to purchase inventory at lower prices.

A variation of forming a coalition is obtaining a *co-optation*. A true co-optation means that somebody who was not on your side does an about-face and becomes your ally. Leaders need all the allies they can find. Obtaining a co-optation requires even more finesse than forming a coalition. A frequent form of co-optation in business is for a company facing financial trouble to invite one of its bankers to sit on the board. As a board member, the banker then works to get the bank to act mercifully. Suggestions for creating a co-optation include:

➤ Offer your potential enemy an opportunity to gain additional status. For example, ask him or her to become a member of your team or group's advisory board.

➤ Ask your enemy or potential enemy for advice. For example, suggest "I know you have had some reservations about our operation. That is why I am coming to you for some constructive criticism. What should we be doing differently?"

Co-optation is a high-level tactic. After all, converting enemies or potential enemies to your side requires talent.

Key Word

A **co-optation** is a situation in which a potential adversary is brought into the fold. A co-optation thus prevents an erosion of your power as a leader.

Be Your Group's Publicity Director

An informal route to gaining power for yourself and your group is to publicize the efforts of your group to the rest of the organization. The intent of publicizing your group's accomplishments is to enhance your visibility to powerholders within the organization. As your group becomes more visible, you and the group are perceived as more powerful.

Publicizing your group has another potential advantage. With the right exposure, you might get the opportunity to work on critical problems. As you work on more critical problems, you and your group acquire more power.

How Does Increasing the Visibility of Your Group Work in Practice?

Several years ago Alberto Chavez, the human resources director at the El Paso, Texas, processing plant of a large food company, organized a community project day for the plant. A large number of company volunteers built a playground in a poor neighborhood. The event received appropriate mention in the local newspaper. The plant also received a formal letter of appreciation from community leaders and the mayor.

Alberto sent photocopies of the article to key people throughout the company. Soon he and several members of his staff were invited to serve as consultants to the rest of the corporation in establishing community development programs. Alberto's action created benefits for himself and his group by doing good for the community. Alberto was ultimately promoted to a corporate position as community relations director. In his new position, Alberto was able to exercise leadership over a wider sphere of influence.

Here's How You Can Do It, Too

The following tips will help you gain *visibility* for your group—and, therefore, for you:

➤ Prepare a written or oral presentation about something unusual your group has done lately—such as achieving an extraordinarily high productivity or quality standard. Present the information to the editor of the company newsletter, mentioning that perhaps these accomplishments are newsworthy. Do not make the judgment for the editor. News editors are sensitive about being pressured into declaring something newsworthy. Just let the facts speak for themselves.

➤ Publicize the event directly by widely distributing a summary on company e-mail. However, getting a second party to publicize you carries more weight.

➤ Give anybody in the company you meet a 30-second rundown on the activities and accomplishments of your group. Enough people may repeat the essence of what you said to help your group become well-known.

Key Word

Visibility refers literally to making your good works and yourself visible (or seen by) influential people. Unpublicized work usually goes unnoticed. You need to find a professional way of publicizing your accomplishments. Acquiring visibility is not blatant self-promotion.

➤ When an individual or group within the corporation accomplishes something exceptional, have your organizational unit celebrate the accomplishment. Widely distribute an e-mail message to the effect that, "The corporate packaging design team takes this opportunity to congratulate Mary Kane for having won the national packaging design contest." Many people might forget who won an award—Mary Kane or the packaging design group!

Gaining visibility for yourself and your group is a major strategy for gaining power, advancing your career, and demonstrating to group members that you are a strong leader.

"If You Don't Believe Me, Listen to Our Consultant"

To help legitimatize their position, executives often hire a consultant to conduct a study or cast an opinion. With outside support, the executive is more likely to be authorized to move in a direction he or she thinks is desirable. The link between using this tactic and acquiring power is that each time a major initiative of yours is implemented, your power is increased.

An example of using the outside expert technique occurred at a fledgling manufacturer of NetTVs—television sets that enable users to access the Internet. Although the company's product held great promise, initial sales were so slow that the company could not meet its payroll or pay its other bills. The marketing vice president recommended that the company outsource its manufacturing. In this way, the company would eliminate most of its fixed manufacturing costs and only pay for manufacturing when it received orders.

The marketing vice president believed strongly that unless his plans were implemented, the company could not survive. He hired a consultant whose lengthy report concluded that outsourcing manufacturing was a sensible alternative for the problems facing the company. The other principals (except for the head of manufacturing!) agreed. Within a few months, the company sold its manufacturing facilities and located an Asian company to make the NetTVs according to their

Watch Out!

Tooting your own horn must be done softly. Ostentatious or repeated self-puffery makes you suspect. An effective power-grabber is subtle and sensitive enough to know how much is enough.

Watch Out!

Consciously or unconsciously, many consultants are hesitant to "bite the hands that feed them." Keep in mind that the busier, more professional, and emotionally secure the consultant, the more likely he or she will furnish a truly objective opinion. A consultant will therefore often support the executive's position. In turn, the executive will use the consultant's findings to prove that he or she is right.

specifications. As the company soon broke even, the marketing vice president became the second most powerful executive in the company.

An expert does not necessarily have to be an outside consultant. The opinion of an in-house expert might also carry weight. Another alternative is to find an article or book supporting your opinion. You then present the information to the people who have the authority to support your initiative.

Avoid Political Blunders to Prevent Power Erosion

A strategy for not losing the power you have accumulated is to refrain from making power-eroding blunders. Shooting yourself in the foot is not only uncomfortable, it creates a power leak. The accompanying Blunder Quiz will get you to start thinking about blunders. Several leading blunders are described next.

The Blunder Quiz

Indicate whether you agree or disagree with the following statements.

	Agree	Disagree
1. It's fine to criticize your manager or team leader as long as the criticism is valid.	❏	❏
2. Dressing for success is a sham. You should wear to work whatever clothing you find most comfortable.	❏	❏
3. I am willing to insult any co-worker or manager if the insult is deserved.	❏	❏
4. I don't see a problem in using competitors' products services and letting my superiors know about it.	❏	❏
5. If I thought the CEO of my company was way overpaid, I would send him or her an e-mail making my opinion known.	❏	❏
6. Never bother with company-sponsored social events, such as holiday parties, unless you are really interested.	❏	❏
7. If I disagreed with something my employer did, I would voice my opinion in a letter to the editor or via intracompany e-mail.	❏	❏
8. I'm very open about passing along confidential information.	❏	❏
9. I openly criticize most new ventures my company or department is contemplating.	❏	❏
10. I avoid going out of my way to be nice to people just to develop a network of allies.	❏	❏

Scoring and interpretation: The greater the number of statements you agree with, the more prone you are to political blunders that can damage your interpersonal relationships and your career. You need to raise your awareness level of blunders on the job.

Criticizing Your Manager or Other Key Person in a Public Forum

The oldest saying in human relations is to "praise in public and criticize in private." Yet in the passion of the moment, you may surrender to the irresistible impulse to criticize your manager or some other powerful person publicly. As a result, that person will harbor resentment toward you and perhaps block your chances for advancement.

Bypassing the Manager

Many people believe that because most organizations are more democratic today, it is not important to respect the layers of authority (or chain of command). In reality, etiquette is highly valued in most firms. Going around your manager to resolve a problem is, therefore, hazardous. Upper management will usually side with the boss unless his or her behavior has been outrageous and also reported by others. Your career could be damaged and your recourses limited. It is politically wiser to work out differences with your manager using standard methods of resolving conflict.

Overt Displays of Disloyalty

Being disloyal to your organization is a basic political blunder. Making it known that you are looking for a position elsewhere is the best-known form of disloyalty. Criticizing your company in public settings, praising the high quality of competitors' products, and writing angry, internal e-mail messages about your company are others. You may not get fired, but overt signs of disloyalty may place you in permanent disfavor.

Being a Pest

Common wisdom suggests that diligently pressing one's demands is the path to success. This is true up to a point, but when assertiveness is used too often it becomes annoying to many people. The over-persistent person comes to be perceived as a pest, and this constitutes a serious political blunder. An example of being a pest would be asking your manager every month when you are going to receive the raise you deserve.

Burning Your Bridges

A potential political blunder is to create ill will among former employers or people who have helped you in the past. Bridge-burning is most frequent when a person departs from an organization. A person who leaves involuntarily is especially apt to express anger toward those responsible for the dismissal. Venting your anger may give a temporary boost to your mental health, but it can be detrimental in the long run.

Advisor

What can be done to remedy a blunder? Avoid defensiveness. Demonstrate that you are more interested in recovering from the blunder than sharing the blame for what happened. Focus on solutions to the problem rather than faultfinding. Suppose you have been too critical of your team leader in a recent meeting. Explain that your attempts to be constructively critical backfired and that you will choose your words more carefully in the future.

Another way to patch a blunder is to stay poised. Admit that you made the mistake and apologize, but don't act or feel inferior. Avoid looking sad and distraught. Instead, maintain eye contact with the people when you describe your blunder.

The Least You Need to Know

➤ Develop a network of people with the power to help your own power flourish.

➤ Work on critical organizational problems to acquire power.

➤ Perform well on a small project to help you gather power in the long run.

➤ Forming coalitions is a sophisticated method of becoming more powerful.

➤ If an outside expert agrees with your position, you may be able to exert more power.

➤ Be aware of the possibility of making political blunders, and then watch yourself to minimize that happening.

How to Choose the Right Leadership Style

Industrial sales rep Brett rushed into his boss's office at 4:00 on a Thursday afternoon. "I'm so glad I found you here, Courtney," said Brett. "Please help me decide what to do. I just got off the phone with Walworth Industries, a new customer in North Dakota. Two weeks ago, the company bought a $6,000 piece of peripheral equipment from us. The company owner said it's not working properly and that I should fly right out there at our expense and fix it. I just don't know what to do."

"What is it that you don't know what to do?" asked Courtney.

"I don't know whether to make the trip at our expense. Sending a technician to North Dakota would cost about $1,500—unless he stays the weekend so the fare is reduced a few hundred dollars. Either way, the travel costs would wipe out our profit on the deal. Who knows if Walworth would become a repeat customer to justify the loss on the first sale?"

"What have you told the customer so far?" asked Courtney.

"I suggested that the service technician and I get on a conference call with their equipment operator. We could probably resolve the problem over the phone. The owner told me that the equipment is definitely defective and cannot be fixed over the phone. He demands an in-person visit by a company representative."

"What do you intend to do?" asked Courtney.

Getting red in the face, Brett said, "I don't know what to do. I can't handle this problem alone. You tell me what to do. You're the boss."

"True, I am your manager," replied Courtney. "That's precisely why I'm not going to tell you what to do. Part of my job is helping sales representatives grow in decision-making ability."

Is Brett a wimpy sales rep? Is Courtney a wimpy leader/manager? The most critical question here is whether Courtney is using the right style of leadership to fit the occasion. She believes that only by granting considerable decision-making authority to Brett will he become a fully professional sales representative. On the other hand, Brett feels the need for decisive leadership from Courtney.

In this chapter, you will learn about various leadership styles and how to choose the best one to fit the occasion. A starting point is to take the following quiz, which will help you examine your own tendencies toward being the participative or team leader so widely recognized today.

What Style of Leader Are You or Would You Like to Be?

Answer the following questions, keeping in mind what you have done or think you would do in the scenarios and attitudes described.

	Mostly True	Mostly False
1. I am more likely to take care of a high-impact assignment myself than turn it over to a group member.	❏	❏
2. I would prefer the analytical aspects of a manager's job rather than working directly with group members.	❏	❏
3. An important part of my approach to managing a group is to keep the members informed almost daily of any information that could affect their work.	❏	❏
4. It's a good idea to give two people in the group the same problem and then choose what appears to be the best solution.	❏	❏
5. It makes good sense for the leader or manager to stay somewhat aloof from the group, so you can make a tough decision when necessary.	❏	❏

6. I look for opportunities to obtain group input before making a decision, even on straightforward issues. ❏ ❏

7. I would reverse a decision if several of the group members presented evidence that I was wrong. ❏ ❏

8. Differences of opinion in the work group are healthy. ❏ ❏

9. I think that activities to build team spirit, like the team fixing up a poor family's house on a Saturday, are an excellent investment of time. ❏ ❏

10. If my group were hiring a new member, I would like the person to be interviewed by the entire group. ❏ ❏

11. An effective team leader today uses e-mail for about _____ percent of communication with team members. ❏ ❏

12. Some of the best ideas are likely to come from the group members rather than the manager. ❏ ❏

13. If our group were going to have a banquet, I would get input from each member on what type of food should be served. ❏ ❏

14. I have never seen a statue of a committee in a museum or park, so why bother making decisions by committee if you want to be recognized? ❏ ❏

15. I dislike it intensely when a group member challenges my position on an issue. ❏ ❏

16. I typically explain to group members how or what method they should use to accomplish an assigned task. ❏ ❏

17. If I were out of the office for a week, most of the important work in the department would get accomplished anyway. ❏ ❏

18. Delegation of important tasks is something that would be (or is) very difficult for me. ❏ ❏

19. When a group member comes to me with a problem, I tend to jump right in with a proposed solution. ❏ ❏

20. When a group member comes to me with a problem, I typically ask that person something like "What alternative solutions have you thought of so far?" ❏ ❏

Scoring: The answers in the participative/team-style leader direction are as follows:

1. Mostly False	8. Mostly True	15. Mostly False
2. Mostly False	9. Mostly True	16. Mostly False
3. Mostly True	10. Mostly True	17. Mostly True
4. Mostly False	11. Mostly False	18. Mostly False
5. Mostly False	12. Mostly True	19. Mostly False
6. Mostly True	13. Mostly True	20. Mostly True
7. Mostly True	14. Mostly False	

If your score is 15 or higher, you are most likely (or would be) a participative/team-style leader. If your score is five or lower, you are most likely (or would be) an authoritarian-style leader.

Skill development: The quiz you just completed is also an opportunity for skill development. Review the 20 questions and look for implied suggestions for engaging in participative leadership. For example, question 20 suggests that you encourage group members to work through their own solutions to problems. If your goal is to become an authoritarian leader, the questions can also serve as useful guidelines. For example, question 19 suggests that an authoritarian leader looks first to solve problems for group members.

Going North, South, East, and West to Learn About Your Style

A good starting point in choosing an effective *leadership style* is understanding how others perceive your present style. Even if you are not currently occupying a managerial position, it is still possible to obtain some feedback on how you come across as a leader. Perhaps others have observed you in a temporary leadership assignment such as heading a committee or chairing a meeting. Maybe you have had some leadership experience in a religious, community, or sports group. Maybe you have been a Little League coach where other parents have observed your coaching style. Parents are likely to have strong opinions about the leadership skills of anybody privileged enough to coach their offspring, and they might not be diffident about expressing their opinions.

A starting point in understanding your style is asking people who have seen you in any type of leadership role to describe how you act as a leader. (The quiz earlier in the chapter also provides potentially useful

Key Word

Leadership style is the typical pattern of behavior the leader exhibits when dealing with group members. Styles are typically described by such terms as autocratic, participative, task-oriented, and people-oriented.

information.) Tell them that you are thick-skinned and you are not looking for compliments. You just want to know how you come across to others as a leader. If asking open-ended questions does not furnish you the information you need, try these probes:

➤ In your opinion, do I put more emphasis on the relationships with people, or do I focus more on the task at hand?

➤ Do I come across as a taskmaster?

➤ Do I come across as too easy-going with people?

➤ How much direction do I provide?

➤ How responsive am I to the needs of the group members?

➤ As a leader, am I an SOB?

➤ As a leader, am I a pussycat?

➤ Does my leadership inspire you or anybody else?

➤ As a leader, do I come across as a hard-core bureaucrat?

➤ How warm and supportive am I as a leader?

A more systematic method of understanding how you come across as a leader is to use *360-degree feedback*. This technique developed at the Center for Creative Leadership is now used in thousands of organizations.

The technique can be used both to help evaluate performance and to understand a person's leadership style. The leader-manager can use this technique to obtain insight into the effectiveness of his or her leadership behavior. Using the 360-degree technique, feedback is systematically derived from a full sampling of parties who interact with the leader. Feedback is thus derived from a full circle (360 degrees) of observers.

If your company uses the 360-degree technique, you can use it to fine-tune your leadership attitudes and behavior. Workers who interact with the manager review a broad range of management practices. An analysis examines any gaps between what you as a leader should be doing and what you are doing. For example, you might rate yourself 8 on a 1-to-10 scale in "empathy toward group members." If the average rating you receive from the 10 people who evaluated you is 1.5, the big gap suggests you have a problem.

Key Word

360-degree feedback is a formal evaluation of superiors based on input from people who work for them and with them, sometimes including customers and suppliers. Such multiple input is valuable because it gives you a clearer picture of how you operate than if only one person provides feedback. Dozens of consulting firms now offer 360-degree feedback programs, and many human resources departments are prepared to establish such a program.

Gaps can also indicate that you are too self-critical. Suppose you rate yourself 9 on a 1-to-10 scale for being highly critical, yet the average rating you receive is 3.4. You might then conclude that you don't have a problem as a leader in being too critical of group members. The following table illustrates the type of feedback on leadership practices a person might gather from the 360-degree technique. As you can see, the leader in question thinks more highly of his effectiveness than does the group.

Manager Evaluated: Bob Kendig			
Behavior or Attitude (10 is highest)	Self-Rating	Average Group rating	Gap
1. Gives right amount of structure	9	7.5	-1.5
2. Considerate of people	10	6.2	-3.8
3. Sets a direction	9	3.9	-5.1
4. Sets high standards	7	9.0	+2.0
5. Gives frequent feedback	10	6.3	-3.7
6. Gets people pulling together	9	5.1	-3.9
7. Inspires people	10	2.8	-7.2
8. Gives emotional support	8	3.7	-4.3
9. Is a helpful coach	10	4.5	-5.5
10. Encourages people to be self-reliant	6	9.4	+3.4

Note: A negative gap means you rate yourself higher on the behavior or attitude than does your group. A positive gap means the group rates you higher than you rate yourself.

360-degree feedback chart.

The feedback from a 360-degree evaluation is communicated to the leader (as well as others being evaluated) and interpreted with the assistance of an industrial/organizational psychologist or other human resources professional. Professional feedback is often necessary because of the emotional shock that significant gaps can carry. How would you feel if you perceived yourself as a warm, caring, likable leader, yet those evaluating you perceived you as cold, uncaring, and disliked?

Who's in Charge Here?

In choosing a leadership style, a foundation step is deciding how much authority to retain for yourself versus how much to hand over to the group. A completely boss-centered leader holds on to most of the authority and makes most of the decisions alone. At the other extreme, a subordinate-centered leader turns over almost all decision-making authority to the group. A boss-centered leader is labeled as authoritarian or authoritative. A subordinate-centered leader is labeled as free rein. The *participative* leader falls into the middle of these two extremes; a participative leader shares decision-making with group members. The same style is also referred to as participative/team.

To decide how much authority to retain (or how much to be in charge), examine the factors described in the next sections. Understanding these factors will help you make the best choice in a given situation.

Authority Vested in the Leader

Managers and leaders who believe that group members should have a say in decision-making will move toward being subordinate-centered. Managers who have confidence in the capabilities of group members grant them more freedom.

Your natural inclinations are also important. Some people are more directive by nature, whereas others feel more comfortable sharing decision-making.

Authority Vested in the Group Members

Generally speaking, group members can be granted more decision-making latitude if they ...

➤ Are independent.

➤ Can tolerate ambiguity such as an unclear task.

➤ Are competent to perform the task at hand.

➤ Identify with the goals of the unit and the organization.

➤ Expect to share in the decision-making process.

Key Word

In general, the **participative** leader is more in vogue these days because this style is well suited for team leadership.

Watch Out!

Even if the group members don't appear capable of participating in an important decision, find some area for using their input. If your job is to contribute input to a strategic plan (and you feel you have the best vantage point), say: "I have to submit our unit's contribution to the strategic plan. I welcome your input on anything I should tell top management."

One reason that granting group members decision-making authority has merit is that it helps establish a partnership between the leader and group members.

Authority Vested in the Situation

If groups within the organization are accustomed to participating in decisions, the leader should move toward being subordinate-centered. Work groups with a history of effectiveness can handle more decision-making freedom. At times, the group has enough information to deal with the problem at hand. At other times, only you, as the leader, have sufficient information to handle the problem. In the latter circumstance, you act more boss-centered. For example, you might have the right network contact to get a budget issue resolved.

Advisor

When faced with an emergency or crisis, make the decision yourself as the team leader. An alternative is to call a meeting within a couple of hours. Any group member in the office that day is invited. Meet for a maximum of 60 minutes to discuss the problem, and get some input. Then make your decision immediately. Part of being an effective leader is the ability to make quick decisions under fire.

Time Pressures

The more you as the leader-manager need an immediate decision, the more difficult it is to involve others in decision-making. Employee-centered leadership is time-consuming despite its merits. For example, have you ever seen how long mature adults can haggle over deciding how to spend a department budget?

Key Word

Synergy is a combination of people's efforts whereby the output is greater than the sum of the parts. Five people working together to build a house represents synergy. Building a house by yourself takes more than five times as long. In fact, it is virtually impossible unless your arms extend 12 feet in length.

Are You a Member of the Band or a Soloist?

Another way of understanding leadership styles is classifying them as team leadership versus solo leadership. Team leaders share power and de-emphasize individual glory. They are flexible and adaptable, thus welcoming change. Team leaders function as facilitators who bring out the best in others while still being inspirational.

Team leaders place considerable emphasis on team building. In their way of thinking, if the team has done well, they have done their job well. Team leaders recognize intuitively that the whole is greater than the sum of the parts. They search for *synergy* by getting team members working together to multiply their productivity. A team leader believes that as they share power, they become more powerful. This attitude makes sense because if an empowered group performs well, the leader shares credit for some of their accomplishments.

The solo leader is more of the traditional leader in a bureaucracy. Basically an autocrat, the solo leader receives a lot of the credit for the group's accomplishment. Some of the credit is frequently undeserved because the solo leader does not recognize how dependent he or she is on the team.

"Help Me, Help Me" vs. "Please Get Out of My Light"

An anecdote about Pablo Picasso tells us a lot about how much structure, guidance, and help leaders should give team members. By retelling this story, I run the risk of making the mistake mentioned in Chapter 5, "Communicate Like a Leader," of using tired old anecdotes. Picasso was allegedly asked by a wealthy patron what she could best do for the famous painter. He replied, "Please stand out of my light." The best a boss (or patron) could do for Picasso was give him the resources he needed and then stand out of the way. However, not every person you will lead is as self-sufficient as Picasso. Many group members need considerable help and guidance.

The major factor in deciding how much supervision, management, and leadership a group member needs is his or her ability to work independently. In short, the stronger the person, the less guidance and structure he or she needs. Conversely, the weaker the person, the more guidance and structure he or she needs to perform well.

> **Another Perspective**
>
> The description of the solo leader presented here might seem harshly negative. You might say the solo leader is a glory seeker who is out of tune with the times. Before you write off entirely the merits of being a solo leader, recognize that many successful entrepreneurs and financiers are the solo type— nothing like being a rich, self-centered autocrat.

Orientations for Providing Guidance

The two key aspects of leadership for providing structure and guidance are task orientation and relationship (or people) orientation. Using a task orientation, you give the person guidance about the task such as technical instructions and goals and deadlines. You might also help with work scheduling. Using a relationship orientation, you focus on such activities as giving encouragement, listening to problems, calming down an anxious person, and reducing causes of work stress.

Guidelines Help You Decide How Much Guidance to Provide

The following guidelines will help you decide how much structure and guidance people will need, including both a task and a people orientation:

➤ When a group member is new to the task, unsure, low in self-confidence, and not strongly motivated, he or she requires close supervision. Focus on the task to get the person going, but do not neglect giving considerable reassurance and encouragement.

➤ When a group member appears interested in avoiding hard work and has questionable ethics, the person will need close supervision and considerable follow-up. Use a task orientation by asking for progress reports. Work hard at inspiring the person, thus also emphasizing a relationship orientation.

➤ When a group member is eager to be a high producer but is not very skilled, emphasize helping with the task. At the same time, show appreciation for the person's effort.

➤ When a group member is strongly motivated but less competent than he or she recognizes, encourage the person's good deeds. Also hold frequent review sessions to monitor how well the person is performing.

➤ When a group member is obviously competent, well-motivated, well-trained, and experienced, provide a minimum of structure and hand-holding. However, do not ignore a star performer. Give occasional recognition for his or her independence. Make statements such as, "Because I don't touch base with you frequently, don't think I do not recognize and appreciate your accomplishments. You're a wonderful contributor to the team. What can we do for you in return?"

Key Word

A **servant leader** serves constituents by working on their behalf to help them achieve their goals, not the leader's own goals.

"I'm Here to Help You"

During his two runs for the presidency, prominent business executive H. Ross Perot emphasized that he would be a *servant leader*. If elected, he would help people accomplish what they think is important. A genuine servant leader should, therefore, seek leadership not for glory and power but to better the lot of constituents. At their best, "public servants" such as members of Congress are servant leaders. As formulated by Robert K. Greenleaf, the idea behind servant leadership derives naturally from a commitment to service.

Servant leaders are found in universities, research laboratories, and hospitals where the managers see their role as handling administrative tasks for the professionals. Many professors view being a chair or department head as a service activity. In industry, servant leaders are less common because top-level managers have more authority, prestige, and income than people who are not managers. Business leaders may serve the needs of people, but they also emphasize pursuing their own agendas.

If you want to be the servant-style leader in a business setting, here are several suggestions (with a few ideas from Greenleaf included):

➤ Place service before self-interest. A servant leader is more concerned about helping others than acquiring power, prestige, financial reward, and status. The servant leader seeks to do what is morally right, even if not financially rewarding. (Aren't these leaders wonderful?)

➤ Frequently ask group members such questions as "How can I help you?" and "What can I do in my position to make life easier for you?"

➤ Listen first to express confidence in others. The servant leader emphasizes listening to get to know the concerns, requirements, and problems of group members. He or she listens carefully to understand what course of action will help others accomplish their goals.

➤ Mention frequently, "I'm in this job to help you." Also, use the term "servant leader" when talking about your position or role.

➤ Downplay any talk about your own ambitions. Remember, you are only in this job so you can help others.

➤ Collect data frequently about the needs and concerns of your constituents.

➤ Focus on what is feasible to accomplish. Even though the servant leader is idealistic, he or she recognizes that one individual cannot accomplish everything. So, the leader listens carefully to the array of problems facing group members and then concentrates on a few.

Another Perspective

As pioneering leadership authority Ralph Stogdill wrote 30 years ago, "The most effective leaders appear to exhibit a degree of versatility and flexibility that enables them to adapt their behavior to the changing and contradictory demands made on them."

A More Elastic You

A major requirement for effective leadership is the ability to adapt your style to meet the demands of a given situation. Style flexibility means that you fine-tune your leadership approach as the people and task demand change. If you are ordinarily a consensus-style decision-maker, you quicken your pace during a crisis. Assume your characteristic leadership style is to isolate yourself from the group while performing analytical work and developing strategy. This style might work well in managing a group of self-reliant professionals. Now assume that the scenario changes to leading a group of workplace neophytes who were previously welfare recipients. You must shift to a more intense person-to-person leadership.

Becoming an adaptable leader requires the realization that style flexibility is important for effectiveness. Understand that you have a characteristic approach to leadership, but it must be adapted to the circumstances. When placed in a new or modified leadership situation, seek answers to questions such as …

➤ What style of leadership do these people need to perform best?

➤ Considering the capabilities of these people, how much guidance, support, and structure do they need from me?

➤ What is it about my core approach to leading people that is helpful for these people?

➤ What can I do to establish better rapport with this group?

➤ What help does this group really need from me to succeed?

➤ Should I act as though I am here to serve these people or as though they are here to help me?

The Least You Need to Know

➤ 360-degree feedback can help you understand your leadership impact by providing multiple input on how you come across to people as a leader.

➤ Decide how much authority to retain for yourself.

➤ Understand the difference between solo and team leadership.

➤ Decide how much guidance and structure your group members need.

➤ Become a servant leader, and help people achieve their goals.

➤ Become adaptable to the leadership situation.

Chapter 10

Become a Multicultural Leader

In This Chapter

➤ Developing your cultural sensitivity

➤ Learning to appreciate the diversity umbrella

➤ Recognizing cultural attitudes and values you need to know

➤ Motivating people from different cultures

Sales manager Ken said to Judy, who was headed for a business trip to the Dominican Republic, "Brush up on your Spanish until you can speak it *bien* (well). It could really help negotiations if you speak a little Spanish."

Judy replied, "It's true that the native Dominican language is Spanish. Maybe you don't realize that all the business people down there speak English also. If I run into any trouble, I'm sure the company will have an interpreter available. In fact, Kerry, from our sister division, had a great business trip to the Dominican Republic recently, and she doesn't speak a word of Spanish."

Ken then explained, "Judy, there is a big difference between Kerry's trip and yours. When Kerry went there, she was negotiating with a Dominican company to be a supplier. She was buying. You are going there to *sell*."

"When you are buying, showing your appreciation of another country's culture is less important. When you are selling, it's a different situation. You are trying to please them. Showing your appreciation of another culture is extra important."

Ken is showing good cultural sensitivity. He recognizes the importance of showing your interest in another party's culture when you want to please that person. In this chapter, you will learn about one of the most exciting challenges facing leaders today—working well with people from different cultures. Different cultures are found within one's own country as well as in other countries. In addition to learning about the basics of working well with people from other cultures, you will also read about some bloopers to avoid.

To get you mentally prepared to study this important information, take a candid look at your current propensities toward being multicultural. The following quiz is designed for that purpose. *Voilà!*

Cross-Cultural Skills and Attitudes

The following are various skills and attitudes that some employers and cross-cultural experts think are important for relating effectively to co-workers in a culturally diverse environment.

	Applies to Me Now	Not There Yet
1. I have spent some time in another country.	❏	❏
2. At least one of my friends is deaf, blind, or uses a wheelchair.	❏	❏
3. Currency from other countries is as real as the currency from my own country.	❏	❏
4. I can read in a language other than my own.	❏	❏
5. I can speak in a language other than my own.	❏	❏
6. I can write in a language other than my own.	❏	❏
7. I can understand people speaking in a language other than my own.	❏	❏
8. I use my second language regularly.	❏	❏
9. My friends include people of races different than my own.	❏	❏
10. My friends include people of different ages.	❏	❏
11. I feel (or would feel) comfortable having a friend with a sexual orientation different from mine.	❏	❏
12. My attitude is that although another culture may be very different from mine, that culture is equally good.	❏	❏
13. I would be willing to (or already do) hang art from different countries in my home.	❏	❏
14. I would accept (or have already accepted) a work assignment of more than several months in another country.	❏	❏
15. I have a passport.	❏	❏

Interpretation: If you answered "Applies to Me Now" to 10 or more of the preceding questions, you most likely function well in a multicultural work environment. If you answered "Not There Yet" to 10 or more questions, you need to develop more cross-cultural awareness and skills to work effectively in a multicultural work environment. You will notice that being bilingual gives you at least five points on this quiz.

Now I Know Why You Act the Way You Do

To be a *multicultural leader,* you must be able to work well with people from several cultures. So important is this ability that people with overseas business experience are favored to fill many executive positions in large organizations. Furthermore, an increasing number of American business leaders are bilingual, such as Carlos Guttierrez of Kellogg Company.

To relate well to someone from a foreign country, a leader (or any other person) must be alert to possible cultural differences. When working in another country, you must be willing to acquire knowledge about local customs and learn to speak the native language. Saying even simple phrases in the language of the people you want to lead adds to your charisma. When working with people from different cultures, it is important for you to be patient, adaptable, flexible, and willing to learn and listen. The same principle applies as well in working with diverse people from your own country.

The two most important words in becoming a multicultural leader are *cultural sensitivity,* or an awareness of and a willingness to investigate the reasons why people from another culture act as they do. If you develop cultural sensitivity, you recognize certain nuances in customs that will help you build better relationships with people from cultural backgrounds other than your own.

Developing cultural sensitivity takes time, much like becoming a more intuitive decision-maker. You need experience combined with penetrating observations of that experience. Assume Jeff is the manufacturing manager at the Ohio plant of an American company. His company expands its presence in Asia by building a manufacturing plant in Bombay, India. Jeff spends the first two weeks in December visiting the new plant. Slowly it dawns on Jeff that very few people wish him "Merry

Key Word

A **multicultural leader** has the skills and attitudes to relate effectively to people of different races, sexes, ages, social attitudes, and lifestyles. He or she can motivate them and conduct business in a diverse, international environment.

Key Word

A leader with good **cultural sensitivity** usually develops the ability to feel comfortable leading diverse groups of people.

Christmas" as he prepares to return home. Assuming the workers from Bombay are being timid, he takes the initiative to wish many of them "Merry Christmas."

Instead of reciprocating his greeting, Jeff encounters many quizzical glances and a few giggles. A lightbulb finally flashes in Jeff's head: "My Bombay associates are not exchanging Christmas greetings with me out of shyness or rudeness. It's just that most of them are Hindi, not Christian. They don't celebrate Christmas." Jeff learned the general lesson that not everybody in the world shares his same religious holidays.

Jeff rethinks his interpretation of why some people in Japan and China often celebrate Christmas. To them it is a fun-filled American custom that does not have religious significance.

Advisor

To be an effective cross-cultural leader you also have to learn about many cross-cultural differences in communication. (Several nonverbal differences were described in Chapter 3, "How Do Leaders Think?") Here are a few cross-cultural differences to keep in mind:

➤ Members of Asian and some Middle-Eastern cultures consider direct eye contact rude.

➤ When Japanese people say "We'll consider it," they probably mean "No."

➤ British people understate praise and compliments. If your work associate from England says your idea has "a bit of merit" he or she is probably ecstatic or at least enthusiastic. (Oops! I hope I haven't angered the British Anti-Defamation League.)

Described next are some everyday suggestions for developing the cultural sensitivity you need to add to your leadership tool kit. All but the last suggestion are inexpensive with respect to money and time:

➤ Talk to workers from different cultural groups in your company. Ask them what's important to them about their work.

➤ Talk to your customers from different cultural groups. Observe carefully their customs and behavior.

➤ Invite several people from other cultures to your next house party. Chat with them and observe their customs and manner of speech.

➤ When dining out, occasionally choose a neighborhood ethnic restaurant that caters to a clientele from that ethnic group. Carefully observe the customs of the clientele. How do they greet strangers? How do they greet each other?

➤ Devote 15 minutes per day to upgrading your skill in another language. Resuscitate whatever knowledge you acquired in school. Gradually learning another language helps you be more sensitive to the ethnic groups who speak that language.

➤ Purchase travel videos and books about your target country or countries. These information sources are filled with a lot of useful information about the customs and values of other countries.

➤ While surfing the Internet, click the version for your target country. For example, the search engine Yahoo! has versions for about 10 different countries. This cross-cultural experience might not be intense, but it's a start. Similarly, set up your Internet so a newspaper in your target foreign language appears when you first access the Net.

➤ Take a vacation in a country representing the culture you want to know. Disengage yourself from a group of tourists, and don't seek people from your own country. If you can speak the language at all, minimize the time you spend speaking your native tongue. Carry a phrase book of the language, and fumble, struggle, and stutter. It will do you good.

Advisor

Watch a foreign-language television channel for your target culture. For example, Spanish TV channels are omnipresent in the United States, and the same is true for French TV channels in Canada. Attend foreign films on your target culture. See what makes the audience laugh; watch how actors in the film greet each other; note the level of formality or informality of dress. While you're at the cinema, take some time to observe the audience. It might be heavily populated with people from the ethnic group featured in the film.

We're All Different; We're All Okay

Improving your ability as a cross-cultural leader includes learning the true meaning of appreciating diversity. To appreciate diversity, a person must go beyond tolerating and treating people fairly from different racial and ethnic groups and the two sexes. The true meaning of valuing diversity is respecting and enjoying a wide range of cultural and individual differences. To be diverse is to be different in some measurable way. A multicultural leader enjoys differences just as a music lover might enjoy a variety of music, all offering their special delights.

Advisor

Multicultural leaders are politically correct in a natural way. They don't use phrases that sound as if they are bending over backward to recognize differences or soften the fact that they dare mention a person's group characteristics. A manager, asked if the company had a culturally diverse professional staff, responded, "Absolutely. A good example is one of our new electronic engineers, Chandra Jones. She's black." This statement helped the leader sound more comfortably multicultural than if he'd said, "Chandra Jones is an electronics engineer in our company who happens to be a woman and who happens to be black."

To be highly skilled in interpersonal relations, a leader must recognize and appreciate the ways in which people are distinct. Some people are more visibly different than others because of their physical features or disabilities, yet the diversity umbrella includes everybody in an organization. To value diversity is, therefore, to appreciate individual differences among people.

A foundation principle for being a multicultural person is to show respect for all workers. The key attitude is to regard other cultures as *different* from yours, but not *inferior.* A widely used comment that implies disrespect is to say to a person from another culture, "You have a funny accent." Should you be transferred to that person's culture, you would also have a "funny accent."

The diversity umbrella continues to include more people as the workforce encompasses a greater variety of people. An important goal for the multicultural leader is to enable people of all cultural backgrounds to achieve their full potential. They should not be restrained by group identities such as sex, nationality, age, race, or religion.

Following is a broad sampling of the way in which workplace associates differ from one another. Studying this list can help you anticipate the types of differences to understand and appreciate in a diverse workplace. The differences include cultural as well as individual factors. Individual factors are also important because people can face discrimination for personal characteristics as well as group factors. Many people, for example, believe they are held back from promotion because of their weight-to-height ratio. Here are some of the differences that fit under the diversity umbrella:

➤ Race

➤ Sex

➤ Religion

➤ Age (young, middle-aged, old)

➤ Ethnicity (country of origin)

➤ Education

➤ Job-relevant abilities

➤ Mental disabilities (attention deficit disorder)

➤ Physical disabilities (hearing impairment, wheelchair use)

➤ Values and motivation

➤ Sexual orientation (heterosexual, homosexual, bisexual)

➤ Marital status (married, single, cohabitating, widow, widower; and don't forget polygamous)

➤ Family status (children, no children, two-parent family, single parent, grand-parent)

➤ Personality traits (introverted, extroverted, conscientious)

➤ Functional background (area of specialization)

➤ Technology interest (high-tech, low-tech, technophobe)

➤ Weight (average, obese, underweight, ano-rexic)

➤ Hair (full head of hair, bald, wild hair, tame hair, long hair, short hair)

➤ Tobacco use (smoker versus nonsmoker, chewer versus nonchewer)

➤ Gum use (use versus nonuse)

➤ Styles of clothing and appearance (dress up, dress down, professional appearance, casual appearance)

As a leader, you should welcome all of these differences, However, when certain individual differences create productivity, quality, and morale prob-

Watch Out!

Be careful not to attribute a cultural characteristic of a group to every individual in that group. For example, Chinese people in general are more concerned with group than individual recognition, but this characteristic might not be true of your new Web site design specialist.

lems, you might have to intervene. An example is if a person smokes in the office or is not conscientious about producing high-quality work. Hair length can have safety implications, such as long hair being a hazard around machinery, and no hair leading to heat stroke for a life guard. Wearing a hat takes care of both problems.

Vive la Différence in Cultural Values

Another Perspective

Cross-cultural differences in risk-taking are often subtle, and some get confounded with ethical issues. Some American sales managers risk shipping a customer more product than was ordered, figuring that the customer will go along. In one situation an American manager was upset with a Japanese sales rep who said that doing this was too risky. The American manager should have realized he was dealing with cultural differences and not insubordination.

If you as a leader understand certain major cultural differences, you lay the groundwork for developing effective cross-cultural relations. Research has identified eight values that are reasonably reliable in differentiating one culture from another. Use these values as starting points in understanding people, but confirm them later by observing the person's actual behavior.

Individualism vs. Collectivism

At one end of the continuum is individualism, a mental set in which people see themselves first as individuals and believe that their own interests take priority. Collectivism, at the other end of the continuum, is a feeling that the group and society receive top priority.

Highly individualistic cultures include the United States and Canada, whereas Japan and Greece are more collectivistic. A worker who believes in collectivism is a strong team player.

Acceptance of Authority and Status

People from some cultures readily accept the fact that some people in the organization have more authority and carry higher status than others. According to this belief, the boss has the right to make certain decisions. In other cultures, employees do not readily accept hierarchy. Cultures with high acceptance of authority and status include France and Mexico. People from the United States and Scandinavian countries are less accepting of authority. As a leader, you will find it easier to control people from cultures where authority is readily accepted.

Risk-Taking Attitude

In some cultures, people are more willing to take risks and engage in unconventional behavior. These people are not afraid to face the unknown. Cultures with a greater propensity for risk-taking include the United States and Canada. Workers in Israel and Japan are more conservative with respect to risk-taking.

Materialism vs. Caring for People

People in some cultures focus heavily on acquiring money and material objects and at the same time de-emphasize caring for others. In contrast, some cultures place a high emphasis on caring for people and are less concerned about materialism. Japan and Italy are rated as highly materialistic. The United States rates average on materialism, whereas Scandinavian nations all emphasize caring as a national value.

Long-Term Thinking vs. Short-Term Thinking

Workers from a culture with a long-term orientation maintain a long-range perspective. Such individuals are thrifty, do not demand quick returns on their investments, and patiently wait for a job promotion. Short-term thinking is characterized by a demand for immediate results, a propensity not to save, and impatience for promotion. Inhabitants of Pacific Rim countries are noted for their long-term orientation. In contrast, the cultures of the United States and Canada are characterized by a short-term orientation.

Watch Out!

Differences in time orientation often cause cross-cultural clashes. A small-business owner went to Mexico to close a huge deal on fiber-optic cables with a Mexican telephone company. The Mexican company owner kept the American waiting three hours in the company office. The American was so frustrated, he was rude to the Mexican executive. As a result, the relationship between the two soured, and the deal fell through.

Formality vs. Informality

A country that values formality attaches considerable importance to tradition, ceremony, social rules, and rank. At the other extreme, informality refers to a casual attitude toward tradition, ceremony, social rules, and rank.

Workers in Latin countries highly value formality, such as lavish public receptions and processions. Americans, Canadians, and Scandinavians are more informal. Have you noticed that some servers in American restaurants greet guests by saying, "Hi, guys, what can I get you?" As a manager, you might have to coach an informal person on how to behave when visiting a formal country.

Urgent-Time Orientation vs. Casual-Time Orientation

Individuals and nations attach different importance to time. People with an urgent-time orientation perceive time as a scarce resource and tend to be impatient. People with a casual-time orientation view time as an unlimited and unending resource and tend to be patient. Americans are noted for their urgent-time orientation. They frequently impose deadlines and are eager to start doing business. Asians and Middle Easterners, in contrast, are patient negotiators.

High vs. Low Emphasis on the Surrounding Situation

Cultures differ in how much importance they attach to the surrounding circumstances, or the context, of an event. High-context cultures make extensive use of body language. Some cultures, such as the Asian, Hispanic, and African-American cultures, are high context. In contrast, northern European cultures are low context and make less use of body language. The Anglo-American culture is considered to be medium-low context. People in low-context cultures seldom take time in business dealings to build relationships and establish trust.

Advisor

Cultural differences in values make good reading and discussion, but effective leaders realize that cultural values are only a starting point in working with people from other cultures. You must still focus carefully on the individual's values. For example, many Japanese workers seek individual glory and are high risk-takers.

The United States vs. the Rest of the World

A good way to appreciate differences in national values is to compare U.S. values to the collective values of many Western and Eastern countries. You can use this information as a general stereotype of how Americans are likely to differ from people in other countries. If you are aware that such differences exist, you might be able to better understand and lead people from diverse cultures. As researched by International Resources, the major differences are presented as follows:

In the United States	In Many Other Countries
Time is to be controlled	Time is fluid, malleable
Emphasis on change	Emphasis on tradition and continuity
Individualism	Group orientation
Personal privacy	Openness, accessibility
Informality	Formality

In the United States	In Many Other Countries
Individual competition	Cooperation
Equality/egalitarianism	Hierarchy/authority
Short-term emphasis	Long-term emphasis
Work emphasis ("One lives to work")	Leisure plus work emphasis ("One works to live")
Task emphasis	People emphasis
Direct/explicit communication style	Indirect/implicit communication style
Action bias or emphasis	Planning and preparation emphasis

Where Do I Find a Multicultural Carrot?

A highly practical application of being a multicultural leader is that it enables you to motivate and influence people from different cultures. Much of what is said about motivation and influence previously in this book and in Chapter 13, "The People Side of Team Leadership," can be used to motivate people from different cultures. The big difference, however, is that you must identify rewards that are usually valued by people in that culture.

Another way of looking at the same challenge is that the "What" in "What's in it for me?" will differ across cultures. For example, the majority of Americans might want an individual reward, whereas most Taiwanese are likely to favor a group reward. French people, as well as many other Europeans, value vacations as a reward more than do most career-oriented Americans.

Link Rewards to What People Want

The rewards considered important by people from different cultures are usually linked to their cultural values.

Ron, a manager from San Francisco, discovered this through firsthand experience. His company purchased a manufacturing firm located in southern California with a predominantly Mexican-American workforce. One of Ron's responsibilities was to boost productivity and quality at the new company.

Working with the former company owner (now division president) and the human resources department, he established a suggestion system. By submitting money-earning ideas to the program, employees could receive substantial cash rewards running as high as $5,000. Despite what Ron thought was a fabulous motivator, few suggestions were submitted. Ron then conferred with Wanda, one of the highly regarded supervisors at the company. Wanda gave Ron a good lesson in cross-cultural motivation. She explained:

133

"Ron, I mean no offense to your program. Thank you for wanting to give our workers money for being smart. The problem is that our Latino workers are closely knit. They are embarrassed to accept rewards that would isolate them from their friends. Offer rewards that people can share with their close friends here in the plant; then you'll see some action."

Ron did change the reward structure to include rewards that could be shared by team members. For example, if one worker won a large reward, other workers in the immediate group also received a small cash award. In addition, the company sponsored a party for the work group. Ron reworked the rewards but not the total cost to the company because the size of individual rewards was decreased. Revamping the suggestion system quadrupled the number of ideas that were submitted.

Find Out What People Want

The general guideline for motivating people from different cultures is that you should investigate which rewards might be effective. Ask the workers themselves and their supervisors and consult with specialists in the culture such as foreign language professors and anthropologists. An especially effective approach for approaching the workers is conducting small-group discussions.

Watch Out!

The issue of bribery versus rewards often surfaces when attempting to motivate people from other cultures. A bribe centers around offering another individual something of value to get them to do what you want. A reward is more ethical. It involves giving another person something of value for performing well. A reward can be publicly discussed while a bribe is more secret.

A study conducted with Russian cotton mill workers illustrates the principle of investigating the most effective rewards. Three different approaches were used to motivate the 99 workers in the study. One approach involved giving the workers American goods such as jeans for producing high-quality fabric. The second approach required that supervisors give praise and recognition for engaging in the right behaviors. The third approach had supervisors solicit input on work procedures from the workers.

The Russian workers performed better when they were rewarded with American goods or received praise and recognition. Encouraging the workers to participate in decision-making not only failed to improve performance, but also actually contributed to a performance decline. The workers seemed to say "Nyet" to participative management because it was a poor cultural fit.

The Least You Need to Know

➤ Develop your cultural sensitivity by observing and understanding cultural differences.

➤ A winning cross-cultural attitude is to show respect for people of all cultures.

➤ Appreciate the wide variety of people who fit under the diversity umbrella, such as recognizing that workers differ from one another in dozens of tangible and intangible ways.

➤ Recognize the differences in cultural attitudes and values in such dimensions as formality versus informality and attitudes toward time.

➤ Establish a good strategy for motivating people from different cultures, including identifying their motivators.

Chapter 11

You Can Become a Visionary and Transformational Leader

In This Chapter

➤ Establishing super values

➤ Creating inspirational vision statements

➤ Acting and talking like a strategic leader

➤ Setting the direction for large-scale change

➤ Becoming a revolutionary thinker

➤ Being a knowledge manager

➤ Managing the change you've created

A large multinational conglomerate was holding its annual stockholders' meeting. Profits had been down for three years. The stock price had plunged 25 percent below its peak of 5 years ago. Many shareholders were disappointed and restless.

During the question-and-answer period, a major stockholder asked the CEO, "Mr. Sommer, could you please tell us shareholders precisely what this company is doing? What is the nature of our business?"

CEO Sommer said hesitatingly, "It's hard to say that we are doing one thing in particular. We are in a variety of businesses in seven different countries. Before I became CEO seven years ago, our firm was basically a holding company. We buy and sell companies, almost as if they are pieces of real estate. We own oil wells, restaurants, tanning salons, a manufacturer of windshield wiper blades, and three small retail chains. Another example of our diversification is that we own and operate two lumber mills."

"Looking into the future, I hope we can continue to squeeze good profits from our holdings and make life pleasant for our shareholders. I also hope we can create a large number of jobs."

"Aha!" said the shareholder. "I appreciate your candor, Mr. Sommer. You have practically admitted that Accelerated Industries is a hodgepodge of loosely connected businesses. Our problem is that you provide no vision for the company. I hope that you will create a vision for us by the second quarter of this year."

The irate shareholder has a point. A vision can help turn around a floundering organization and improve profitability.

Visions and transformations are not just for CEOs. You can also be a visionary and transformational leader of a small chunk of the organization or of a small business. In this chapter, you will learn how to create visions and how to make transformations. If all goes well, after reading this chapter you will be able to say triumphantly, "I do visions." You will also receive suggestions for managing the change that your visionary and transformational leadership creates.

You, Too, Can Make Management Gurus Weep with Joy

During the last decade, advisors to top management have emphasized the importance of *values* in providing visionary leadership to workers. According to this line of thinking, if the leader articulates the right values, many good results flow naturally. Workers at all levels will work in unison to increase productivity, quality, and profits and to advance the cause of humanity. Thumb through the *Harvard Business Review* for the last 12 years, and you find dozens of articles extolling the wonders of corporate values.

Key Word

A **value** is the importance a person attaches to something that serves as a guide to action. For example, if a person values the scientific method, he or she carefully researches the facts before submitting a recommendation to management.

Inspiring others to adopt high productivity and ethical behavior through value-driven leadership requires that you articulate specific values. To say, "Our company is driven by values" is not specific enough to guide the behavior of group members. The statement is true because values do influence all behavior. One of the reasons people stop at red lights even when no other cars are in sight is that they value obeying the law. However, you must clarify the general term "values" by pointing to specific values.

Here is a sampling of values that can be useful for guiding people toward the type of behavior that helps a vision come true:

➤ Profit; creating shareholder wealth

➤ High-quality goods and services; customer satisfaction

➤ Becoming a technology leader

➤ Continuous improvement

➤ Respect for people; helping employees grow and develop

➤ Job security for employees; brand recognition by millions of consumers

➤ Being a good neighbor; patriotism to the country

➤ Ethical behavior in dealing with workers, suppliers, and customers

➤ Providing a workplace free from physical and sexual harassment

The types of values illustrated here do not change behavior if they simply rest in corporate policy manuals, mission statements, and vision statements. You must discuss them regularly in staff meetings and address them when facing ethical dilemmas.

A manufacturing supervisor might ask the plant manager, "Do you think we can get by with inserting a few remanufactured (used) parts in these new machines? Our parts inventory is low, and we have to meet a tight deadline." The plant manager can point to the corporate value of complete honesty to guide this decision.

Another way in which a leader's values influence behavior is that the leader repeats the value at all opportune times. Jack Welch, the legendary former chairman and CEO of General Electric, places a strong value on quality as implemented through the Six Sigma program. In daily interactions with employees and in discussions with outsiders, Welch repeatedly mentions quality and how GE is still working hard to achieve Six Sigma (close to perfect quality). As a result, high quality is pursued in all GE business units.

Another Perspective

Values might not be taken as seriously as some management gurus believe. Many workers think corporate values state the obvious and fail to influence behavior because they seem more like lip service than a guide to action. As a union leader said, "If management believes that the company's most important asset is people, why don't they do more to prevent repetitive motion disorders?"

Oh, What a Beautiful Future!

Establishing a *vision* is a starting point in building a glorious future for your firm or your organizational unit. To form a vision, you must look beyond the immediate future to create an image of what the organization or unit can become. A vision highlights the discrepancy between present and ideal conditions and provides people with

139

something important to strive toward. Being able to articulate a vision is another important leadership behavior.

A common assumption is that an effective leader is supposed to be a visionary possessing a storehouse of fabulous ideas. The leader's own imagination is only one source of ideas for formulating a vision. You can gather information from many sources to create a vision:

➤ **Your intuition.** Listen to your own intuition about developments in your field, the markets you serve, and the preferences of your constituents.

Key Word

Create a **vision**—an idealized scenario of what the future can be—for your organization or an organizational unit. In contrast, a mission usually refers to the organization's purpose and its place in the world.

➤ **Your team.** Speak to group members individually and collectively to learn of their hopes and dreams for the future.

➤ **Your organization.** Study the entire organization's vision and develop a vision for your organizational unit that is compatible.

➤ **Your customers.** Hold group discussions about what it takes to please the people your group serves.

➤ **Research.** Read the work of futurists (specialists in making predictions about the future) as it relates to your type of work. Don't neglect annual reports, management books, and Web sites that describe the vision statements formulated by others.

Some firms spend six months to one year, part-time, agonizing over the construction of a vision statement. Sometimes the vision task force collects input from a thousand employees. My opinion, based on leadership workshops, is that after collecting the information such as that just outlined, you can usually formulate a vision in one meeting with a two-hour deadline. Here are three sample visions:

Microsoft Corporation: Give people the power to do anything they want, anywhere they want, and on any device.

Apple Computer (in its early days): We don't want to make computers. We want to change the world.

Tommy Hilfiger: Be whatever our customers want us to be.

Morgan Stanley, Dean Witter, Discover & Co.: We are bent on creating the preeminent financial services firm globally.

Public relations firm in New York: Be the leading African-American–owned promotional and public relations firm in the USA.

Advisor

A widely circulated misunderstanding about creating a vision is that it is a full-time job. Top executives often say that their main job is creating a vision for the organization, yet in reality they spend about 99 percent of their time engaged in other activities. Creating a vision is a high-impact activity, but leaders also have dozens of important responsibilities as described throughout this guide. A vision needs renewal only every few years, so, in my opinion, developing visions does not take much time, despite the importance of the activity.

Think, Talk, and Act Big

A distinguishing characteristic of strategic, or visionary, leaders is that they think and talk in terms of the big picture. Such mental activity adds to their charisma.

To gain a quick assessment of your current level of strategic thinking, take the following quiz. Indicate your strength of agreement with each of the following statements: strongly disagree (SD), disagree (D), neutral (N), agree (A), or strongly agree (SA). Circle the correct number for each question.

Scoring and interpretation: Obtain your total score by adding the point values for each question. A score of 42 to 50 suggests that you already think strategically, which should help you provide strategic leadership to others. Scores of 20 to 41 suggest a somewhat neutral, detached attitude toward thinking strategically. Scores of 10 to 19 suggest thinking that emphasizes the here and now and the short term. People scoring in this category are not yet ready to provide strategic leadership to others.

Thinking strategically requires high-level mental skills. Of prime importance are the ability to think conceptually, absorb and interpret a multitude of trends, and condense all of this information into a straightforward plan of action. Many people refer

Watch Out!

Thinking strategically will help you be a visionary and transformational leader, but don't go overboard. Avoid giving others the impression that talking about present work problems is too mundane to merit your attention. If you are a full-time visionary, your constituents do not receive the direction and guidance they need to handle present-day realities.

to this activity as "systems thinking." A key part of strategic thinking is understanding how your organization or unit can successfully interact with the outside environment.

Are You a Strategic Thinker?

Indicate your strength of agreement with each of the following statements: strongly disagree (SD), disagree (D), neutral (N), agree (A), or strongly agree (SA). Circle the correct number for each question.

	SD	D	N	A	SA
1. Every action I take on my job should somehow add value for our customers, clients, or public.	1	2	3	4	5
2. Let top management ponder the future; I have my own job to get done.	5	4	3	2	1
3. Strategic thinking is fluff. Somebody down in the organization has to get the job done.	5	4	3	2	1
4. A company cannot become great without an exciting vision.	1	2	3	4	5
5. What I do on the job each day can affect the company many years into the future.	1	2	3	4	5
6. It's rather pointless to develop skills or acquire knowledge that cannot help you on the job within the next month.	5	4	3	2	1
7. Strategic planning should be carried out by a separate department, rather than involving people throughout the firm.	5	4	3	2	1
8. It makes good sense for top management to frequently ask themselves the question, "What business are we really in?"	1	2	3	4	5
9. If a company does an outstanding job of satisfying its customers, there is very little need to worry about changing its mix of goods or services.	5	4	3	2	1
10. Organizational visions remind me of pipe dreams and hallucinations.	5	4	3	2	1
TOTAL					

A basic example is a product manager of diapers studying demographic data and observing that many more people are living much longer. A nonstrategic, nonsystems thinker might reflect, "Oh, well, this has no relevance for me. Our group makes diapers for babies." In contrast, a strategic systems thinker would say, "What a great opportunity for us. Our core business is serving the needs of people who cannot control the timing of eliminating bodily wastes. Let's start producing diapers for older people who might need them for personal use."

Creative problem-solving is also important for strategic thinking because the leader must develop alternative courses of action for shaping the organization. One such search for alternatives is, "How else can we make money besides what we are already doing?" Furthermore, asking "What if?" questions requires imagination. For example, when Navistar was still called International Harvester, the CEO asked the question, "What if we got out of the farm equipment business?" (That was akin to GM thinking of exiting the auto business.) The company then exited from its core business to concentrate on trucks, a decision that helped the company survive.

Can You Bring About Some Really Big Changes?

A major component of being a *transformational leader* is direction-setting, which involves anticipating and sometimes creating a future for the enterprise or organizational unit.

For example, IBM CEO Lew Gerstner told his managers during the mid-1990s that the company should gain a large share of revenues from providing services (such as maintaining computer systems) instead of relying so heavily on selling products. That move has been a dynamic success for IBM.

To set a productive direction for the future, the leader must accurately forecast or anticipate the future. Insight into tomorrow can take many forms, such as a leader making accurate forecasts about consumer preferences and customer demands. Understanding the future can also involve recognizing the skill mix required to operate the future organization.

Key Word

A **transformational leader** is one who helps organizations and people make positive changes in the way they conduct their activities. The changes are often large-scale and dramatic.

A truly visionary leader anticipates a future that many people do not think will come to pass. A classic example is that in the early days of xerography, market research indicated that most of the people polled saw no need for a product to replace carbon paper. (If you are unfamiliar with the term carbon paper, find somebody over 45 to explain what it means.)

Creating the future is a more forceful approach than anticipating the future. The leader, assisted by input from many people, creates conditions that do not already exist. He or she must ask questions about the shape of the industry in 5 to 10 years and decide how to ensure that the industry evolves in a way that is highly advantageous to the company.

The coffee-shop business is a good example of creating a future or reinventing an industry. Before the Starbucks chain, the upscale coffee-shop business was almost exclusively run by independent operators. Starbucks was soon joined by Timothy's World Coffee and New World Coffee.

After setting an exciting new direction for a company or reinventing the future, the leader typically chooses among six different methods for bringing about the changes:

143

➤ Changing the organizational culture

➤ Raising people's awareness about rewards

➤ Helping people look beyond self-interest

➤ Helping people search for self-fulfillment

➤ Investing others with a sense of urgency

➤ Committing to greatness

The following sections explain these methods.

Changing the Organization Culture

The most far-sweeping act of a transformational leader is revamping the organizational culture. This means that the values, attitudes, and entire atmosphere of the organization change. The most typical change is to convert the culture from a low-risk-taking, stiff, bureaucratic one to a culture in which people are more adventuresome and less constrained by rules and regulations.

Raising People's Awareness About Rewards

The transformational leader makes group members aware of the importance and values of certain rewards and how to achieve them. He or she might point to the pride workers might experience if the firm becomes number one in its field. At the same time, the transformational leader should point to the financial rewards accompanying such success.

Helping People Look Beyond Self-Interest

The transformational leader helps group members look at the big picture for the good of the team and the organization. Bit by bit, you make workers aware that their actions contribute to broader purposes than satisfying their own interest.

A leader helping workers look beyond self-interest might take this form: The leader tells a group of haggard workers who have put in 65-hour weeks for 2 months, "I know you feel beaten into the ground, and you are upset and angry. Keep in mind that the project you are working on will revolutionize the field, and you will be part of that revolution."

Helping People Search for Self-Fulfillment

The transformational leader helps people move beyond a focus on minor satisfactions to a quest for self-fulfillment. The leader might explain to a group of employees grumbling about the low quality of food served at a retreat, "I agree with you that the food here is disappointing. For a moment, think beyond the food. Every person here is being asked to participate in developing a new direction for the company. I suspect that is really more important to you than the food."

Investing Others with a Sense of Urgency

To create the transformation, the leader assembles a critical mass of managers and other workers and involves them in a discussion about the urgency of change. The critical message must be communicated that "If we don't change now, there may be no future for our organization (or department)."

Committing to Greatness

The ultimate transformational act is to get people excited about the prospects of doing great work and having a great organization. Everything else written in this book about leadership behavior contributes to greatness. Also, consider these suggestions:

> ➤ Have every worker write an essay about what actually constitutes greatness for the unit and the organization. Then hold a staff meeting about the key themes of the essays.

> ➤ Include a "greatness goal" in each worker's goal statement.

> ➤ Answer this question: "What would I have to do to feel like a great leader?"

Why Not Create a Revolution?

Another useful perspective on becoming a visionary and transformational leader is that you must think like a revolutionary. Suggesting useful, incremental changes or interesting tweaks might help the organization, but it does not constitute visionary or transformational leadership. Incremental changes include lowering the price of a product, modifying a product, shortening delivery time, or beginning a day-care program for employees.

What kind of a revolution can a leader create? Leading business strategist Gary Hamel notes that revolutionary thinking must seriously challenge the status quo. Overturning the way a product or service is manufactured or delivered can be classified as revolutionary thinking. An example is how Michael Dell, the founder of Dell Computer, revolutionized the marketing of computers to businesses and individuals by selling over the phone. Ted Waitt at Gateway Computer can be considered a co-revolutionary in the same domain.

What constitutes a revolutionary idea is subjective, especially because what some people call revolutionary is really recycling an old idea. For example, large-ticket items (such as mattresses) were sold by telephone long before the sale of computers by phone.

Learning how to become a revolutionary thinker is as complex as learning how to become more creative. Here are a few suggestions for getting started:

➤ Hold fantasy-brainstorming sessions in which you challenge a group of your brightest people to "be wilder than you have ever been before."

➤ Look at products, services, and work methods that are successful outside your field, and stretch your mind to find an application to what you are doing. The owner of a restaurant chain might ask, "Many large retailers run restaurants in their stores. What nonfood items could we profitably sell in our restaurants?"

➤ Read stories about breakthrough businesses in such magazines as *Entrepreneur, Success,* and *Working Woman.* Reading these stories might trigger your thinking about new possibilities for your firm.

➤ Develop a long list of the markets you do not serve. Ask for each one, "What could we do differently to reach this market?"

➤ Challenge the boundaries of your industry. Ask yourself questions such as "If banks can sell securities, and securities companies can provide banking services, how can we step outside our boundaries?" For example, how about a waste disposal service that also maintains windows and lawns?

Advisor

Many business strategists believe that Jeff Bezos, the founder of Amazon.com, is a revolutionary. His company sells books through the Internet, offering readers a choice of over 2,000,000 titles and allowing readers to browse some of these books. Amazon.com also sells a wide variety of merchandise and has affiliations with hundreds of retailers. The revolutionary thinking is that Amazon.com is a virtual bookstore and general retailer that provides order fulfillment and shipping. Along with a substantial inventory of its own, the company sells books owned by publishers or distributors. Amazon.com receives a commission for each order it places with another bookseller and other affiliated retailers.

Being a Knowledge Manager

A key, new role for transformational and strategic leaders is to create conditions in which the organization can learn and manage knowledge well. To accomplish this feat, a knowledge manager needs to cultivate a *learning organization.* The terms are confusing because they differ slightly from their commonsense meaning. The basic idea is that the leader helps the entire firm or organizational unit adapt well to the environment. To manage knowledge is to facilitate people throughout the organization so that they have the information they need to do their jobs well.

When knowledge is managed effectively, information is shared as needed whether it is printed, stored electronically, or rests in the brains of workers. Managing knowledge well helps an organization learn. A major activity in *knowledge management (KM)* is to take steps to facilitate information-sharing. The accompanying figure sheds light on the problem: Too much information is stored in private CPUs, often referred to as the human brain. It is good to have knowledge in the brain, but it also needs to be disseminated and stored elsewhere. Here, we look at a few effective approaches to knowledge sharing.

➤ Encourage workers to circulate books and articles or bring relevant Net-based information to the attention of each other.

➤ Gather to discuss ways of handling an activity, within a work unit or across divisions. Ask each other to share experiences that relate to the problem at hand.

➤ Work with the information systems department to establish an elegant database of employee knowledge and skills, sometimes referred to as "corporate Yellow Pages."

➤ Offer small rewards to former employees and retired employees who can contribute relevant knowledge. It has often been said that thinned-out organizations suffer from corporate Alzheimer's disease.

Managing knowledge is so important that at least 100 large firms have created positions with a labels such as Chief Knowledge Officer, or Chief Learning Officer. For now, you be your own CKO or CLO. It could help you become a COO or CEO. (Did somebody say business has too many acronyms?)

Key Word

A **learning organization** is one that *is* skilled at creating, acquiring, and transferring knowledge. It also modifies behavior to reflect new knowledge and insights. For example, a learning organization might fire too many talented people during a downsizing and be shorthanded when business conditions improve. The next time business declines, top management would figure out how to find a way to retain a larger number of talented people.

Key Word

Knowledge management (KM) is the systematic sharing of information to achieve such goals as innovation, nonduplication of effort, and competitive advantage. You know you are managing knowledge well when proprietary information is available to those in need.

An example of knowledge management.

(Adapted from The Delphi Group)

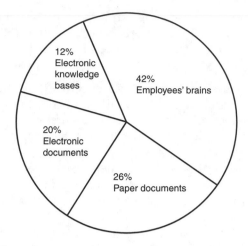

12%
Electronic
knowledge
bases

42%
Employees' brains

20%
Electronic
documents

26%
Paper documents

Now That You've Created This Monster, What Do You Do Next?

As a visionary and transformational leader, assume you create some large-scale changes. Maybe you transform the culture of your organization or department into one that takes greater risks and is more competitive. Maybe you move your company into a new way of doing business. Maybe you are now serving entirely different markets.

You need to overcome heel-dragging in regard to the changes and also ensure that the changes are implemented successfully in other ways. The following sections describe a few suggestions for managing change based on extensive research and opinions.

Helping People Understand the Need for Change

Even though you brought about changes, many people need convincing to sustain the changes. The transformational leader must help group members understand the need for change, both emotionally and intellectually. The problem is that change involves dislocation and discomfort. A big change faced by many middle managers today is that they must shift from the comforts of running a department to being a team leader with much less authority.

An effective transformational leader recognizes the emotional component to resisting change and deals with it openly. Ways of dealing with the emotions and attitudes surrounding change include the following:

➤ Conduct a one-hour discussion about how the change might adversely affect the person.

➤ Hold group discussions about the need for change in a competitive, changing environment.

➤ Conduct a group discussion about the advantages and disadvantages of the change.

➤ Present financial information about the need for change.

Gain Political Support for Change

In practice, few workplace innovations get through firms without the change agent forming alliances with the people who will support his or her proposals. Top management must buy into, and preferably sponsor, the program. Gaining *political support* often means selling the proposed changes to senior executives before proceeding down the hierarchy. It is much more difficult to create change from the bottom up. Even if you are a top-management leader, you need political support at lower levels.

Assume that as a top-management leader, you bring about an organizational change for the company to open its employment doors to disadvantaged people. Because managers at lower levels in the organization handle the recruiting and hiring, you need their buy-in. Like a U.S. president telephoning members of Congress to gain support for a piece of legislation, use your personal influence with managers across the organization.

Point Out the Financial Benefits

Because so many workers are concerned about the financial consequences of work changes, it is helpful to discuss these matters openly. Suppose, for example, that the firm is moving toward becoming a *virtual corporation* for introducing new products. Employees would welcome learning how these strategic alliances might translate into higher employee earnings.

Key Word

Political support refers to a situation in which others support your ideas because they feel a personal allegiance to you and thus become champions of your ideas.

Key Word

A **virtual corporation** is a temporary alliance of independent firms joining forces to share skills, costs, and access to each other's markets. In this way a new company does not have to be formed that would require new office staff, employees, and equipment. And when the joint project is completed, nobody is laid off because nobody new was hired.

Place Adaptable People in Key Spots

An important tactic for effectively introducing change is placing the right people in jobs directly associated with the change. The "right people" in this instance are those with a reputation for being flexible and adaptable.

Assume that the focus of your transformation is to make the company or unit more disposed toward taking risks. You, therefore, plant a person in charge of bidding on contracts who has a track record of taking risks and stretching his or her imagination. This person is likely to encourage others to extend the boundaries of the type of work the company thinks it can handle. An example is a building contractor bidding on a contract four times as big as any project it has handled before.

Allow for Discussion and Negotiation

You can reduce lingering resistance to change by discussing and negotiating the more sensitive aspects of change. The fact that discussion is a form of participation in decision-making contributes to its effectiveness. Discussion also often leads to negotiation, which further involves employees in the change process.

Assume that, as part of workplace innovation, the company wants to disband several departments in favor of forming self-managing teams. Some of the professionals might be concerned about losing expertise because they will be forced to work as generalists. These highly skilled professionals might be reassured by being told that they can still rotate through assignments that call for their professional expertise.

Refer to Your Inspirational Vision

A strategic way of gaining acceptance and implementing change is to inspire people with uplifting statements about the firm's future. Given that you have already developed your inspiring vision statement, refer to it frequently.

Some companies print their vision statement on coffee mugs and key chains. From time to time, broadcast your uplifting message over e-mail. Remind others of the glorious future of your firm. Some cynics will snicker, but do not be perturbed. Even the greatest leaders do not attain the support of 100 percent of their constituents.

How About Some Hard Data About What Transformational Leaders Really Do?

Doing transformations is not as well structured as replacing transmissions in a car or computing the market valuation of a company. However, a recent study on the behaviors of transformational leaders reported in the *Journal of Business and Psychology* provides a few specifics. According to the research reported, transformational leadership consists of seven behaviors. All of these behaviors are covered at some point in this guide. Consequently, you won't be left empty-handed the next time you do a transformation. The seven key behaviors are listed next, along with a simple statement of what these behaviors mean to employees.

1. **Vision.** Communicates a clear and positive vision of the future.

2. **Staff development.** Treats staff as individuals, and supports and encourages their development.

3. **Supportive leadership.** Gives encouragement and recognition to staff.

4. **Empowerment.** Fosters trust, involvement, and cooperation among team members.

5. **Innovative thinking.** Encourages thinking about problems in new ways and questions assumptions.

6. **Lead by example.** Is clear about his or her values and practices what he or she preaches.

7. **Charisma.** Instills pride and respect in others and inspires by being highly competent.

The Least You Need to Know

➤ Incorporate values into your visionary and transformational leadership by including such elements as "profit," "high-quality goods and services," and "helping employees grow and develop."

➤ Create effective vision statements by using such sources of information as your intuition about the future and the hopes and dreams of group members.

➤ Present yourself as a strategic thinker by thinking and talking in terms of the big picture and by interpreting trends in the outside environment.

➤ Set the direction for large-scale change by anticipating and sometimes creating a future for the enterprise or organizational unit.

➤ The revolutionary thinker goes beyond suggesting useful, incremental changes. The revolutionary thinker overturns the way a product or service is manufactured or delivered.

➤ Manage the type of change your transformations create through such means as helping people understand the need for change, gaining political support for change, and pointing out the financial benefits.

➤ Manage knowledge so that people throughout the organization share useful knowledge.

Part 3

You Can Become a Team Leader

The new organizational world with all its downsizing, rightsizing, and streamlining has eliminated many managerial leadership positions. Yet, many new managerial positions have been created, especially the position of team leader. A newly appointed team leader described his new position to his retired father, who had worked as a supervisor in a steel mill.

The father asked, "Do you wear a different-colored hard hat from the others in the group?" The son said, "No, Dad, we're more democratic than that."

The father asked next, "Are you the guy responsible for hiring and firing workers?" The son replied, "No, Dad, those are really team decisions."

Getting a little frustrated, the father said, "Okay, then you must be the one who decides who gets a raise and how much?" The son replied again, "No, Dad. I don't make those kind of decisions myself."

The father then asked, "If you answered 'no' to all my questions, why do they call you a leader?" The son replied, "Because a team leader facilitates. I help the group accomplish work, but I don't give orders. What you did was great in your day, Dad, but times have changed."

In this part, you'll learn about the many exciting activities carried out by team leaders, including assigning roles, enhancing team spirit, and resolving conflict.

Chapter 12

You Can Become a Motivational Force

In This Chapter

➤ Capitalizing on the WIIFM principle

➤ Recognizing what people really want

➤ Setting goals, goals, and more goals

➤ Diagnosing motivational problems

➤ Motivating members of Generation X

➤ Setting up a motivational climate

Paula, the manager of the deli department, was slowly accumulating evidence that Nick, the deli clerk, was lazy. One day Paula watched him interact with a customer who asked for two thirds of a pound of ham. Nick asked the customer, "How about just taking the amount I already sliced? It should be about right." The scale read 0.54 pounds, and the customer grumbled, "I'm not happy, but I'll take it."

Paula thought to herself, "Is Nick so busy he can't go back and slice a little more ham?"

A few days later, Paula observed a similar incident. This time an elderly man asked for three quarters of a pound of pastrami, sliced thin. Nick responded, "Why don't I even off that order to one pound? It saves some time, and then you have some extra pastrami." The customer said, "I don't really want a full pound, but I'll take it if it's the best you can do."

At the end of Nick's shift, Paula called him into the back room for a motivational talk. "Nick," she said, "I've noticed you've been giving customers a hard time when they order various amounts of cold cuts. Are you too lazy to give customers what they want?"

Nick answered, "Paula, you've got me all wrong. I do okay when customers ask me for a full pound or a half pound. Then I give them exactly the amount they ask for. It's just that I have no idea how to convert fractions into the decimals used on the scale."

"I'm sorry, Nick," said Paula. "I was confusing a lack of skill with low motivation. I'll help you by making a chart that converts fractions into decimals and decimals into fractions. Then you'll be able to fill whatever order a customer wants."

The interchange between Paula and Nick illustrates a frequently overlooked point about motivating people. To be a motivational force, a leader or manager must be able to diagnose the motivational situation. In this chapter, you will learn how to diagnose motivational problems and how to apply key methods of motivating workers. Other topics in this book also deal with the perennial challenge of motivation. Among the topics I cover are developing charisma (Chapter 4, "How About a More Charismatic You?"), influencing others (Chapter 7, "Your Tool Kit of Influence Tactics"), empowering yourself and others (Chapter 17, "How to Become an Empowering Leader"), and giving feedback and positive reinforcement (Chapter 23, "Giving Feedback and Positive Reinforcement").

Are You WIIFM or Against Them?

One of a leader's most important responsibilities is motivating people to do things in the interest of the organization. It pays to take seriously a motivational principle that is almost as reliable as the law of gravity: People are motivated by self-interest. This principle is referred to as "What's in it for me?" or *WIIFM* (pronounced *WIFF-em*).

Reflect on your own experience. Before working hard to accomplish a task (including studying this book), you probably want to know how you will benefit. If your manager asks you to work extra hours to take care of an emergency, you will most likely oblige. Yet underneath you might be thinking, "If I work these extra hours, my boss will think highly of me. As a result, I will probably receive a good performance evaluation and maybe a better-than-average salary increase."

Nick, our fractionally challenged deli clerk, will probably be motivated to learn how to use the conversion chart for fractions and decimals. What's in it for him is that he can now avoid embarrassment when a customer requests one third of a pound of Italian salami. He can

Key Word

WIIFM (pronounced *WIFF-em*), or **"What's in it for me?"** is a universal motivational principle indicating that people are motivated to achieve goals to the extent that they think their self-interests will be satisfied. A simpler way of stating this principle is that self-interest is the great motivator.

triumphantly look for 0.333 lb on the butcher scale. Besides, adding to his skill repertoire will add to his job security.

A perplexing issue to ponder is how the WIIFM principle explains why people are motivated to help others. Why would a CEO donate gift baskets of food to the homeless? Why hire a virtually unemployable person for a nonproductive job in the company? People who perform acts of social good receive the reward of feeling better about themselves. In psychological terms, they satisfy their needs to nurture others. A cynical reason is that helping the unfortunate leads to recognition for being a good Samaritan.

If you are interested in seeing how helping others can satisfy self-interest, do the following. Next time you feel down on yourself, do a kind deed for a homeless person or someone in need. You'll undoubtedly experience a quick fix of need satisfaction.

Although the WIIFM principle may be almost as reliable as the law of gravity (well, not exactly), it is not so easy to implement. Part of the problem is that you might not have to offer whatever will satisfy the person's self-interests.

How to Use WIIFM

To use the WIIFM principle in motivating others, you must find out what *needs, desires,* or *motives* a person wants to satisfy. You find out these needs by asking people what they want or by observing what interests them.

Key Word

A **need** is an inner striving or urge to do something, such as an urge to accomplish something worthwhile. A need can be regarded as a biological or psychological requirement. Needs and motives function in about the same way because a **motive** is an inner drive that moves a person to do something. The words "needs" and "motives" are often used interchangeably. A **desire** is like a need but it falls more into the "nice to have" rather than the "must have" category.

For instance, the way you might motivate a recognition-hungry group member is to tell that person, "If you perform 10 percent above quota for 6 consecutive months, we will get you a plaque signifying your achievement to hang on the wall."

Here are some suggestions for identifying the needs, desires, or motives your team members may want to satisfy:

➤ Carefully observe what appear to be the person's spontaneous interests. If the person spends a lot of time searching the Internet, motivate that person by offering the opportunity to do a work-related Internet assignment.

➤ Give the person a chance to discuss goals and aspirations. You might find out, for example, that the person likes the comfort of working at home. Use the opportunity to work at home as a potential motivator.

➤ Ask work associates what they think are the biggest motivators for each group member. Each person writes down what he or she thinks best motivates every other group member. The exercise could be illuminating and could also add to group cohesiveness.

➤ Keep in mind that the WIIFM principle may sometimes be difficult to implement either because you cannot identify what people want or because they are not sure themselves. Some people are not clearly aware of what is in their best interest.

Before digging further into the study of how leaders motivate people (both here and in Chapter 23) take the following quiz. It will give you some gauge of your present level of knowledge about work motivation.

Scoring and interpretation: Add the circled numbers to obtain your score.

90 to 100: You have advanced knowledge and skill with respect to motivating others on the job. Continue to build on the solid knowledge base you have established.

50 to 89: You have average knowledge and skill with respect to motivating others. With additional study and experience, you will probably develop advanced motivational skills.

20 to 49: To effectively motivate others on the job, you need to greatly expand your knowledge of motivation theory and techniques.

Why Are You People So Needy?

To effectively capitalize on the fact that people operate from self-interest, you have to understand which needs (or internal strivings) a person is trying to satisfy. You also have to understand the need cycle.

The Need Cycle

The central idea behind need theory is that unsatisfied needs motivate us until the needs become satisfied. When people are dissatisfied or anxious about their present status or performance, they try to reduce this anxiety.

My Approach to Motivating Others

Describe how often you act or think in the way indicated by the following statements when you are attempting to motivate another person. Scale: Very infrequently (VI), Infrequently (I), Sometimes (S), Frequently (F), or Very frequently (VF).

	VI	I	S	F	VF
1. I ask the other person what he or she is hoping to achieve in the situation.	1	2	3	4	5
2. I attempt to figure out if the person has the ability to do what I need done.	1	2	3	4	5
3. When another person is heel-dragging, it usually means he or she is lazy.	5	4	3	2	1
4. I explain exactly what I want to the person I'm trying to motivate.	1	2	3	4	5
5. I like to give the other person a reward up front so he or she will be motivated.	5	4	3	2	1
6. I give lots of feedback when another person is performing a task for me.	1	2	3	4	5
7. I like to belittle another person enough so that he or she will be intimidated into doing what I need.	5	4	3	2	1
8. I make sure that the other person feels treated fairly.	1	2	3	4	5
9. I figure that if I smile nicely I can get the other person to work as hard as I need.	5	4	3	2	1
10. I attempt to get what I need done by instilling fear in the other person.	5	4	3	2	1
11. I specify exactly what needs to be accomplished.	1	2	3	4	5
12. I generally praise people who help me get my work accomplished.	1	2	3	4	5
13. A job well done is its own reward. I therefore keep praise to a minimum.	5	4	3	2	1
14. I make sure to let people know how well they have done in meeting my expectations on a task.	1	2	3	4	5
15. To be fair, I attempt to reward people similarly no matter how well they have performed.	5	4	3	2	1
16. When somebody doing work for me performs well, I recognize his or her accomplishments promptly.	1	2	3	4	5
17. Before giving somebody a reward, I attempt to find out what would appeal to that person.	1	2	3	4	5
18. I make a policy not to thank somebody for doing a job they are paid to do.	5	4	3	2	1
19. If people do not know how to perform a task, their motivation will suffer.	1	2	3	4	5
20. If properly designed, many jobs can be self-rewarding.	1	2	3	4	5

TOTAL

Assess your motivational skills.

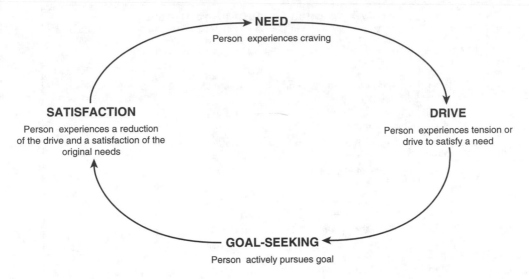

The need cycle.

Assume that you have a strong need for recognition. As a result, you experience tension that drives you to find some way of being recognized on the job. The action you decide to take is to apply for the position of team leader of your group. You reason that your appointment as team leader would provide ample recognition, particularly if the team performs well.

Advisor

The need cycle helps to explain why most people are difficult to satisfy and motivate. You satisfy one of their needs and motives, and they then want a bigger jolt of need satisfaction. Worse, they next shop around to satisfy a higher-level need. The same principle works on and off the job. Have you ever met anyone who seems to have found the perfect pastime and then within a year starts looking for an even more exciting one?

You are appointed to the position, and for now your need for recognition is partially satisfied as you receive compliments from your co-workers and friends. Once you receive this partial satisfaction, two things typically happen. Either you will soon require a stronger dose of recognition, or you will begin to concentrate on another need or motive, such as achievement.

In either case, the need cycle will repeat itself. You might seek another form of recognition or satisfaction of your need for power. For example, you might apply for a position as department manager. Ideally, in this situation your boss gives you more responsibility. You might even open your own business. Either way, your action could lead to more satisfaction of your recognition need and to some satisfaction of your achievement need.

Let's Get Down to Specifics

As a leader or potential leader, you should be aware of some of the more prevalent needs group members probably want to satisfy on the job. Giving people an opportunity to satisfy these needs will improve your motivational force:

➤ **Achievement.** People with a strong achievement drive find joy in accomplishment for its own sake. The achievement need can be satisfied by building something from the ground up or completing a major project.

➤ **Power.** People with a high power need feel compelled to control resources, such as other people and money. To truly satisfy a power need, a person would have to hold a significant managerial or leadership position. However, you might be able to appeal to a group member's power need by giving the person a chance to control a major account. For many people, a taste of power beats the deprivation of having no power at all.

➤ **Affiliation.** People with a strong affiliation need seek out close relationships with others and tend to be loyal as friends or employees. Promising an employee an assignment to a stable work group can appeal to his or her need for affiliation.

➤ **Recognition.** People with a strong need for recognition want to be acknowledged for their contribution and efforts. The recognition motive can be satisfied through winning contests, receiving awards, and seeing one's name in print. Chapter 23 gives you suggestions for recognizing and satisfying the universal need for recognition.

➤ **Dominance.** People with a strong need for dominance want to influence others toward their way of thinking, often by forceful methods. People driven by dominance often take over in meetings and volunteer to be leaders, and they are good at the hard sell. A leader can appeal to a person's need for dominance by rewarding the person with a chance to be in charge of something important.

➤ **Order.** People with a strong need for order have the urge to organize things. They also want to achieve arrangement, balance, neatness, and precision.

Projects abound on any job that might appeal to a person's need for order. Among them are organizing a database or reorganizing a warehouse.

➤ **Thrill-seeking.** People with a strong thrill-seeking motive crave excitement and are driven to a life of stimulation and risk-taking, such as conducting avalanche rescues. Dealing in penny stocks can satisfy the thrill-seeking urge, as can introducing a new product in a highly competitive environment. You might appeal to a thrill-seeker in your group by rewarding the person with the opportunity to repossess company property.

➤ **Security.** Most people have a strong need to work in a safe environment, be free from both physical and emotional injury, and have relatively stable employment. The need for security can be satisfied by a safe, friendly work environment and a full-time, relatively permanent job.

Watch Out!

Most people like to discuss their wonderful high-level needs, such as wanting achievement and power. However, they might also be motivated by more basic needs, such as affiliation and security.

A Four-Letter Word for Focusing People's Energies

The simplest way to be a motivational force in the lives of others is also the most effective. Encouraging and assisting people in establishing goals will help them focus their energy better and elevate their performance. A *goal* is an event, circumstance, object, or condition a person strives to attain. A goal thus reflects your desire or intention to regulate your actions.

Advisor

The contribution of goal-setting to motivation and performance has been documented in literally hundreds of studies. Time and time again when people set goals, they perform better. A common-place example would be to improve customer service performance by establishing a goal of an average two-minute wait for a telephone inquiry, when the present average wait is four minutes.

Despite the many advantages of setting goals, not just any goal will do. Goal-setting is an art, in the sense that some people do a better job of goal-setting than others. A few suggestions follow for setting effective goals—those that lead to achieving what a person hopes to achieve. Helping group members to set goals with these characteristics will enhance your motivational force:

➤ **Set specific goals.** A goal such as "improve performance" is too vague to serve as a guide for daily action. A more useful goal is to express exactly what is meant by improved performance and when it should be achieved.

➤ **Formulate realistically difficult goals.** Goals that stretch people's capabilities are motivational—provided they are not so difficult that frustration over not attaining them is inevitable.

➤ **Write down concise goals.** A useful goal can usually be expressed in a short, punchy statement. An example is "Increase collection of past-due accounts by 50 percent by December 31 of this year."

➤ **Ensure that the person you are attempting to motivate accepts the goal.** The evidence is a little mixed on this point, but for goals to improve performance, the worker must usually accept them. That is why it is often helpful to discuss goals with group members rather than imposing goals on them.

➤ **Describe what you are actually doing if you reach your goal.** An effective goal specifies the behavior that results after the goal is achieved. A useful goal for a sales representative is "Increase the percent of leads I turn into actual sales." Turning more leads into sales is exactly what the rep will be doing upon reaching the goal.

➤ **Set goals for different time periods.** You might have daily goals, short-range goals, medium-range goals, and long-range goals.

➤ **Use progress toward goals as a measure for performance evaluations and other feedback.** When group members know that how well they do in achieving their goals counts when their performance is evaluated, they work even harder to achieve goals.

➤ **Specify what is going to be accomplished, who is going to accomplish it, when it is going to be accomplished, and how it is going to be accomplished.** The *what, who, when,* and *how* of goal-setting covers a lot of ground. It helps people focus their energies on what effective goal-setting really entails.

Another Perspective

Some experts believe that people should set outlandish goals so they can "be all they can be" and attain wild dreams. A good resolution of this problem is to set realistic goals for the most part but also plug in a fantasy goal. For example, a product manager might be motivated by keeping in the back of her mind a goal such as developing a product that will revolutionize the industry.

An example is "The video disk sales manager will increase the number of sales by 40 percent within 15 months by selling to dealers with satisfactory sales records. Returns and nonpayment will be subtracted from the total number of sales."

What's the Missing Link?

Using an explanation of motivation called "expectancy theory," it is possible for managers and leaders to diagnose fairly accurately why motivation is low in a given situation. The expectancy in *expectancy theory* refers to the idea that people will work hard depending on what they expect to receive from their efforts.

According to expectancy theory, a person will be motivated (put forth effort) under three conditions:

1. **The effort-to-performance expectancy is high.** Under this condition, the person believes strongly that he or she can perform the task, such as Nick, the deli worker, being able to convert fractions into decimals or a financial analyst being able to run new software for estimating the true value of a company's stock.

Key Word

The **expectancy theory** of motivation is based on the premise that how much effort people expend depends on the reward they expect to receive in return. (Notice the similarity to WIIFM?) Expectancy theory assumes that people are rational and logical. In any given situation, they want to maximize gain and minimize loss.

2. **The performance-to-outcome expectancy is high.** Under this condition, the person believes strongly that performance will lead to certain outcomes, such as earning more money, getting a promotion, or holding onto a job.

3. **The valence (worth of the outcome) is high.** If the person highly values the outcome, such as a raise, promotion, or job security, the person will more likely be motivated. The intensity of the need satisfaction must also be high. A team member might work harder to receive a $5,000 annual raise than he would to receive a $500 raise.

Assume that you are attempting to motivate a group member in a given situation. Somehow the person is not working as intently as you had hoped. Using expectancy theory to diagnose why the person's motivation is not strong, seek answers to the following questions:

➤ Does the person I am attempting to motivate have the skills and self-confidence to do the job? If the person feels ill-equipped to perform, he or she will be discouraged and show little motivation. You may have to intervene with skills training and self-confidence building.

➤ What assurance does the person have that if he or she performs the work, the promised reward will be forthcoming? Does the company have a decent reputation for following through on promises? What about me? Have I established my credibility as a person who follows through on promises? If you or the company are not trusted, motivation could be reduced substantially.

➤ How badly does the person want the reward being offered in the situation? Am I offering a reward that will make it worthwhile for the person to do what I need done? If the sum of the outcomes in the situation is close to zero (some positive, some negative), motivation will be absent. A negative outcome indicates problems associated with receiving a reward, such as having to travel extensively if promoted.

➤ Are there any zeros in response to the first three questions? If so, motivation will be absent because expectancy theory holds that a zero response to one question wipes out the values of the responses to other questions. As in algebra, when you multiply anything by zero in an equation, the result is zero.

Yeah, but What About Those Gen-X People?

Group stereotypes have their limits for motivation. People within the group are likely to vary considerably among themselves. For example, many senior citizens are not particularly interested in stability and security. They are willing to take a low salary with big stock options just to get in on the ground floor of a high-tech start-up. Despite these reservations about group stereotypes, there are some consistent observations about what makes Gen-Xers (born between 1965 and 1980) tick. The following list of work preferences will give you a few ideas for motivating members of Generation X, including yourself. Or, if you are a member of Gen X who has a Baby Boomer boss, share this list with him or her.

➤ They like variety, not doing the same thing every work day.

➤ Part of their career goals is to face new challenges and opportunities. It's not all based on money, but on growth and learning.

➤ They want jobs that are cool, fun, and fulfilling.

➤ They believe that if they keep growing and learning that's all the security they need. Advancing their skill-set is their top priority.

➤ They have a tremendous thirst for knowledge.

➤ Unlike Baby Boomers, who tend to work independently, Gen-Xers like to work in a team environment.

➤ They prefer learning by doing and making mistakes as they go along.

➤ They are apt to challenge established ways of doing things, reasoning that there is always a better way.

➤ They want regular, frequent feedback on job performance.

➤ Career improvement is a blend of life and job balance.

Like most people, members of Gen X are motivated by exciting, challenging work that provides some opportunity for teamwork and allows for a balanced life. At times, this platitude is easier to articulate than implement.

Think Big and Set Up a Supercharged Atmosphere

The techniques for enhancing motivation mentioned in this chapter and in Chapter 23 work well at an individual and group level. If you want to motivate others from a strategic or macro point of view, however, it is essential to establish an organizational culture that leads to high motivation.

For example, if your job title is "astronaut," you feel compelled to work hard regardless of whether your boss is an effective motivator. The organizational climate surrounding the astronauts assumes that each team member gives his or her all. This supercharged atmosphere among the astronauts still exists despite the many woes of NASA and the space program.

Organizational climate or *corporate culture* is a system of shared values and beliefs that actively influence the behavior of workers throughout the organization. Simply put, the organizational or corporate culture is its norms.

Key Word

The right **corporate culture** can inspire employees to be productive. Similarly, the wrong culture can lead to low productivity. A new corporate culture cannot be implemented as readily as an employee recognition program. It takes a long time to develop a culture that fosters strong motivation and productivity.

An organizational culture that fosters strong motivation has several of the following characteristics reported by psychologist Michael Cavanagh in *Personnel Journal*:

➤ An atmosphere that rewards excellence by giving big rewards to top performers. This characteristic is doubled-edged: Outstanding performers get big raises and promotions, whereas poor performers get few raises and no promotions and may even be terminated.

➤ An atmosphere that rewards creative thought by giving tangible rewards to innovators. At the same time, few penalties are imposed on people whose creative ideas lead to failure.

➤ A pervasive belief that the organization is a winner. If employees believe that they belong to a winning team, many of them will be highly motivated. (Not even the greatest motivation guru can eliminate all the free riders in a company.) Proud organizations such as Cisco Systems, Barnes & Noble, and _____ capitalize on this aspect of culture. (The blank is for the name of your company after you implement the ideas in this book.)

➤ A spirit of helpfulness that encourages employees to believe they can overcome setbacks. Motivation is enhanced when workers believe that when they face job hurdles, the company will provide assistance.

The Least You Need to Know

➤ Use the WIIFM principle by figuring out what people really want.

➤ Recognize that needs determine what motivates people by establishing a driving force within them.

➤ Create goals that are motivational through such means as developing specific, difficult goals that will serve as the basis for performance evaluation later on.

➤ Diagnose motivational problems using expectancy theory and evaluate whether the person has the training and self-confidence necessary to accomplish the job.

➤ Be aware of Gen X work preferences so you can motivate them toward high performance.

➤ Build an organizational culture that motivates people, such as a climate whereby people get caught up in the excitement of performing well.

Chapter 13

The People Side of Team Leadership

> **In This Chapter**
>
> ➤ Establishing a teamwork culture
>
> ➤ Getting team members to treat each other as customers
>
> ➤ Getting people to trust each other and management
>
> ➤ Using terms and phrases that support teamwork
>
> ➤ Establishing characteristics of a winning team
>
> ➤ Getting the team to spend time together

"I'm having a terrible problem," said team leader Larry to an organization development consultant. "I'm trying to get the employees assigned to my team to be better team players. There is no way this crew of prima donnas is going to be a strong team if they don't grow up and see what they are doing wrong."

"Why do they need to be a strong team?" asked the consultant.

"Because without a strong team, we'll never drive a stake through the heart of the competition. It's a dog-eat-dog world out there. My workers had better realize that soon."

"I can tell from the few comments you've made so far," said the consultant, "that it could be you who is blocking teamwork. You think of the team members as subordinates; you describe them in negative terms; and you have an overly harsh view of competition. Instead of wanting to win your share of rewards, you want to drive a stake through the heart of the competition. You say you want teamwork, yet you talk like an authoritarian combatant. Developing better teamwork could start with you."

Another Perspective

Many companies emphasize the team concept. Hewlett-Packard is a good example because their work teams are based on the assumption of egalitarianism rather than hierarchy. Team members generally feel that their contribution is as important as that of the team leader. Of course, in an organization with so much depth of talent (only geniuses need apply at Microsoft), it's easy to implement the team concept.

Key Word

In most situations, **team leaders** have less formal authority than a department head. In some organizations, the team leader position is rotated among group members because it is believed that all members have leadership potential.

The honest and clear-thinking consultant certainly did not tell team leader Larry what he wanted to hear. The consultant points to several attributes of dealing with the human aspects of team leadership.

In this chapter, you will learn various people-oriented techniques for being a good team leader. The next two chapters deal with other aspects of team leadership—developing team spirit and managing the tasks involved in team leadership.

Begin with a Little Brainwashing

A major challenge relating to the people side of team leadership is establishing a culture that fosters teamwork.

This challenge is similar to establishing the right culture for motivating people, as described in the preceding chapter. Although top management has the lion's share of the responsibility for establishing an organizational culture, the team leader also contributes to the development of culture. A *team leader* is a manager who coordinates the work of a small group of people while acting as a facilitator and catalyst. He or she can contribute to a subculture that fosters teamwork. Given that team leaders usually do not have much formal authority, they have to work extra hard at establishing a culture or subculture.

The recommended strategy is for the team leader to promote the attitude that working together effectively is an expected standard of conduct. Developing a culture (or norm) of teamwork is difficult when a strong culture of individualism exists within the larger company. Although the tactics and strategies described in the rest of the chapter support a teamwork culture, here are a few easy-to-implement suggestions to consider:

➤ **Broadcast.** Publicly mention incidents and anecdotes that illustrate teamwork within the group such as, "The other day, Billy's PC crashed and it looked as though his valuable data flew into cyberspace. However, Jackie jumped in and retrieved the information. She saved the day."

➤ **Communicate.** Share with team members your analysis of what makes good teamwork. You might say something to the effect of, "When we first started as a team, we were like a tennis team. We added together the sum of our contributions. Now we are playing as a soccer team—a true collective effort. We are all dependent upon one another."

➤ **Reinforce.** Strengthen the concept of team play with rhetorical questions such as "Because our company now has a team-based organizational structure, I wonder how long it will be before our performance evaluations include a space for evaluating team play?"

Team leaders who themselves believe in teamwork are in a better position to establish a culture of teamwork. Take the following quiz to think through your attitudes toward teamwork.

Team Player Attitudes

Describe how well you agree with each of the following statements, using the following scale: Disagree Strongly (DS); Disagree (D); Neutral (N); Agree (A); Agree Strongly (AS).

	DS	D	N	A	AS
1. I am at my best when working alone.	5	4	3	2	1
2. I have belonged to clubs and teams ever since I was a child.	1	2	3	4	5
3. It takes far too long to get work accomplished with a group.	5	4	3	2	1
4. I like the friendship of working in a group.	1	2	3	4	5
5. I would prefer to run a one-person business than to be a member of a large firm.	5	4	3	2	1
6. It's difficult to trust others in the group on key assignments.	5	4	3	2	1
7. Encouraging others comes to me naturally.	1	2	3	4	5
8. I like the give-and-take of ideas that is possible in a group.	1	2	3	4	5
9. It is fun for me to share responsibility with other group members.	1	2	3	4	5
10. Much more can be accomplished by a team than by the same number of people working alone.	1	2	3	4	5
Total score	—	—	—	—	—

171

Scoring and interpretation: Add the numbers you have circled to obtain your total score.

41 to 50: You have strong, positive attitudes toward being a team member and working cooperatively with other members.

30 to 31: You have moderately favorable attitudes toward being a team member and working cooperatively with other members.

10 to 29: You much prefer working by yourself than being a team member. To work effectively in a company that emphasizes teamwork, you may need to develop more positive attitudes toward working jointly with others.

"I Love Ya, Babe; You're a Customer"

In the eyes of many management specialists, everybody with whom you interact is your customer. Nevertheless, most workers treat external customers with more respect and concern than they do fellow employees. Some team leaders encourage team members to treat each other as if they were external customers, thus fostering cooperative behavior and politeness. Treating team members as external customers involves the following actions:

➤ Take a team member to lunch just to maintain a working relationship.

➤ Ask a teammate if you can help him solve a difficult problem.

➤ Ask a teammate exactly the kind of input she needs so you can do an outstanding job of helping her.

➤ Smile and be pleasantly surprised whenever you have a chance encounter with a teammate.

➤ Open doors for your teammate when walking together into a building. (However, don't set up a politeness struggle where you go back and forth with "After you" or "Go ahead.")

Treating teammates as external customers also involves concern about keeping good working relationships with them. One team member would, therefore, worry if another team member did not consult with him or her for a long time.

Relax—Everyone Around Here Can Be Trusted

You already learned about the importance of credibility as a leadership characteristic in Chapter 6, "How to Develop Credibility." Mutual trust is also a bedrock condition for high levels of teamwork and cooperation. If team members do not trust each other, they hold back on mutual cooperation. Learning to trust one another takes time, but here are a few suggestions for speeding up the process:

➤ Encourage team members to give honest feedback to each other during team meetings. For example, one team member might say to another, "I would be more eager to join your subcommittee if you took deadlines more seriously."

➤ Hold candid team meetings in general. Candor leads to trust because openly expressing one's opinion leads others to think that the person does not hide opinions and information.

➤ Have team members fully disclose the type of work they perform outside of shared team activities. Disclosure of this type helps reduce concerns that team members are doing work that is so competitive it might make somebody look bad. If a team member, for example, is asked by higher management to tackle the same assignment as you, one of you is going to look better.

➤ Perform the widely used "trust fall" exercise in a park or company recreational center. Team members take turns wearing blindfolds and falling backward off a chair into the arms of teammates. A tamer version of the exercise is to fall backward from a standing position. The trust fall exercise is voluntary, so you accept any physical or mental excuse to be excluded. The trust fall inevitably leads to a discussion of the importance of trust. (As a safety precaution, do this exercise over a thickly carpeted floor or one made of rubber. Grass is okay, too, but avoid concrete or hard wood floors.)

Distrust of top management often occurs when team members perceive that their best efforts are not rewarded. In the heyday of quality circles, many members of the circle teams became discouraged because their suggestions were ignored so frequently. Team efforts backfire if the team's productivity increases result in the need for fewer workers and subsequent layoffs.

Advisor

Do not assume that wheelchair users don't want to participate in the trust fall. With help in getting out of the wheelchair and getting launched, wheelchair users can participate in this exercise. However, do encourage any woman who is pregnant or anyone who has an adverse medical condition, such as heart or back problems or weak retinas, to be an observer rather than a participant in the trust fall.

Use Team Terms and Bury the First Person Singular

A team is designed as a democratic structure in which hierarchical rank and other status differences are not so pronounced. Emphasizing the words *team members* or *teammates* and de-emphasizing the words *subordinates* and *employees* help communicate the norm of teamwork and a teamwork culture. Although it is still widely used in professional and technical books about management and leadership, it is also wise to avoid the term *follower*.

A divisive distinction to avoid is "essential" versus "nonessential" work. For example, as a team leader, do not say to the group, "Soon we may have to terminate those among us who do nonessential work." (In the language of the slash-and-burn manager, the only *essential* work deals with making and selling products, thus excluding about two thirds of the workforce.)

A boost to your effectiveness as a team leader is frequently using the terms *we* and *us*. Pepper your conversation with phrases such as …

➤ "Our team."

➤ "We can overcome that hurdle."

➤ "We achieved this."

➤ "Let us do it."

➤ "We work great together."

➤ "We must all share credit for this accomplishment."

➤ "We are looking good in the eyes of management."

➤ "It's inevitable that top management will soon reward us for our outstanding contribution."

The reason that such phrases are important is that language shapes attitudes and lead to changes in behavior. Talking about the group as if it were a team helps make it a team.

Watch Out!

There are still times when individuals deserve to be singled out for exceptional accomplishments. A good team will rally behind a team member who has achieved an outstanding individual accomplishment. For example, teammates cheered when they heard that a team member had saved the life of an employee who had a heart attack in the parking lot. The team member administered CPR while the medics were on the way.

Hey, Gang, We're a Bunch of Winners!

Teams with the best records of accomplishment have the best teamwork. Conversely, teams with the best teamwork have the best records of accomplishment. Whether winning teams create good teamwork or vice versa, it pays to emphasize that yours is a winning team. Remind team members frequently of what your team is doing that is above average and consequently why they belong to a winning team.

Most teams are particularly good at some task. The leader should help the group identify that task and promote it as a key strength. A packing and shipping department, for example, might have the best no-breakage deliveries record in the company. A claims processing unit in an insurance company might have the fewest overpayments. One way in which a manufacturing group can distinguish itself is to remain accident-free for a long time.

Winning teams and effective work groups in general are not just a question of luck and circumstance. Research studies conducted over the years have identified certain characteristics of effective work groups. (These studies appear in organizational behavior research journals such as *Personnel Psychology, Journal of Applied Psychology,* and the *Academy of Management Journal.*) Many of these characteristics relate to the people side of how groups operate, whereas some relate to the task side.

Understanding the characteristics of an effective work group in general will help you do a better job as a team leader. Suppose you notice a characteristic that you think is important for your group yet appears to be absent. You might then develop an action plan to modify your team with respect to that characteristic.

Another Perspective

SEI Investments, with headquarters in Oaks, Pennsylvania, is an outstanding example of the team concept in action. Key SEI services include managing $130 billion in assets, mostly in mutual funds, and managing back-office operations for the trust departments of over 100 leading banks. Most employees are assigned to one base team and three or four *ad hoc* teams.

A few longstanding teams serve major clients or important markets. However, most workers come together to solve a problem and disband when the work is accomplished. Team leaders are not appointed by management. Instead, different people lead during different parts of the process based on their skills and expertise. Leaders must use persuasion to accomplish their objectives because they lack the formal authority present in a traditional hierarchy.

Here's an example: An effective problem-solving group for most purposes includes around five to seven people. If your team has 10 members, you might break into two groups of 5 for solving some problems.

What makes an effective group? Characteristics of effective work groups are described next.

The Right Type of Job Design

Effective work groups are designed so the job to be performed is exciting, challenging, and enriched. An *enriched job* has built-in motivational elements. Effective work groups usually have an element of self-management or at least regular participation of group members in decision-making. Self-managed teams were originally developed as a form of group job enrichment.

The following list outlines the characteristics of an enriched job. The more characteristics that you can build into a job, the greater the enrichment, motivation, and satisfaction:

➤ **Direct feedback.** Team members should receive immediate evaluation of their work. Feedback can be built into a job (such as checking that a new procedure works) or provided by a manager.

➤ **Client relationships.** A job is automatically enriched when a worker has a client or customer to serve, whether that client is internal or external. Serving a client is more satisfying to most people than performing work solely for a manager. A manufacturing engineer who interacts directly with production supervisors is said to have clients.

Key Word

An **enriched job** is one that is motivational and satisfying because it contains variety, responsibility, and managerial decision-making. Team members whose jobs are enriched are usually better motivated and satisfied. As a consequence, they are more productive.

➤ **New learning.** An enriched job allows its holder to acquire new knowledge. The learning can stem from job experiences or from training programs associated with the job. New learning is usually built into jobs in fast-paced, modern organizations.

➤ **Control over scheduling.** The ability to schedule one's work contributes to job enrichment. Scheduling includes the authority to decide when to tackle which assignments and to have some say in setting working hours, such as flex time. For many professionals in organizations, the biggest scheduling issue is whether to stay late at the office or work at home at night after taking care of family responsibilities.

➤ **Unique experience.** An enriched job has some unique qualities or features. A public relations assistant, for example, has the opportunity to interact with visiting celebrities. A field troubleshooting assignment, such as helping a customer through a crisis, can qualify as a unique experience.

➤ **Control over resources.** Another contributor to enrichment is having some control over resources, such as money, material, or people. Giving team members a say in hiring a new member provides them control over resources.

➤ **Direct communication authority.** An enriched job gives workers the opportunity to communicate directly with other people and use their output. A software engineer with an enriched job, for example, might handle complaints about the software she developed. The advantages of this dimension of an enriched job are similar to those derived from maintaining client relationships.

➤ **Personal accountability.** In an enriched job, workers are responsible for their results. They accept credit for a job done well and blame for a job done poorly.

A highly enriched job has all eight of these characteristics and gives the worker an opportunity for self-fulfillment. If you can help team members design these characteristics into their jobs, you take a giant step toward increasing self-motivation.

Advisor

Make up a checklist of the characteristics of an enriched job and bring them back to your place of work. Team or group members rate their jobs on the characteristics. When a job is deficient on a particular characteristic, the group—including the manager—should discuss how a constructive change can be introduced. Assume a cost accountant says her position does not have a client relationship. She might be given the opportunity to receive direct input from the manufacturing people whose costs she is estimating (rather than being handed this input from her manager).

A Feeling of Empowerment

An effective work group believes that it has the authority to solve a variety of problems without first obtaining approval from management. Empowered team members have a confident, can-do attitude. They also think their goals are worthwhile—such as having certain SEI teams manage investments for wealthy clients. Closely related to having worthwhile goals is the feeling of making an impact on the world. Creating even greater wealth for wealthy clients would make many team members feel that their work has an impact.

Interdependence Among Team Members

Effective work groups are characterized by several types of interdependence, involving tasks, goals, feedback, and rewards.

Effective work groups show task interdependence in the sense that members interact and depend on one another to accomplish the work. Task interdependence is valuable because it increases motivation and enhances the sense of responsibility for the work of other members.

Goal interdependence refers to linking individual goals to the group's goals. A member of a sales team might establish a compensation goal for himself, but he can realize his goal only if other team members achieve similar success.

Interdependent feedback and rewards also contribute to group effectiveness. Individual feedback and rewards should be linked to group performance to encourage team play. To avoid hurting the egos of star performers, base compensation on a combination of individual and group accomplishment.

Another Perspective

Although the right size group for many tasks is five to seven members, group activity can sometimes waste considerable time. Experiment with the approach called "brainstorming in twos." Often, two people putting their heads together for 30 minutes will find the right solution. A two-person group also increases the probability that there is no heel-dragging in implementing the solution. Both players will be highly committed to following through.

Group Composition and Size

A group composed of members from varied interests and specialties helps the group perform better when it faces a variety of problems. Members also learn more from each other when the group is diverse. A culturally diverse group generally enhances creativity because of the cross-fertilization of perspectives.

The relative size of the group can be a big factor in creating a winning team. Groups should be large enough to accomplish their work, but when groups become too large, confusion and poor coordination may result. Also, larger groups tend to be less cohesive. As group size increases, more members might think their individual contribution is less important.

A general principle emerging from research on groups is that groups should be staffed to the smallest number necessary to accomplish the work. Downsizing follows this principle, but sometimes it results in groups that are too small to carry the load. Teams, task forces, and committees tend to be most productive with five to seven members.

For those of you seeking technical information about effective work groups, see the article by Brian D. Janz,

Jason A. Colquitt, and Raymond A. Noe, "Knowledge Worker Team Effectiveness: The Role of Autonomy, Interdependence, Team Development, and Contextual Support Variables," *Personnel Psychology*, Winter 1997, pp. 877 to 904.

The Right Environment and Resources

The environment in which the group works and the resources available to the group have a major impact on its effectiveness. Receiving the right training can get the group on a winning track. Managerial support from you and the next level of management in the form of investing resources and believing in group effort boosts effectiveness. An effective group also communicates and cooperates well with other groups in the organization.

Activities Within the Group

Many activities (or processes) that happen within the group influence effectiveness. One of these activities is fostering team spirit or the group's belief that it can be effective. Team spirit is such an important part of work group success that the next chapter describes how a leader can give it a boost. Group effectiveness is also enhanced when workers provide *social support* to each other through such means as helping each other have pleasant interactions.

An example of the potential value of social support took place in a re-manufacturing company (one that basically salvages devices like single-use cameras). The productivity in one department was consistently low. After analyzing the situation, a consultant observed that the group members were not receiving enough social support from each other. A new group was formed composed mostly of friends, and productivity increased to above the plant average. Nobody was fired. Instead, the group in question traded members with two other departments.

Workload sharing is another activity that contributes to an effective work group. By sharing the workload equitably, a group can minimize free-riding. The leader may have the major responsibility for encouraging workload sharing, but members of high-performing groups often take the initiative to spread the work evenly. For example, one member of the group might be overloaded with customer inquires. Spotting the situation, another member of the group would volunteer to handle a few of the inquiries.

Communication and cooperation within the group also contribute to effectiveness. In fact, a work

Key Word

Social support within a group is where group members voluntarily encourage each other and make life pleasant for each other. When members offer mutual social support, bonds within the group strengthen and the group usually becomes more united.

group cannot be effective without good communication and cooperation. In the work group just cited, one member communicated to the others that she was over-loaded. The member who had some slack in her schedule stepped in to assist.

Familiarity with Jobs, Co-Workers, and the Work Environment

Another important set of factors related to work group effectiveness is familiarity. It refers to the specific knowledge group members have of their jobs, co-workers, and the work environment. Familiarity is not the same thing as seniority or experience. Some people work a long time at the same job without absorbing much knowledge about what is going on around them. Have you ever met somebody at a business party who can hardly remember the names of his or her co-workers when making introductions?

Group members are more likely to get to know each other and also become familiar with their jobs and work environment if they are well-motivated and satisfied. This basic observation is another example of how the characteristics of effective work groups are interrelated. In this case, team spirit can enhance familiarity, and familiarity can enhance team spirit.

How About a Retreat at Lake Tahoe?

A team becomes more cohesive as a result of spending time together. Team meetings are obviously important, as are group breakfasts, dinners, and after-hour gatherings. Team leaders must be careful, however, not to intensify the ever-expanding work week for work group members who are exempt from overtime pay regulations. A financial specialist on a cross-functional team said, "A Friday evening drink together with the team is yet another meeting on my cramped schedule. It's one more early evening away from the family."

In addition to working together face-to-face, e-mail and telephone interactions can also help build teamwork. Hundreds of companies also use outdoor training as another approach to getting the team to spend time together. The trust fall is a typical outdoor training exercise—so is scaling a wall or traversing from one tree to another on a pulley.

A newer trend for getting the team to spend time together and developing teamwork is engaging the group in volunteer activity on a weekend. For example, the group might refurbish a senior citizen's house or a playground in a poor neighborhood. The company supplies the material, and you and the other team members supply the sweat.

The Least You Need to Know

➤ Foster a teamwork culture by establishing an atmosphere that emphasizes teamwork.

➤ Encourage team members to treat each other like customers by being extra-pleasant toward each other.

➤ Improve the chances that team members will trust each other and management through such means as giving honest feedback to each other.

➤ Terms and phrases that support teamwork include "the team" and "Here's what we accomplished."

➤ Characteristics of a winning team include enriched jobs, team members dependent on each other, and a team of about five to seven members.

➤ Sensible methods of getting a team to spend time together include a community service activity.

Chapter 14

Techniques for Enhancing Team Spirit

> ## In This Chapter
>
> ➤ Promoting a mission that binds the group
>
> ➤ Fostering interaction through physical proximity and encouraging people to share ideas
>
> ➤ Rewarding contributions to team goals
>
> ➤ Engaging in tasks performed by the team and creating rewarding opportunities for others
>
> ➤ Encouraging the use of in-group jargon and introducing humor with appropriate frequency

Jill, the recently appointed manager of product planning at a food manufacturer, was invited to visit a staff meeting of the packing design team. She welcomed the invitation because packaging design was an essential part of launching a new product.

Reggie, the team leader, introduced Jill to the group with these words: "Good morning, team. As I communicated by e-mail last week, today is very special. Jill Longenmuth, the new manager of new product planning, has generously accepted our invitation to meet with us."

"Jill comes to the company with great credentials. We welcome her as a key partner in our operations. Okay, Jill, you start the dialogue."

At that moment, all six members of the packaging design team waved hello to Jill and started to clap. During the meeting nobody yawned, nobody left the room, and everybody was kind to each other. The team also mentioned several ways in which they want to more closely coordinate their efforts with product planning. As each suggestion was offered, the other team members nodded in agreement.

After the one-hour meeting, Jill said to Reggie, "Hey, thanks for pumping up the group. They sure put on a great show. It made me feel welcome. I can't remember many meetings like that."

Reggie smiled and said, "Jill, we didn't put on a special show for you. What you saw today is an example of why we're a high-performing group with such low turnover. We've got great team spirit."

In this chapter, I describe additional leadership behaviors aimed directly at enhancing team spirit and teamwork. If you can facilitate good team spirit, your team will be much more successful. Team spirit and teamwork go hand-in-hand as do physical exercise and health. Exercise helps you stay healthy, and when you are healthy, it is easier to exercise.

We're Destined for Greatness

Team spirit is a driving force in creating good teamwork, high performance, and high morale. A starting point in developing team spirit and teamwork is specifying a team's mission. Even though many people think missions are idealistic, commitment to a clear *mission* is a key practice of a highly effective team. The *mission statement* for the group helps answer the question, "Why are we doing this?" To answer this question, the mission statement should contain a specific goal, purpose, and uplifting tone. The mission statement helps the team find its niche.

Key Word

A **mission statement** defines the general field in which a firm or organizational unit will operate. The **mission** is the unique purpose that sets a business or organizational unit apart from others of its type.

Here are three examples of mission statements:

➤ To enhance our Web site development capability so we can provide business units throughout the organization with assistance in developing Web sites that exceed the state of the art. (For an e-commerce services group.)

➤ To plan and implement new manufacturing approaches to enhance our high-performance image and bolster our competitive edge. (For a team of manufacturing engineers.)

➤ To provide innovative packaging designs that will give our company's product a competitive edge and place our group in the forefront of the industry. (For a packaging design group.)

As a leader, you can specify the mission when the team is formed or at any other time. Developing a mission for a long-standing team breathes new life into its activities. Committing to a mission improves team spirit and teamwork, as does formulating a mission. The dialogue necessary for developing a mission establishes a climate in which team members can express feelings, ideas, and opinions.

Advisor

To formulate a mission statement, get the team together for a problem–solving or brainstorming session. Develop several different mission statements and put them on a flip chart, chalkboard, computer slide, or overhead projector. Then decide which one is best. The best mission statement can be chosen by consensus. In reality the one that grabs the interest of the group best is the winner. Shoot for a 25–word limit. If your mission statement could fit any group, anywhere, it needs to be stated more specifically.

Don't Be Bashful; Let's Hear What You Have to Say

Team spirit increases when every member contributes to the team effort. It is especially important for you as the team leader to avoid letting other contributors carry one or two people on the team. Unfortunately, not every member of the team has the talent to contribute as much as the stronger members. To gain broader input, try these techniques:

➤ Ask questions of the more diffident members, such as "Chris, what is your opinion of the best approach to dealing with this problem?"

➤ Comment on the positive aspect of even the least valuable contribution with a statement such as "You say that the only way we can succeed is to fire the CEO. Our team doesn't have that much authority, but you have sparked my thinking. Maybe we could ask our CEO for more clarification about the flaws he sees in our project."

➤ When an infrequent contributor offers useful input, offer praise such as "Thanks for your contribution. You are moving us in the right direction."

➤ Solicit input on some issues by going around the table. Tell the group that the issue at hand is so important that each person should contribute. This is a powerful technique for getting input from everybody.

➤ If you have held two or more meetings where someone has not contributed, send that person an e-mail message to the effect, "Good to see you at today's meeting. In the future, I would like to receive more of your input during the meeting." The e-mail approach can work well because it is less embarrassing than a face-to-face confrontation.

The common thread to the techniques just mentioned is that the team leader facilitates widespread communication among team members. Team members should communicate with each other as well as with the team leader.

Advisor

Do not be concerned about making shy people uncomfortable by asking for their input. My experience is that deep down, most people want to contribute to a group meeting. With a little encouragement in getting started, they are likely to turn into regular contributors.

It's Difficult to Ignore Somebody Six Inches Away

You can enhance group cohesiveness, and, therefore, team spirit and teamwork, when team members are located close together so they can interact frequently and easily. Frequent interaction often leads to camaraderie and a feeling of belonging.

One way to achieve physical proximity is to establish a shared physical facility, such as a conference room, research library, beverage lounge, or company athletic facility. Create a temporary common work area in the office by rearranging cubicle walls and modular furniture; use office landscaping rather than offices with doors (as has become almost standard practice except for executives). Conduct brainstorming sessions in relatively small conference rooms. Visit a customer or company facility as a group, riding together in a company van or bus.

Do I Have an Idea for You!

Idea-sharing is a heavy-duty tactic for developing team spirit and teamwork because the exchange of information requires a high level of cooperation. Idea-sharing is particularly attractive to intellectually curious workers. Keep the following idea-sharing techniques on file:

➤ **Show and tell.** Reserve a portion of each group meeting for idea-sharing or information exchange. During this portion of the meeting, the members might also be encouraged to provide constructive feedback to each other.

➤ **Clip file.** Maintain a mutual clipping service where group members send copies of highly relevant newspaper and magazine articles to each other periodically.

➤ **Book club.** Start a team book club that meets about six times a year. Each team member takes a turn leading a discussion on a book he or she thinks is useful for improving group performance. The book could also be enlightening in general ways, such as broadening the thinking of group members. Each member of the team is responsible for reading the book ahead of the meeting. Many companies use the book club idea as a training technique in such areas as leadership, quality improvement, and diversity.

Another Perspective

Close physical proximity may facilitate team spirit, but some people regard such close contact as an invasion of their space. Also, many creative people still prefer to work in isolation rather than in view of others. A major theme of the ubiquitous *Dilbert* cartoons is the discomfort associated with working in cubicles and having little privacy. A good compromise might be that group members spend only part of their time in physical proximity.

➤ **E-mail action.** Encourage team members to send their "best idea of the week" to each other via e-mail. At the same time, discourage team members from sending cyberspace filler. Most people receive more low-value e-mail messages than they can absorb.

Idea sharing builds team spirit. At the same time it may enhance creative thinking because intellectual stimulation is enhanced.

Have a Nice Reward; You Helped the Group

For the group to develop a strong team spirit, individuals must feel a sense of mutual accountability. Team members should be given frequent reminders of what they are doing right and encouraged for actions that contribute to team goals. Almost any constructive action by a team member contributes to group welfare. Nevertheless, some actions are geared more toward helping the group than individual productivity. Here is a sampling:

➤ A sales representative cuts back on making easy sales of hot-selling items to foster the group goal of penetrating new markets.

➤ During a group meeting, an effective idea generator on the team encourages another person to contribute rather than make the contribution himself or herself.

➤ In a research laboratory, a scientist temporarily puts away a project that could lead to a patent (and, therefore, individual glory) to help on a pressing group project.

➤ A member of a work group who is not interested in a new technology takes a course in the technology just because the group is moving in that direction.

➤ A team member who is overdue for vacation postpones the vacation to help the group get through a crash project.

When a team member achieves a group-oriented goal, he or she should be rewarded as much as or more than if an individually oriented goal were achieved. Doing so contributes to team spirit and teamwork.

How About Team Coffee Mugs and Matching T-Shirts?

A key strategy for encouraging team spirit is rewarding the team as well as individual members. The most convincing team incentive is calculating compensation partially on the basis of team results. For example, one half of merit or bonus pay might be attributed to group accomplishment and one half to individual output. (Base pay, however, should not be affected by group performance; tampering with base pay can lead to riots!) Group incentives build teamwork because the team must perform well for individual members to receive their share of the merit pay.

Watch Out!

External rewards are necessary for motivation, but establish a limit as to how much time will be invested in this activity. If too much time is invested in developing effective rewards and involving many meetings, the activity will become unrewarding.

An effective application of team incentives is rewarding a group partially on the basis of customer satisfaction. One bank executed such a program because when individual incentives alone were used, customers complained that bank employees were more interested in sales than service. The team payouts drained some profits, but the team incentives proved a good investment. That approach reduced the costs of closing accounts and replacing customers who defected to other banks.

Giving rewards for group accomplishment reinforces teamwork because people receive rewards for what they achieve collaboratively. The recognition accompanying the reward should emphasize the team's value to the organization rather than to the individual. Examples of team recognition could be …

➤ Display walls or electronic bulletin boards for postings related to team activities, such as certificates of accomplishment, schedules, and miscellaneous announcements.

➤ Team logos on items such as T-shirts, athletic caps, mugs, jackets, key rings, sports bags, and business cards.

➤ Celebrations to mark milestones, such as first-time activities, quality improvements, productivity improvements, cost savings, and high levels of customer satisfaction.

➤ Asking the group to give itself a nickname—a widely used yet still effective gimmick for boosting team spirit. Examples include the Zebras (a well-known Eastman Kodak Company team), the Wall Street Bulls, the Factory Critters, the East End Gang, the Bay Street Bandits, and the Cybernauts.

➤ End-of-year memos to the team, and to top management, summarizing the team's accomplishments for the year.

You Know Who the Enemy Is

One of the best-known methods of encouraging team spirit and teamwork is rallying the support of the group against a real or imagined threat from the outside. Beating the competition makes sense when the competition is outside your organization. When the enemy is within, the team spirit within may become detrimental to the overall organization and the we-they problem may arise. As a consequence of outsourcing some manufacturing, many domestic groups perceive themselves to be in intense competition with foreign affiliates who are making the same product. The domestic group should focus on improving productivity and quality rather than harping on the issue of "slave labor."

Watch Out!

When encouraging competition with another group, you should encourage rivalry, not intense competition that might lead to unethical business practices. It is good to encourage rivalry with a formidable opponent but not to bash the competition.

No Job Is Too Dirty for Me

An effective team leader performs many of the tasks performed by team members, including analyzing data, calling on accounts, and crunching numbers. Especially important is for the team leader to solve some of the most demanding technical problems facing the group, such as troubleshooting why a piece of equipment is not working in a customer setting.

The idealized version of a leader who spends all of his or her time formulating visions, crafting strategic plans, and inspiring others through charisma does not fit team leadership. It boosts team spirit if the leader decreases the distance between himself or herself and the group by engaging in some of the tasks ordinarily performed by the group.

The team leader does engage in some work that is strictly the leader's responsibility, such as arriving at a final decision after listening to group input. However, much of a team leader's job overlaps with that of team members, at least in groups where team spirit or productivity is high.

You Won't Hear Me Go "Oink, Oink!"

If the team leader hogs the best opportunities, assignments, and credits, it dampens team spirit and performance. One of a leader's biggest challenges is to provide opportunities for group members to perform well. The challenge is more acute when the leader is a person with a strong track record and the other team members are at an earlier career stage. An outstanding sales representative who gets promoted to sales manager should avoid holding onto the biggest accounts and calling on the big prospective accounts.

Consider these ideas for creating opportunities for others:

Watch Out!

An effective team leader helps team members with difficult tasks but still does not take over the team member's job. Specifically, the team leader should avoid agreeing to take over a team member's job because the latter finds it too difficult or too frustrating. Say, "I'm here to help, but not to take over your job."

➤ If you have an opportunity to visit a top executive or a key customer, bring along a team member. Assign him or her a meaningful role such as presenting technical details.

➤ Grant authority to the group to work on a major problem with a minimum amount of input and direction from you.

➤ Welcome all input from team members to encourage even modest contributions (as described earlier in the chapter).

➤ Introduce team members to some of the strongest people in your internal and external network when it seems appropriate. If you do this too often, it will seem like you are running a networking club.

Sorry, Rest of the World; You're the Outgroup

Conventional wisdom is that jargon should be minimized in business. However, liberal use of jargon among team members enhances team spirit because it sets the team apart from others in the organization. When dealing with outsiders, on the other hand, team members can follow the principle of minimizing jargon.

Teams performing specialized work are likely to use jargon:

➤ A team performing legal work might refer to a knowledgeable judge as a "jurist." (Most outsiders think a jurist is a member of the jury!)

➤ A team member from a quality-improvement team returned from vacation. Asked about his golf game during vacation, he replied, "Far too much variation to achieve zero defects." (In this situation, jargon was used with humor. Outsiders probably wouldn't understand.)

If you happen to occupy an executive position, you might encourage groups throughout the organization to be proud of their jargon. Explain that you want to develop team spirit and camaraderie.

Introduce Humor with Appropriate Frequency

Humor and laughter are excellent vehicles for building team spirit when used with appropriate frequency. The group needs to laugh enough to raise morale, increase the fun associated with the team task, and stimulate creativity. An effective team leader, therefore, has a good sense of humor but avoids the immaturity of a nonstop office clown.

For building team spirit, the most effective humor is linked to the situation in the form of a humorous comment. Bringing rehearsed jokes into team meetings is much less effective. Following are two examples of humor that worked in specific situations. Recognize that outside the context, a statement might not appear so humorous.

Watch Out!

Humor and the many other attempts to build team spirit mentioned in this chapter are important. However, there is a risk in so strongly emphasizing team spirit and morale that you lose focus on task accomplishment. High performance allows the firm to achieve its objectives and contributes to team spirit. This is true because feeling like a winner elevates team spirit.

➤ A team member explained how he tricked a supplier into granting the company an extra 15 percent reduction on the price of a component by exaggerating the significance of a minor blemish on the inside. The team leader commented, "Thank you, Sal, for explaining to us how you stole 15 percent from Baxter Metal Finishing."

➤ A fastidious executive toured the company's office facilities. During her trip, she noticed several coffee pots and small microwave ovens in the work area—a violation of safety regulations. The executive commented to the office manager, "In general, I like what I see, but why have our employees set up light housekeeping? Are you keeping them here all hours of the night?" Shortly thereafter, the gear for food and beverage preparation disappeared outside of the employee lounge. The humor had achieved its purpose.

Now that you have dug deeply into the factors that contribute to team spirit and teamwork, run through the following checklist. It is designed to help you diagnose the level of team spirit in your own work group.

How Are We Doing, Gang?

Yet another approach to building team spirit is for the team to receive feedback on how well it is performing. You set the performance standards at the outset. Then establish a critique procedure, including self-evaluation by the team and evaluation by those who use the team's output, such as other units and customers. Once a month, set aside about one hour for the team to evaluate its progress and compare its work to expectations.

When the feedback is positive, the team may experience a spurt of energy to keep working together well. Negative feedback, so long as it is not hostile, might bring a team together to develop action plans for improvement. The head of a maintenance team in a nuclear power plant told his team, "The ratings I have here tell us our performance on making repairs on time is next to last in the region. Will you join me in the challenge to improve?" His challenge was greeted with cheers of approval.

The Team Spirit and Teamwork Checklist

The following checklist can serve as an informal guide to diagnosing team spirit and teamwork. All members of the team, including the leader, should complete the checklist. Indicate whether your team or group has the following characteristics:

	Mostly Yes	Mostly No
Frequently helping a member who is overloaded with work.	❏	❏
A reasonable amount of laughing, kidding, and joking together.	❏	❏
Open communication in an atmosphere of trust and respect.	❏	❏
Frequently mentioning the word "we" when talking about group accomplishments.	❏	❏
A tendency for group members to lunch together rather than with outsiders.	❏	❏
A self-adopted nickname for the team.	❏	❏
Affectionate nicknames given to each team member, such as "Terminator Terri."	❏	❏

	Mostly Yes	Mostly No
Frequently sharing knowledge and skills.	❑	❑
Frequently using in-group jargon in a natural manner.	❑	❑
A strong interest in orienting new members to the group.	❑	❑
Toleration for the unintended mistakes of each other.	❑	❑
Almost no back-stabbing.	❑	❑
Voluntary effort to bring reticent group members into the mainstream of group activities.	❑	❑
Spontaneous clapping when learning of a team member's exceptional individual accomplishment.	❑	❑
Spontaneous consultation with other team members about technical problems.	❑	❑
A tendency to give an emotional boost and encouragement to a member who is experiencing work or personal problems.	❑	❑

Scoring and interpretation: The larger the number of statements answered "Mostly Yes," the more likely team spirit and teamwork is present, thus contributing to productivity. The answers can serve as discussion points for improving team spirit, teamwork, and group effectiveness. Negative responses to questions can be used as suggestions for taking action to improve teamwork in your group.

The Least You Need to Know

➤ Prepare an effective mission statement by getting the group together in a problem-solving session.

➤ Obtain input from all group members through such means as going around the table in a meeting to gather each team member's suggestions.

➤ Encourage group members to share ideas through such means as having an information-exchange portion of group meetings.

➤ Reward contributions to team goals by using both financial rewards and symbolic rewards such as T-shirts and coffee mugs.

➤ As a team leader, you should engage in tasks performed by the team because your role is that of a collaborator and facilitator, not an executive who delegates most of the work to the group.

HEY GUYS, LOOK WHAT I FOUND FOR YOU.

NEW DATA

Chapter 15

The Task Side of Team Leadership

In This Chapter

➤ Establishing demanding tasks for the group

➤ Clarifying access to resources

➤ Challenging the team with fresh facts and information

➤ Assigning task roles to team members

➤ Using input from peer evaluations

➤ Minimizing micromanagement

The CEO at an electronics company formed a six-person task force to study the interaction between the organization and the environment. The group was allocated $15,000 for expenses incurred in executing its mission. In accepting the assignment, task force leader Darryl asked the CEO, "Precisely what is it you want us to accomplish?"

The CEO answered, "This is high-level stuff. I want us to be the modern type of firm that adapts well to a rapidly changing environment. Do what you think is best."

For the first four meetings, the group conducted long, intellectual discussions about what it means for a firm to adapt well to its environment. The members finally arrived at six different interpretations of what adaptation to the environment means in practice. The group then decided to conduct a study of the environment to discover what forces they must adapt to.

Three months after forming the group, the CEO asked Darryl how much progress the group had made. With some hesitation Darryl said, "It's hard to say whether we have made much progress. We really don't know what we are trying to do, so we don't know if we've accomplished much. I do notice that the task force members enjoy our intellectual discussions. They say it's a refreshing change from taking care of day-to-day details. Once we get rolling, I know we can make a great contribution to company strategy."

This task force might be functioning well from the standpoint of interpersonal relations. However, it is suffering from a common malady of group effort. The work group lacks enough task structure to perform anywhere close to potential. In this chapter, you will learn many of the task-related actions a leader can take to help a group achieve high productivity. (The discussion of goal-setting in Chapter 12, "You Can Become a Motivational Force," can also be considered a way of focusing on the task side of team leadership.) As a starting point in thinking about the task aspects of leadership, take the self-quiz at the end of this chapter.

Let Them Sweat a Little

A major driving force in team success is for the leader to establish demanding tasks for the team. An equally good alternative is for the leader to facilitate any group that establishes demanding tasks for themselves. Either way, the result is the same. With tough work facing them, group members are likely to pull together and perform well.

High performance stems from the team facing a realistically tough challenge that is a combination of a difficult task and a sense of urgency. The phenomenon is simply an issue of rational adults responding well to reasonable work pressure. The pressure creates enough stress so group members are revved up rather than immobilized.

An effective team leader urges the group to raise its sights and discard old notions of what constitutes good performance. The leader of a product development group at an industrial products division of GE told the team, "Six months might be the old standard for developing a new product in the past. With the ever-increasing competition, development time for our type of products must decrease to a maximum of three months. I won't accept approaching problems with standards from the past. I know we can do better."

Part of establishing a demanding task is imposing a deadline or having the group impose one of its own. A team without a deadline can drift into lengthy discussions about both central and tangential issues and philosophical debates. During a fashion design meeting at a clothing manufacturer, a team member leaned back in her chair and asked the group, "Before we set the hem length for this year, let's look at a bigger issue. Are we serving the best interests of society by adjusting hem lengths so frequently? Are we only contributing to the problem of making life more complex for women? Should our company be going against the grain of simplifying life?"

The designer in question may have had a point, but management had already decided to change the hemlines to increase demand for a new fall line. Her questioning the team's purpose was, therefore, too late.

Here are several examples of challenging tasks based on a combination of task difficulty and time pressures:

➤ A consumer products company gave its product development group six months to design an entry into the rapidly growing market for women's razors.

➤ A marketing group at Gateway 2000 Computers had several months to develop a strategic plan for increasing the company's share of the industrial market.

➤ A curriculum committee at an American university (usually a slow-moving mechanism) had four months to design an MBA program to be offered in Europe and Asia.

➤ A task force at a medical insurance company had 30 days to reduce the average wait time for a response to a customer's phone inquiry from 3 minutes to 45 seconds.

In each of these situations the time constraints placed on the group created a useful degree of challenge and pressure.

The goal of creating pressure is to create the right amount of stress. Remember that stress is an internal reaction to a force a person thinks he or she cannot cope with well. If you apply too much pressure, the amount of stress might be overwhelming, leading to poor performance.

Do What Needs to Be Done If It Doesn't Cost Money

An important part of the task aspect of team leadership is clarifying *access to resources*. For group members to accomplish their goals, they need the right backing from the leader and the organization. A potent way to dampen morale is to give group members a seemingly important assignment and then later inform them that the project is too expensive.

In one company, a group was told to investigate whether corporate headquarters was a sick building (one with a variety of pollutants in the air). Furthermore, the group was told to rectify the problem if the building were, indeed, sick. Diagnosing the problem was relatively inexpensive. The report recommended that the company take such expensive measures as installing new windows to cure the problem. The CEO rejected the recommendations as unrealistically expensive. As a result, the team members felt they had wasted their time. They were also concerned that if the results of the study became public knowledge, the company could develop a bad reputation as socially irresponsible.

Key Word

Access to resources refers to workers being able to get the money, personnel, equipment, and supplies they need to accomplish their work. Giving group members proper access to resources shows that the leader is serious about backing up the group.

To deal with the problem of clarifying access to resources, inform the team at the outset of the size of budget they are allocated. You might inform the team, for example, "Our goal is to reduce mortgage approval time by 15 days with an investment in software and consulting fees at a maximum of $150,000."

Advisor

It's stylish to consume few resources to get a lot accomplished. Serve as a model of efficiency by demanding a minimum of resources for your own work. Ask yourself, "Do I really need a large travel budget and extensive secretarial help to accomplish my work?" The intent is not to look like a cheapskate, but to demonstrate that financial extravagance is not necessary for business success. Top executives at two industry leaders, Wal-Mart and Southwest Airlines, work out of spartan headquarters.

Your group members will regard you as an effective leader if you also give them access to nonfinancial resources. In a team-based and trimmed-down organization, many new ventures are started without hiring new staff. As one middle manager described working conditions in his company, "We're a do-it-yourself company, even though we don't operate a chain of home-improvement centers." The team starting a new activity must, therefore, use existing company personnel on a part-time or temporary basis. Staff support in the form of clerical workers is also often in short supply. To avoid disappointments and missed deadlines, the team should know in advance the limits to the personnel they will have available to support the project.

Not to Upset You, but Here Are Some Facts to Digest

As a team leader, you can enhance group effectiveness by feeding the team valid facts and information that motivate team members to work together to improve the status quo. New information prompts the team to redefine and enrich its understanding of the challenge it faces. As a result, the team is likely to focus on a common purpose, set clearer goals, and work together more smoothly. Focusing on a purpose and setting clear goals are directly related to the task side of leadership. This is true because "purpose" and "goals" usually are linked directly with task accomplishment. For example, a team goal might be to decrease errors in fulfilling orders.

Feeding fresh facts to rev up performance might take this form: Imagine that you are in charge of the United Way program in your company. The level of voluntary compliance (with plenty of arm twisting by supervisors) has reached 94 percent. You then learn that the average for other companies in the industry is 95 percent, and you feed this statistic to the group. The team might work furiously to move your company's compliance to surpass 95 percent.

Feeding relevant facts and information to the team is also valuable because it helps combat *groupthink*, or a tendency to be too agreeable even on bad ideas.

The team might be prompted by new facts to re-examine a decision it is about to make. An office equipment company was faced with declining profits and sales. The executive group decided that if the company laid off its own sales force and sold only through the Internet and distributors, it would save enough money to reestablish high profits. The marketing vice president presented a study showing that selling only through the Internet and distributors makes it extremely difficult to penetrate further into the industrial market. Losing out on the industrial market was in conflict with the company strategy of increasing sales to the industrial market.

Key Word

Groupthink is a deterioration of mental efficiency, reality testing, and moral judgment in the interest of group cohesiveness. The group tries so hard to get along with each other that they accept outrageous ideas such as hiring a corporate spy to steal trade secrets from a competitor.

If We Play Our Roles Right, We'll Be Successful

One of the most powerful task actions you can take as a team leader is to assign *roles* (or prescribed activities) to members. The tactic is to assign roles related to task accomplishment. The team members assigned these roles might not have exclusive responsibility for them, yet they should be mindful that their particular talents suit them for fulfilling certain roles.

Assigning roles contributes to task accomplishments and teamwork. Instead of competing against each other, each member contributes in a different way as defined by the role. Roles are not necessarily fixed, and the same team members occasionally occupy more than one role simultaneously. As reported in *Supervisory Management*, April 1989, you can find the following task roles in an effective team:

➤ An *ideator* is good at generating ideas.

➤ An *inventor* translates ideas into tangible realities, thus serving as the implementor on the team.

➤ A *champion* has an impatience for seeing his or her vision become a reality. As the leader, you might assign this role to yourself. In your quest to be a great leader, don't forget to look out for number one!

➤ A *sponsor* has the power to protect, shield, and encourage both the project and the champion. A sponsor is usually a senior executive who might not be a team member. You probably need to recruit a company executive to be your sponsor. You need political skills to attract and retain a sponsor.

➤ A *technical gatekeeper* is a team member who assimilates, accumulates, organizes, and disseminates technical information, such as what new technologies could help the group.

➤ A *market gatekeeper* assimilates, accumulates, organizes, and disseminates market information, such as the likely demand for a product.

At the start of a project, team members should be encouraged to play multiple task roles because so much learning needs to take place. By occupying more than one role, the team members can magnify their capacity to learn. As the project matures, roles tend to become more defined with team members gravitating toward their roles of greatest expertise. For example, most teams have one member with the strongest grasp on information technology. That person becomes the team's computer guru.

Watch Out!

Proceed with caution in keeping group members with specified roles. A few of the roles may appear natural, whereas others may appear stiff. In rare occasions, the team members might be so involved in attempting to carry out their roles that it could become difficult to accomplish the task at hand. If the roles are too confusing, revert back to a few of the clear-cut (or more understandable) roles, such as "ideator."

Now I Have to Kiss Up to Co-Workers as Well as the Boss

Another task-related activity for leading the team is encouraging high performance by peer evaluations. Depending on your authority as a team leader, you might have the primary responsibility for evaluating the contribution of each team member. If team members know they also have responsibility for evaluating each other, they might work even harder. The reason is that team members are often in a better position than the leader to evaluate individual performance within the group. Peer evaluations can take several forms, including the following:

➤ Teammates rate each other on a standard rating form, such as that used in individual evaluations.

➤ Teammates write brief narrative descriptions of significantly good or bad instances of job performance they have observed during the evaluation period:

"One night at 5:30, I was tearing my hair out preparing some overhead transparencies for a presentation due the next day. Jackie came over to my desk and in reassuring tones asked me if I needed help. I said 'Yes,' and she got me on the right track in 20 minutes."

"I also observed Jackie doing something quite negative. During a group meeting with the vice president of finance, she took credit for ideas she borrowed from Gerry, who was not present at the meeting."

➤ During a group discussion, each team member is evaluated by all the other team members on key dimensions of job performance such as productivity, creativity, quality, and cooperation. You, as the team leader, serve as the moderator. A session of this nature can get quite intense.

Input from peer evaluations is usually combined with the manager's observations for a total performance evaluation. A more specific use of peer evaluations is giving them a certain weight, such as 20 percent, in the total evaluation. In this way, 20 percent of merit increases might be based on peer evaluations.

Practice Open-Book Management

Earlier, we mentioned *open-book management* as a way of developing trust within the organization. Sharing information about the company will often foster teamwork throughout the firm. As employees share information, they become business partners and perceive themselves as members of the same team.

In a full form of open-book management, workers share strategic and financial information. Responsibility for the success of the firm is shared between top management and other workers. The company also shares risks and rewards based on results, so workers are likely to pull together as a team for the company to succeed.

An important goal of open-book management is to have a well-informed, partner-oriented, high-performance company. Part of keeping workers informed is for company leaders to host round-table discussions about company financial information. Another approach is to regularly disseminate information through e-mail about the company's financial progress.

Open-book management may help in building teamwork, but it is not as effective as some of the more direct techniques described in this and the previous chapter. Also, open-book management may work better in small and medium-size firms than it might in behemoths. An entry-level worker at Oracle Corporation is unlikely to become a better team player because he learns that the company earned 25¢ per share in the last quarter. Knowing that that CEO Larry Ellison just became the world's richest man might not be a great team-spirit builder either.

Key Word

Under a system of **open-book management,** every employee is trained, empowered, and motivated to pursue the company's business goals.

Why Did You Select That Font, and Why Is Your Left Shoelace a Little Loose?

A final aspect of task leadership is that the leader should avoid closely monitoring the minor details of team member activities. To achieve outstanding results, the leader must give team members the opportunity to manage their own work. What constitutes *micromanagement* depends on team members' perceptions of the leader's actions. As a tentative guideline, you know you are micromanaging when you regularly do such things as …

➤ Ask a group member to change the font he or she chose for writing a report.

➤ Ask to review the To Do list of team members.

➤ Require that team members sign in and sign out for lunch.

➤ Require daily progress reports from each team member.

➤ Ask for the raw data behind reports from each team member.

➤ Edit and proofread all reports sent outside the team.

➤ Visit each member of the team at his or her work area at least once per day.

➤ Ask team members to return from trade shows or professional meetings with a written summary of what they learned.

➤ Almost always accompany a team member when he or she visits a client or customer for the first time.

➤ Conduct daily staff meetings before the start of each workday.

➤ Ask team members for a log of time spent on the Internet and sites visited.

➤ Investigate, in person, a site chosen for a team party before giving approval.

➤ Make food and exercise recommendations to team members.

➤ Give unsolicited child-rearing suggestions to team members.

Key Word

Micromanagement is the close monitoring of most aspects of group member activities by the manager or leader. Many micro-managers resemble anal-retentive personalities because they closely observe, and want to modify, the smallest details around them.

Minimizing micromanagement helps maximize the contribution of team members. Teams are organized with autonomy for the team members. If you as a leader micro-manage the group, team members will become disgruntled. As a result, they might not be as productive and creative as they would if they had more latitude.

Now it's time for a quiz to get you started thinking about the task aspects of leadership.

The Leadership Task Scale

Respond to the following statements as they relate to your leadership experience. If you do not have leadership experience, on or off the job, imagine how you would act if you were a team leader. Indicate the extent to which you perform (or would most likely perform) the actions described in the following statements: very infrequently (VI); infrequently (I); sometimes (S); frequently (F); very frequently (VF). Circle the number under the most accurate answer for each question.

	VI	I	S	F	VF
1. I state explicitly what the team is attempting to accomplish.	1	2	3	4	5
2. I work closely with team members in translating the mission into goals.	1	2	3	4	5
3. I'm a "hands off" leader who lets team members figure out how to do things on their own.	5	4	3	2	1
4. I carefully schedule work activities for the team.	1	2	3	4	5
5. I involve myself with the people aspects of the group and let alone the technical details of team activities.	5	4	3	2	1
6. I help others plan their work down to the intimate details.	1	2	3	4	5
7. Before I leave work, I check to see how much the team has accomplished for the day.	1	2	3	4	5
8. I worry a lot about the details of what the team is working on.	1	2	3	4	5
9. I use a computerized file to check on the status of team projects.	1	2	3	4	5
10. I use charts to follow the progress of team activities.	1	2	3	4	5
11. I try out new ideas for work improvement.	1	2	3	4	5
12. I point out errors when I see them.	1	2	3	4	5
13. I assign tasks to team members.	1	2	3	4	5
14. My team members assign tasks to themselves without my assistance.	5	4	3	2	1
15. Team members decide on their own deadlines.	5	4	3	2	1
16. I maintain a file of updated job descriptions.	1	2	3	4	5
17. I encourage team members to decide for themselves what is a fair day's work.	5	4	3	2	1
18. I encourage team members to figure out the best method for accomplishing work.	5	4	3	2	1
19. I set quantity standards for work.	1	2	3	4	5
20. I set quality standards for work.	1	2	3	4	5

TOTAL

Scoring and interpretation: Add the numbers you circled, and use the following guide to evaluate the extent to which you emphasize the task aspects of leadership.

85 to 100: You place considerable emphasis on the team achieving its intended tasks. You could be entering the danger zone where you place so much emphasis on task accomplishment that your style is incompatible with team leadership and empowerment. Try chilling out and backing off a little, and see what happens. Team productivity might increase.

65 to 84: You place reasonable emphasis on the task side of team leadership. You are concerned about team productivity, but you give team members enough breathing room so they feel they are part of an empowered team. The balance you achieve may be just right for effective team leadership.

20 to 64: You might be neglecting the task side of leadership in an attempt to boost team spirit and show that you are a modern, empowering, and people-oriented leader. Watch out; your boss might think you are too laid back and uninvolved. You might need to become more involved in goal-setting, planning, scheduling, and controlling.

The Least You Need to Know

➤ Assigning demanding tasks for the group is important because group members are likely to pull together and perform well.

➤ Showing the group how it can obtain necessary resources is important because for group members to accomplish their goals, they need the right backing from the leader and management.

➤ Challenge the group with fresh facts and information because the information might serve as group targets.

➤ Assign task roles to group members such as ideator (idea generator) and market gatekeeper (collects market information).

➤ Improve task accomplishment by use of peer evaluations that give group members an opportunity to point out each other's strengths and areas for improvement.

➤ Minimize micromanagement to avoid being a pest and interfering with group members accomplishing their work.

Chapter 16

Managing Conflict

In This Chapter

➤ Understanding that leaders need to be good at resolving conflict

➤ Resolving conflict with confrontation and problem-solving

➤ Inventing options for mutual gain

➤ Letting both sides exchange images

➤ Using cognitive restructuring

➤ Handling criticism constructively

➤ Asking good questions to resolve complaints

Returning to the office from an overseas business trip, CEO Byron said to Amy, his executive assistant, "I took the last few days for a vacation swing through London, so I haven't checked my e-mail. What's new?"

Amy replied, "A human rights advocate group discovered that our line of fishing poles is made by adolescents in Pakistan who are overworked and underpaid. The group is threatening a boycott of the major stores that carry our fishing equipment. We're facing a big hassle with the stores and the human rights group."

"Tim (the head of manufacturing) and Carolyn (the head of finance) have been at loggerheads again. Tim says that Carolyn is overestimating manufacturing costs just to make him look bad. Carolyn said she has had it with Tim's lack of cooperation and demands that the three of you meet together."

"Any other pressing developments?" asked Byron.

"Come to think of it, yes," said Amy. "Four branch managers who were released during our downsizing claim they are victims of age discrimination. They said that if you don't meet with them by next week to discuss the problem, they will initiate a lawsuit."

"Thanks for the rundown, Amy," said Byron. "But you didn't exactly answer my question. I asked 'What's *new*?' Conflict and hassles are *old*. Dealing with conflict is the single most time-consuming part of my job."

CEO Byron might have a pessimistic view of his role as a leader, yet he is correct in saying that dealing with conflict is a substantial part of a leader-manager's job. Several studies estimate that managers invest about 20 percent of their workweek in resolving conflict. For example, according to an Accountemps study, managers spend roughly nine work weeks a year resolving employee personality clashes. In this chapter, you will learn about several effective methods of resolving conflicts with others. You will also learn the high-level leadership skill of helping two people resolve their conflict.

What You Rarely Read About in the Annual Report—Conflict

Please don't think this is some kind of wimpy chapter pleading for harmony, peace, and love in the workplace. Researchers studying behavior in the workplace have known for years that the right amount and type of conflict has positive consequences. The right amount of *conflict* refers to the idea that conflict in moderate doses is akin to a healthy spurt of adrenaline. It can do wonders for your ability to solve problems and your competitiveness. The right kind of conflict refers to conflict directed at issues (such as the best method for achieving a goal) rather than personalities.

Key Word

The opposition of forces that gives rise to tension is **conflict.** It occurs when two or more parties perceive mutually exclusive goals, values, or events. Each side believes that what it wants is incompatible with what the other wants.

The focus of this chapter deals with how a leader resolves conflict that typically has negative consequences to the organization. Awareness of these negative consequences leads naturally to an appreciation of the leader-manager who can resolve conflict.

Conflict Consumes Considerable Leadership Time

As noted, managers spend as much as 20 percent of their time dealing with conflict and its consequences. The net result might be lower managerial productivity because less time is spent on problems that can increase profits or save money. A related problem is that dealing with conflict can be so draining that it temporarily lowers a person's ability to think creatively about major problems.

Conflict over Goals Can Result in Extreme Self-Interest

Organizational units and individuals in conflict often place their personal welfare ahead of the rest of the firm. A manager at a telecommunications company offers this example: "We have a few managers who will fight for the continuation of their project even if they know deep down the project is a loser. They also know the company is better off investing that money in a winning project. However, the managers hang on because they don't want to lose the status of a project leader."

Prolonged Conflict Is Detrimental to Your Health

Many individuals suffer a stress-related disorder as a consequence of the intense disputes that occur within their company. A production supervisor in Ohio had a heart attack on the shop floor in the middle of an argument with his boss over the necessity of replacing a machine. The supervisor might have been experiencing stress at home as well, but the job altercation put him over the edge. Less dramatic are the daily cases of people who leave work feeling depressed, anxious, and fatigued because they absorbed hostility during the day. Such people ultimately become despondent and hardly make joyful family members.

Time and Energy Can Be Diverted from Reaching Important Goals

Instead of working on tangible company problems, people in conflict often divert time and energy into their conflicts. It is not uncommon for two managers in conflict to spend time sending e-mail messages proving each other wrong in a particular dispute. Each message prompts a clever response in turn. Sometimes the distribution list for the message includes others not directly involved in the dispute. The outsiders receiving the messages often feel compelled to send messages expressing their viewpoints. As a result, more time is wasted.

> **Watch Out!**
>
> Conflict creates stress, and just like stress, it should exist in optimum amounts. With too little conflict, workers might become complacent. Yet constant, intense conflict can be disruptive; it might interfere with concentration and cause mental health problems.

Conflict Can Lead to Employee Sabotage

The computerization of the workplace has increased the consequences of employee sabotage. Angry professional, technical, and support workers have been known to destroy databases and shut down company operations. In one company, a suspended computer operator entered a number of unauthorized commands, taking 32 tape drives offline. The communications company where he worked was unable to service its customers the next day.

Another Perspective

In San Diego, California, an aerospace production worker shot and killed his supervisor and wounded an industrial relations representative. The violent worker had been fired after 25 years of service with the company. We cannot assume that if the worker's supervisor had been skilled in resolving conflict, the supervisor would have been spared. Nevertheless, the consequences of unresolved conflict can be so great that learning to resolve conflict is a good investment of time and energy.

Worst of All, Conflict Can Lead to Workplace Violence

Workplace violence is a dysfunctional consequence of growing concern. Violence has become so widespread that homicide is the leading cause of workplace death. Currently about 1,000 workers are killed on the job in the United States each year.

Most of these deaths result from robbery or commercial crime. Many of these killings, however, are perpetrated by a disgruntled worker or former employee harboring an unresolved conflict.

In short, a leader who can resolve conflict effectively can save the company time, money, and other resources. At the same time, the leader can prevent more people from getting sick and a few people from dying.

Let Me Tell You What's Really Bothering Me

You can employ a variety of different methods for resolving conflict on and off the job. Several of them are described in this chapter. The most useful, general-purpose approach for resolving conflict between yourself and another person is confrontation and problem-solving. *Confrontation and problem-solving* is a method of identifying the true source of conflict and resolving it systematically. True source refers to the underlying problem such as the other party not respecting your authority or a team member not showing a responsible attitude toward the job.

The confrontation should be gentle and tactful rather than combative and abusive. Being reasonable is important because the person who takes the initiative in resolving the conflict wants to maintain a harmonious relationship with the other party. Confrontation and problem-solving involves five steps:

Step 1: Recognize that the conflict warrants action. You decide that your conflict with another person is serious enough for you to seek resolution. At the same time, you think that it is counterproductive to let the conflict fester. Assume that Jessica, the manager of human resources, thinks that Ralph, the manager of manufacturing, does not appreciate the contribution of her group. In fact, Jessica has some evidence that in meetings with other managers, Ralph makes snide comments about the human resources group.

Step 2: Make the confrontation. Jessica decides to work cooperatively with Ralph. She sends him an e-mail requesting an appointment in his office at his convenience. She says she wants to discuss "an issue of mutual concern." Ralph and Jessica agree to a mutually convenient time in his office. After the ceremonial exchange of pleasantries and shop talk, Jessica begins the confrontation. She says, "I wouldn't waste our time if I didn't have an important issue. My concern is that you do not take seriously the contribution of the human resources group. I have heard you refer to us as 'record keepers' and 'happiness merchants.' It's important that we discuss this problem."

Key Word

A major advantage of the **confrontation and problem-solving** approach *is* that you attempt to deal with the real underlying problem. Because you get at the true problem, the conflict is likely to stay resolved.

During the confrontation stage, the other party might indicate a willingness to accept the confrontation or might decide to gloss over its seriousness. In some instances, the conflict is resolved at this point. The party being confronted might decide that he or she is at fault and show a permanent change in behavior. For example, Ralph might become apologetic and exclaim, "You're 100 percent right, Jessica. I've been narrow-minded, unappreciative, and just plain wrong. From now on, your group will receive from me the complete respect you deserve." Unfortunately, one confrontation is usually not that powerful. When the problem is not too serious and complicated, it has the best chance of being resolved with one brief confrontation.

Step 3: Determine the cause of the conflict. In this step, the two parties discuss their own opinions, attitudes, and feelings in relation to the conflict and attempt to identify the real issue. The root problem in this situation might be that Ralph does not understand how a human resources group contributes to the good of the organization. He does not understand, for example, how Jessica's programs can increase the job satisfaction of production employees and reduce turnover. Another example is that he needs to see evidence that the diversity initiatives spearheaded by Jessica can make the company more competitive. Jessica might learn through discussion how she contributes to the conflict with the heavy-handed approach she sometimes takes in gaining acceptance for her programs.

Step 4: Develop approaches to reducing the conflict. In this step, the parties attempt to develop specific means of reducing or eliminating the cause of the conflict. Ralph agrees to give Jessica or another representative of the human resources department more time to explain the potential contribution of human resources programs. He also agrees to study a few selected articles about human resource initiatives. Jessica, in turn, agrees to be less heavy-handed in implementing human resources programs in manufacturing. For example, she will stop sending e-mail messages to Ralph's boss about his poor cooperation.

Suppose the cause of the problem cannot be changed, such as Ralph's limited perception of the contribution of human resources. In that case, develop a way of working around the cause. For example, Ralph might exercise self-control to suppress snide remarks about human resources in public. He might make a few more concessions to allow the implementation of more human resources programs in his area. Jessica might also exercise more self-control about zapping Ralph with e-mail messages to his boss.

Step 5: Monitor progress. After the solution is implemented, both parties should check periodically to ensure that their agreements are being met. In this case, Ralph and Jessica might have brief follow-up discussions to discuss the level of cooperation they experience with each other.

Advisor

You sometimes need the assistance of a third party (such as an external or internal consultant or a common boss) to effectively use the confrontation and problem-solving approach. The two parties in conflict might be so emotional about the conflict that they cannot see the issues clearly. The consultant will work hard to get the two people in conflict to fully express their concerns and also to listen to the other side. One approach is to have each person write down what he or she wants the other person to do.

Let's Make Everybody a Winner

The ideal aim of confrontation and problem-solving, as well as other methods of conflict resolution, is for both sides to gain something of value. This philosophy of conflict resolution has sparked use of the catch-phrase *win-win conflict resolution*.

Inventing options for mutual gain is a high-level skill because most people are poor at resolving conflict. If you need convincing, read or watch today's news. Look at all the disputes in various spheres of life that go unresolved for a long time, including domestic disputes, long-standing conflicts between countries, and extensive violence in hockey. Your leadership stature will be greatly enhanced if you can find options for mutual gain.

Finding win-win solutions to conflict should receive high priority because it builds the basis for good long-term working relationships. For example, if a company in dispute with a supplier over price finds an equitable way to resolve the conflict, the two of them can work together harmoniously in the future. If the supplier feels defeated by a solution to the problem, however, the supplier will look for ways to retaliate in the future.

A powerful negotiating tactic is generating several workable options before entering into the heat of the actual negotiation session. Emotions might interfere with your thinking if you try to select an option in the presence of your adversary. When the stakes are high, the stress created by the negotiation session can dampen creativity. As a result, you might not arrive at creative alternatives.

Key Word

Win-win conflict resolution is a method of resolving conflict that finds solutions that result in both sides meeting an important need. The win-win philosophy of conflict resolution is also referred to as inventing options for mutual gain.

Under ideal circumstances, the two parties brainstorm together to arrive at options that are mutually satisfying. Both parties might engage in brainstorming separately and then bring the new options to the negotiating session or bargaining table. However, both sides must overcome a major hurdle before a systematic search for options is possible. Both sides must realize that the outcome of negotiation is not a victory for one position over the other.

To adopt the right outlook for developing options for mutual gain, check out the following examples of win-win solutions to conflicts:

➤ The leader of a local labor union wanted a 3 percent across-the-board wage increase in addition to whatever merit pay the members earned. Management explained that a 3 percent increase in salary was too expensive. The win-win solution was for the company to grant the increase if the employees agreed to increase their productivity by 5 percent. The union members dutifully accepted the challenge, and the across-the-board increase paid for itself.

➤ A new vice president of procurement decided that all the company suppliers must reduce their prices by 10 percent. A key supplier said that reducing its prices by 10 percent evaporated almost all its profits. A joint problem-solving session led to an agreement whereby the company ordered the supplies in quantities that were large enough for the supplier to charge 10 percent less.

➤ A group of nonsmokers objected to the fact that smokers were allowed to exit the building several times a day for 15-minute smoking sessions. The nonsmokers called these sessions "productivity breaks." Weeks of haggling produced a win-win solution. Nonsmokers were allowed two 10-minute "fresh-air breaks" during the day, and all workers cut their lunch periods by 10 minutes for four out of five weekdays to make up the lost time. The company believed that ending this dispute might lead to at least a slight gain in productivity.

Here's What I Think You Think of Me

It's time to assume a slightly different mental set. Two people reporting to you are experiencing conflict, and they come to you for help in resolving it. The easy way out is to play the role of judge. Using your great storehouse of wisdom, you decide who is right. The problem with this approach is that one side will think he or she was treated unfairly. To avoid playing the judge role, get the two sides to better understand their conflict and, therefore, find a solution themselves.

The essential point of image exchanging is that the two sides make it clear that they understand the other person's point of view. Empathy of this kind then leads to a useful and productive compromise. A convenient application of this method is to get each person to write his side of the argument along with what he thinks is the other person's side of the argument. Each side first constructs an image sheet without consulting the other person. After exchanging the images, the discussion (and sometimes fireworks) begins. Here is an example of these image sheets based on the dispute between Jessica and Ralph.

Jessica's page might look like this:

My Side of the Story	**What I Think Is Ralph's Side of the Story**
I suggest human resources are highly useful to the organization.	I don't have many useful methods that methods or techniques to offer manufacturing.
Human resources activities are key to the organization's success.	Human resources activities provide little value to the organization's success.

Ralph's page might contain the following:

My Side of the Story	**What I Think Is Jessica's Side of the Story**
I'm a very busy line manager who doesn't have time for staff programs.	I'm hostile toward human resources programs, and I personally dislike her.

I'm somewhat of a joker who will poke fun at anybody including myself.	I'm badmouthing her at every available opportunity.

As a third-party in the image exchange, you play a vital role. You can help the parties in dispute look upon their differences as work-oriented rather than personal. Your contribution is maximized if you can be an objective listener rather than take sides. Keep encouraging the parties to arrive at a workable compromise after they develop a clear perception of their different viewpoints. Laying out differences on a sheet of paper lets people step back and assume a detached viewpoint about their disputes. Many parties in dispute who go through image exchanging often conclude, "Now that I see our problem laid out so clearly, I see room for working out an agreement."

In this situation, Ralph decided to pay more attention to Jessica's human resources initiatives and to discontinue his hostile jokes about human resources. Jessica, in turn, decided to be more patient about implementing human resources programs in manufacturing. She also asked for less of Ralph's time. Ralph agreed to delegate to his assistant some of the responsibility for working with Jessica.

Being Fired Isn't So Bad; It Helps Me Develop Job Search Skills

An indirect way of resolving conflict between people is to lessen the conflicting elements in a situation by viewing them positively. Through *cognitive restructuring,* you mentally convert negative aspects into positive ones by looking for the positive elements in a situation. How you frame or choose your thoughts can determine the outcome of a conflict situation. Your thoughts influence your actions. If you search for the beneficial elements in the situation, there is less area for dispute. Although this technique might sound like a mind game, it can work effectively.

Advisor

You can use the image-exchanging technique to resolve conflict between you and another person, such as your boss or a co-worker, or in your personal life. Although image exchanging takes a little time, the majority of career-minded workers will see its relevance. Bringing in a respected third party can help you achieve the objectivity you need. Above all, seeing your dispute in writing can help you take a detached overview of the elements of the conflict.

Imagine that your manager has repeatedly asked you to work all day on Saturdays to lead the company through a crash project. You are ready to tell your manager, "I'm being treated unfairly. Ask a larger number of people to work on Saturdays. In this way, I could work fewer Saturdays." Instead, you look for the positive elements in the situation. You say to yourself, "My boss has asked me to work an unreasonable number of Saturdays, which is putting a lot of pressure on me and my family. If I want to make it to the next level, however, the experience of helping the company through a crash project is valuable."

Key Word

Cognitive restructuring is a method of softening conflict by mentally converting negative aspects into positive ones. You do so by looking for the positive elements in an otherwise difficult and negative situation. An example is to appreciate a micromanaging boss because you can profit from his technical expertise.

After completing this cognitive restructuring, you can then deal with the conflict situation more positively. You might say to your boss, "I welcome the opportunity to play a key role on a high-priority project, but I also need to maintain a healthy family life. Maybe some aspects of my work could be delegated to several other managers. In this way, I could spend more Saturdays with my family."

For a warm-up on cognitive restructuring, do the accompanying exercise.

Cognitive Restructuring

The following are negative statements about work associates. In the space provided, cognitively restructure (reframe) each comment in a positive way.

Negative: Nancy is getting on my nerves. It takes her two weeks longer than anyone else on the team to complete her input.

Positive:

_____

_____

Negative: My boss is driving me crazy. He is forever telling me what I did wrong and making suggestions for improvements. He makes me feel like I'm an absolute neophyte at my job.

Positive:

_____

_____

You're Right; I Am Kind of Sloppy and Stupid

Learning to profit from criticism helps you benefit from conflict. People who benefit from criticism are able to stand outside themselves while being criticized. They watch the criticism from a distance and look for its possible merits. People who take criticism personally are in anguish when they receive negative criticism. Leaders need to handle criticism well because they are criticized so frequently by others who think they can do the job better.

In some situations, you will decide to agree with the criticizer because the person has a legitimate complaint about you. If you deny the reality of that person's complaint, he or she will continue to harp on that point and the issue will remain unresolved. By agreeing with that criticism of you, you might set the stage for true resolution of the problem.

Agreeing with a superior or constituent, or *disarming the opposition,* is effective because you are then in a position to ask for the other person's help in improving the situation. Imagine that your department has been late in delivering reports on competitive information to your boss during the last six months. It is time for a performance review, and you know that you will be reprimanded for your tardiness. You hope that your boss will not downgrade all other aspects of your performance because of your tardy reports. Here is how disarming the opposition works in this situation:

Your boss: Have a seat. It's time for your performance review, and we have a lot to talk about. I'm concerned about some things, especially the delays on your reports.

You: So am I. It appears that our group has a difficult time submitting our competitive reports on time. It could be creating some delays for our product design and development groups. I wonder if we are being too thorough. Do you have any suggestions?

Your boss: Well, I like your attitude. Maybe you *are* trying to make your reports too thorough before you turn them in. I think your team can improve in finishing the competitive analysis more quickly.

Watch Out!

Too much cognitive restructuring can lead you to Pollyanna thinking in which you find good in all conflict situations. As a result, you might gloss over the importance of resolving negative conflict.

Key Word

Disarming the opposition is a technique of conflict resolution in which one person disarms another by agreeing with his or her criticism. The other side is disarmed because he or she was ready to dig in and clobber you if you disagreed with criticism. Because you agree, there is no room to clobber you.

Try not to gather information for such a wide range of products. Focus on the closest competitive products. We need thorough reports around here, but we can't overdo it.

Disarming is effective because it takes the wind out of the other person's sails and has a calming effect. The other person is often waiting to clobber you if you deny guilt. If you admit guilt, you are more difficult to clobber.

Another Perspective

You might find the occasional successful leader who disagrees that conflict must be resolved constructively to build workplace partnerships. Such a leader blasts the opposition and doesn't worry about consequences. A prime example is Frank Lorenzo, the controversial executive who led both Eastern Airlines and Continental Airlines into bankruptcy. In recent years, he was denied permission by the FAA to launch another airline.

So What Do You Want Me to Do?

A simple, yet powerful, approach to resolving conflict involving a complaint is to ask the complainer, "So what do you want me to do?" The technique has a disarming effect: Your adversary is stopped in his or her tracks and must now clearly articulate the problem. This technique is particularly effective for minor complaints, such as a customer who is dissatisfied with a service or someone who dislikes a report you prepared.

After the complainer articulates what the real issue seems to be, the demand often diminishes. A customer might be ranting and raving about a 10-day delay in shipment of valuable merchandise. When you ask the customer what he really wants you to do, the customer might say simply, "Well, how about a small discount on my invoice?"

A larger conflict, such as a labor union demanding a greater share of a company's profits from investing pension money, might not be as easy to resolve with the magic question. The union leader might reply, "We want 50 percent of those profits distributed to our retired workers." Your generosity just reduced company profits by about $10 million for this year alone.

The Least You Need to Know

➤ Leaders need to be able to resolve conflict because unresolved conflict has so many negative consequences such as lost time, money, and, sometimes, sabotage.

➤ Confrontation and problem-solving is a major method of resolving conflict that includes being assertive about the problem facing you, finding its causes, and developing approaches to reducing the conflict.

➤ Developing options for mutual gain is a high-level method of resolving conflict (win-win) in which both parties satisfy an important demand or need.

➤ Exchanging images helps reduce conflict because each side puts both sides of the story in writing.

➤ At times you can reinterpret conflict situations through cognitive restructuring or looking for the potential benefits in the conflict situation.

➤ Accept criticism constructively by standing outside yourself when criticized, and sometimes get the criticizer to help you.

➤ Remember to ask, "So what do you want me to do?" when attempting to resolve a relatively minor complaint.

Part 4

How to Help Groups Lead Themselves

A few years ago, a stunning advertising billboard was installed in the Times Square area of New York City. Thirty feet up in the air, the living billboard consisted of a 10-seat section of an airplane with the fuselage open so passers-by could see flight attendants and passengers. The people on board waved like celebrities on a parade float. Those on the ground waved and took photos.

The creative genius behind this ad for Delta Airlines was not one person but a brainstorming group. Forty people at Saatchi & Saatchi Advertising arrived at the living billboard idea to help revitalize Delta's business class and international service. By using a standard method of group problem-solving, the leader was able to unleash the creativity of group members.

This part of the book might be considered a continuation of the part you just completed. The emphasis here as well as in the previous five chapters is helping group members bring out their potential. You will also learn about the related topics of helping groups through a crisis and turning around problem people.

How to Become an Empowering Leader

Business executive Kevin had been troubled by a sharp pain that extended from the right side of his neck to the middle of his scalp. For six weeks, Kevin denied that this pain was serious enough to warrant medical attention. When he began to think that he might have a brain injury or a tumor, he scheduled a medical examination.

Kevin was first examined by Nicholas, a physician's assistant. Kevin described his symptoms, including the fact that he was least likely to feel the pain when drinking hot coffee.

Kevin asked Nicholas, "Do you think I have a brain tumor?" Nicholas replied in a matter-of-fact manner, "You could be right. The symptoms you describe do fit the picture of a tumor-like condition. Our neurologist Dr. Carter should be able to see you this morning. Can you wait about an hour and a half?"

Kevin sat in the waiting room for the most agonizing 90 minutes of his life. He attempted to read a newspaper but couldn't concentrate. He began constructing a To Do list for getting his affairs in order, including updating his will.

Five minutes into the examination, Anna Carter, the neurologist, said to Kevin, "I don't know where this tumor idea came from. It's pretty obvious you have a pulled neck muscle that is causing some referred pain into the scalp. If you insist, we'll do a brain scan."

"Oh, no," said Kevin, "I'll take your word for it. Why would a physician's assistant tell me that he suspected I had a brain tumor?"

"It's part of our empowerment philosophy," said Dr. Carter. "Everybody on the medical team has more power than they had in the past. Maybe the physician's assistant went too far this time."

Key Word

People are empowered when they are able to more freely exercise whatever power they possess, such as using their own expertise. **Empowerment** refers to liberating people from constraints such as checking with the boss before taking action.

Poor Kevin had worried needlessly, based on a tentative diagnosis from a person who took empowerment too far. Although an empowered team member, Nicholas was not authorized to offer tentative diagnoses to patients.

As this unusual story illustrates, empowerment must be appropriate so it doesn't backfire. In this chapter, you will acquire the information you need to empower others effectively. You will also learn to avoid common empowerment mistakes, such as letting people assume too much authority. To start thinking about how empowerment applies to you as a leader, take the following self-quiz. To empower employees successfully, the leader has to convey appropriate attitudes and develop effective interpersonal skills. To the best of your ability, indicate which skills and attitudes you now have and which ones will require further development.

I Hear the Word "Empowerment" Every Day— What Does It Really Mean?

The term *empowerment* is widely used in business, government, politics, and education. Empowerment refers to passing decision-making authority and responsibility from managers to group members. Most people consider empowerment a positive force because it means that leaders and managers share or turn over some of their power to people with less formal authority. Simply put, instead of being an authoritarian who hogs most of the power, you pass some power along to others. An empowering leader is at least participative and moves toward being free rein. (Participative management refers to allowing group members to participate in decisions. A free rein style refers to letting group members do what they want within broad limits.) Almost any form of participative management, shared decision-making, or delegation can be considered empowerment.

Empowerment is such an important part of leadership and management that it has been researched extensively. Some of these studies are particularly helpful because they dig deeply into the meaning of empowerment. Knowing more about the nature of empowerment can help you in your quest to be an empowering leader. Or do you prefer to keep as much power as you can?

Are You Ready to Empower Others?

To empower employees successfully, the leader has to convey appropriate attitudes and develop effective interpersonal skills. To the best of your ability, indicate which skills and attitudes you now have and which ones will require further development.

Empowering Attitude or Behavior	Can Do Now	Would Need to Develop
1. Believe that management should share financial information with workers throughout the company.		
2. Believe that teams of workers are likely to be creative problem-solvers.		
3. Very patient with even fairly slow workers.		
4. Think that most customer problems can be solved by workers themselves without having to consult management.		
5. Believe that entry-level workers have much more problem-solving ability than management usually believes.		
6. Willing to give group members the information and tools they need to get their jobs done right.		
7. Enjoy teaching group members skills even if it takes a lot of my time.		
8. Believe that many rules and regulations constrain rather than help employees.		
9. Willing to divulge information about company financial situation with group members.		
10. Regard most mistakes by group members as investments in their learning.		
11. Believe that almost all workers are experts at something.		
12. Willing to quickly forgive honest mistakes made by group members.		
13. Listen patiently to explanations of what went wrong after group member makes a mistake.		
14. Show genuine concern for personal welfare of workers.		
15. Like to be empowered myself.		

Interpretation: The more statements you check as "Would Need to Develop," the farther you are away from being an empowering leader. The suggestions in this chapter should help you position yourself to empower others.

The Psychological Dimensions of Power

A study published in the *Academy of Management Journal* indicates that empowerment really has four psychological dimensions. Full-fledged empowerment includes all four dimensions:

➤ *Meaning* is the value of a work goal evaluated in relation to a person's ideals or standards. Work has meaning where there is a fit between the requirements of a job and a person's beliefs and values. A person who designs accessories for Barbie dolls finds the work meaningful if she believes the work fits her value that bringing happiness to thousands of children is important. Another person doing the same work might find it meaningless because it conflicts with her belief that Barbie dolls perpetuate harmful stereotypes about female beauty. A person who is doing meaningful work is likely to feel empowered.

➤ *Competence* is an individual's belief in his or her capability to perform a particular task well. Workers who feel competent believe they have the capability to meet the demands of a job in a given situation. A credit analyst might say to himself, "I've been given the authority to evaluate credit risks up to $20,000, and I know I can do it well." Feeling competent feeds feeling empowered.

➤ *Self-determination* is an individual's feeling of having a choice in initiating and regulating work activities. Self-determination is especially high when a worker feels he or she can choose which is the best method to solve a particular problem. Self-determination also involves such considerations as choosing the work place and work site. A highly empowered worker might choose to perform the required work on a cruise rather than remain in the office.

➤ *Impact* is the degree to which the worker can influence important outcomes and results on the job, such as the way the company is organized or the products and services it offers. Instead of feeling helpless in following the company's course, the worker has a say in the future of the company. A middle manager might say, "Here's an opportunity to recruit former welfare recipients."

Advisor

The services of a job design specialist would be required to determine if all four dimensions were present. But not to worry, almost all exciting and responsible jobs are likely to have these dimensions built-in.

To have full-fledged empowerment, all four dimensions must be present. Being aware of these dimensions will help you keep in mind the point that empowerment involves more than merely handing any assignment over to a group member.

Give Away Power to Gain Power

Another important part of the nature of empowerment is a paradox. By giving away power, the leader usually gains power in the long run. The paradox occurs for several reasons:

➤ As group members become more empowered, they gain competence and accomplishments. As the group accomplishes more, the leader becomes more powerful.

➤ As group members take over more of the manager's former responsibilities, the manager can focus on those aspects of the job that add more value to the organization. For example, a leader who empowers group members to make more decisions by themselves has more time to search for breakthrough projects for the group.

➤ Empowered workers are better motivated. As they produce more, the leader is perceived as more powerful.

➤ Empowered workers are usually more satisfied. Satisfied workers are more likely to accept a leader's authority, thus enabling him or her to function with more power.

Watch Out!

Empowering people involves a lot more than simply telling them they are empowered. You must also engage in a variety of empowering practices and establish the boundaries (or limits) of empowerment.

Like most paradoxes, the empowerment paradox is difficult for most people to believe. Yet if you implement empowerment successfully, in the long run you will experience the exhilaration of gaining power yourself.

As Grand Master of the Universe, I Now Empower Thee

Now that you know what empowerment really means, it helps to know which specific leadership and management practices lead to empowerment. Empowerment is more likely to be successful when the leader engages in practices that support empowerment, such as the following:

➤ Practice participative leadership regularly by asking for group member input on important decisions.

➤ When asked a question about dealing with a particular problem, respond, "That's not my job. It's yours, and you are better qualified than I am to find a solution."

➤ Train a replacement for yourself, and while training that person, find other constructive work for yourself. In this way, you expand the scope of your job and the job of your potential replacement.

➤ Express confidence in team members' abilities. Pepper your talk with phrases such as, "You are really talented" and "I know you can do it."

➤ Praise initiative. To reinforce empowerment, praise workers who take risks and initiate actions that lead to success. Also recognize workers who make honest and thoughtful efforts yet fall short of achieving worthwhile results.

➤ Liberate people from overly restrictive rules and regulations. My apologies to modern-day hippies reading this book, but some rules and regulations actually help an organization. Don't you think it's a good idea that food preparers and operating-room staff are required to wear hair nets? Nevertheless, some rules and regulations interfere with people using their power. An example is prohibiting business-class air travel even when a trip is urgent and only business-class seating is available.

Another Perspective

An extreme position taken by some empowerment advocates is that hierarchy is incompatible with empowerment. Self-managing teams should, therefore, replace such structures as departments headed by a manager. Empowered teams not only recommend, but they also make and implement decisions and are held accountable. At Food Corp., for example, empowered teams act as managers. They hire and fire people, appraise performance, schedule work, and manage a budget.

You will notice that these empowering practices support the four psychological dimensions of empowerment described previously. For example, if you liberate people from overly restrictive rules and regulations, they can be more self-determining.

➤ Share information widely. Unless workers have useful information about the nature of the company's operations, they are not likely to take advantage of their increased authority. It has been found, for example, that most workers have limited awareness of profit margins. If employees know that the company only keeps about 10¢ on each dollar of sales, they are less likely to squander supplies and money. (We are referring to open-book management again.)

➤ Train people in the skills they need to be empowered. For example, if you empower group members to settle complaints with irate customers, it helps to offer assertiveness training!

For many forms of empowerment, teams are useful because workers like to act as a team in making important decisions. Instead of deferring to a manager, they consult with each other. An empowered team is less likely to make a major blooper than is an individual. Be prepared to shift from hierarchical to team structures. Nevertheless, many employees are intelligent and self-reliant enough to operate independently without the support of a team.

Allow Group Members to Choose Methods

Another empowering practice is so important it requires separate mention. Under ideal conditions the leader/manager explains to the individual or group what needs to be done (sets a direction) and lets the people involved choose the method. Explaining why the tasks need to be performed is also important.

One of the hallmarks of a true professional is to choose the method for accomplishing a task, such as a tax consultant deciding how to prepare taxes for a business owner. Consultant Norman Bodek explains in *Managers Edge:* "What irks people the most is to be told how to do something. Allowing people to determine the most efficient work technique is the essence of empowerment."

Good Morning Ladies and Gentlemen—Your Flight Captain Today Is an Empowered Baggage Handler

The opening case history hints at a principle of effective empowerment that requires separate mention because it is so important—yet so often ignored. Empowerment works best when the people chosen to be empowered have the right training, skill, talent, and motivation to perform the task. Despite the importance of this principle, many empowerment evangelists assume that every worker has the talent and desire to be empowered. Desire without talent can be a devastating combination. Would you want an eager but mechanically maladroit person assembling the antilock breaks on your car?

A frequent manifestation of glossing over worker ability when empowering others is to assume that as long as people work in teams, they don't need input from professionals. Instead of consulting a highly trained and highly skilled professional, you might empower a group of eager entry-level workers to tackle a difficult problem by themselves. A better approach is to ask a professional specialist to join the empowered team as an internal consultant.

Don't Overlook Expertise

An ideal example of infusing an empowered team with the right kind of professional specialist occurred at Valeo Wipers and Motors when it was ITT Automotive. The challenge facing the team involved a windshield wiper system for a new line of Chrysler minivans. An unacceptable 6.5 percent of the wiper systems manufactured at an ITT automotive plant were defective, and nobody knew why. All the components met specifications, the parts were assembled correctly, and engineers could not spot a design flaw. Nevertheless, in a test run, a small number of wipers failed to make a complete sweep across the windshield. Chrysler would not ship minivans with this small defect.

A cross-functional team was empowered as a detective force to find answers to the problem. The team consisted of a manufacturing general supervisor, a quality technician, a quality analyst, and two engineers. After considering the problem for many months, the team found unintentionally serrated edges on the drive shaft of the motor running the wiper blades. The key to solving the problem was that one of the engineers invented a gauge for measuring the crank's movement. Before even one minivan was shipped, the system had no detectable defects. Without an engineer on the team, it is doubtful the problem would have been solved. My point is that an empowered team should include the right technical expertise—an obvious truth that is often overlooked.

Advisor

An important principle of empowerment must be emphasized again. If you want highly productive empowered teams, team members must be selected carefully. Companies with the most successful experiences in empowerment carefully screen team members. Among the factors used in selecting employees are work ethic, versatility in handling work assignments, self-starting ability, cooperativeness and team work, and tact and sensitivity. And don't forget to add to the list technical skill.

To Empower or Not To Empower

This section outlines some additional suggestions for deciding who to empower. Choosing not to empower an employee does not mean the person is denigrated or downgraded. He or she simply does not receive significant new authority and responsibility until ready.

➤ In general, look for employees who are a cut above average at their level of responsibility. Capability and motivation are key success factors for empowerment.

➤ Look for some evidence of good self-discipline, such as not getting discouraged in completing a long-term project. Empowered employees must be self-disciplined because they are expected to work with limited supervision.

➤ Look for evidence of self-confidence in handling past assignments. It takes self-confidence to handle decisions on your own. (Of course, you could argue that being empowered builds self-confidence. Look for at least *some* past displays of self-confidence.)

➤ Make sure the empowered person is conscientious by reflecting on the person's past behavior. Empowered workers who are not conscientious often take advantage of their liberated status and expect other team members to take over part of their responsibility. As one laggard said to a complaining teammate, "I'm empowered to decide how much work to do each day."

Advisor

The most frequent complaint workers have about delegation is that their boss "dumped" on them, meaning that at the last moment, the boss threw them an unpleasant or confusing (or both) assignment. Avoid dumping as part of your empowerment strategy, particularly as you are on your way out of town. Instead, discuss in advance with the group member which activities you will be delegating. Notify in advance about the unpleasant tasks that will be included among the plum assignments.

Now That You're Empowered, I Don't Have to Work So Hard

A practical way of implementing empowerment is delegating tasks to group members. *Delegation* is more narrow than empowerment because delegation deals with a specific task, whereas empowerment covers a broad range of activities and a mental set about assuming more responsibility. Delegation is the assignment of formal authority and responsibility for accomplishing a specific task. Getting back to basics, here are a few major suggestions about delegating effectively:

Key Word

Delegation entails assigning duties, granting authority, and creating an obligation. For delegation to be effective, all three components must be present.

➤ When feasible, delegate the whole task. In the spirit of making jobs more meaningful, a manager should delegate an entire task to a group member rather than divide it among several people.

➤ Give as much instruction as needed, contingent upon the characteristics of the group member. Some people require highly detailed instructions, whereas others can operate effectively with general instructions.

➤ Step back from the details. Many managers are poor delegators because they get too involved with technical details. If a manager cannot let go of details, he or she will never be effective at delegation or empowerment.

➤ Obtain feedback on the delegated task. A responsible manager does not delegate a complex assignment to a group member and then wait until the assignment is complete before discussing it again. Managers must establish checkpoints and milestones to obtain feedback on progress.

➤ Delegate both pleasant and unpleasant tasks to group members. Who wants to be empowered with only junk assignments? When group members are assigned a mixture of pleasant and unpleasant tasks, they are more likely to believe they are being treated fairly.

➤ As a leader or manager, retain some important tasks for yourself. Managers need to retain some high-output (major significance) or sensitive tasks for themselves. In general, the manager should handle any tasks that involve the survival of the unit.

➤ As in virtually all leadership endeavors, it is important to evaluate and reward performance. As the task is completed, the manager should evaluate the outcome. Favorable outcomes should be rewarded, and unfavorable outcomes might either be punished or be denied a reward. It is important, however, not to discourage risk-taking and initiative by punishing all mistakes.

Watch Out!

At this point you may have observed a seeming contradiction between being a charismatic and decisive leader on the one hand and an empowering leader on the other. How do you deal with this contradiction? The answer is to find the right balance. Empower people, but *still inspire* them with your magnetic personality and visionary thinking. Or, at least contribute a few productive ideas.

During the next several times when you have the opportunity to delegate, keep track of which of the preceding delegation suggestions you implement. Perhaps you will identify an area for improvement.

Sorry, You Can't Decide on the Size of My Bonus

Empowerment has much to offer as a strategy for improving productivity and motivation, but it can create problems. Empowerment can create disharmony, dissatisfaction, and dysfunctions when workers do not have a clear perception of the boundaries of empowerment. Limits on empowerment might mean explaining to employees that they have more authority than before but still cannot engage in such activities as the following:

➤ Set their own wages.

➤ Set the wages of top management.

➤ Decide your wages and bonus.

➤ Make downsizing decisions.

➤ Hire mostly friends and relatives.

➤ Work less than 40 hours for full pay.

➤ Take two-hour lunch breaks regularly.

➤ Ignore company policy.

➤ Spend company money beyond certain limits.

As facetious as a few of these guidelines might appear, many employees justify dysfunctional actions by saying, "I'm empowered to do what I want." It is management's responsibility to guide empowerment toward activities that support the organization. Even in an era of empowerment, people still need decisive leadership.

The Least You Need to Know

➤ Empowerment is passing along decision-making authority and responsibility from managers to group members. People are empowered when they are able to more freely exercise whatever power they possess, such as using their own expertise.

➤ Leadership and management practices that lead to empowerment include using participative management, liberating people from bothersome rules, training people in the skills they need to be empowered, and using team structures.

➤ Before empowering others, look for employees who are a cut above average at their level of responsibility. Ability and motivation are key success factors for empowerment.

➤ Use delegation to facilitate empowerment by such means as assigning duties to the right people and delegating the whole task, and delegate both pleasant and unpleasant tasks.

➤ Set limits to empowerment by giving group members a clear perception of the boundaries of empowerment.

Chapter 18

Helping Groups Make Decisions

In This Chapter

➤ Deciding how much to involve the group in decision-making

➤ Setting up the right climate for group decision-making

➤ Taking the group through the problem-solving steps

➤ Getting fancy: using the nominal group technique

➤ Using word processing to enhance group decision-making

Vice president of administration Emily decided to plan a year-end holiday party for the departments reporting to her. They had exceeded productivity and quality quotas, but upcoming salary raises barely matched inflation. Finding that most party houses were already booked for weekend nights in December, Emily booked a party house 25 miles away from the office for the Friday night preceding Christmas. Guests would have a choice of entrée: beef, chicken, or fish. The company would pay for wine, but hard liquor would be served only at a cash bar.

Proud of planning the party in such a short time span, Emily and her assistant mailed party invitations to all department members and their spouses or guests. Three days after the mailing, complaints started pouring in by telephone and e-mail:

➤ "Why in the world did you pick a party site so far from the office?"

➤ "Why are you only serving food derived from animal flesh? Not every person in this department is a carnivore."

➤ "A cash bar? I didn't know the company was broke."

➤ "Friday night is terrible if you have young children. We have to rush home from work, feed the kids, and hurry off to the party. It's no treat."

➤ "I'm concerned that the party has a distinct Christian bias, placed so close to Christmas. You must remember that the department has people of diverse faiths."

➤ "I notice a heterosexual undercurrent in your invitations—something about the way they are worded. It just seems as though same-sex partners aren't welcome."

➤ "Thanks for the invitation, but the holiday season is already too crowded with parties. If you had asked me, I would have suggested January. That's when we really need a party."

Key Word

As they refer to decision-making, **unilateral, individual,** and **authoritarian** are synonyms. All refer to a person making a decision without relying on input from others. In contrast, group decision-making, participative decision-making, and consensus decision-making all refer to receiving input from group members before making a decision.

After reviewing the responses, Emily said with a sigh to her assistant, "So much for planning parties myself. From now on, I'm going to involve everybody in making decisions about the party even if it takes three months."

Emily encountered a classic leadership and management dilemma: whether to make a decision quickly on one's own or to invest the time to involve the group. Unfortunately for Emily, *unilateral* decision-making about planning a party backfired. In this chapter, you will acquire information to help you choose between *individual* and group decision-making. You will also learn how to use several potent methods for making group decisions.

Before you delve further into this chapter, take the accompanying quiz about problem-solving tendencies. It will help you think through how you really, really feel about group decision-making.

My Problem-Solving Tendencies

Describe how well you agree with the following statements. Use the following scale: Disagree Strongly (DS); Disagree (D); Neutral (N); Agree (A); Agree Strongly (AS).

	DS	D	N	A	AS
1. Before reaching a final decision on a matter of significance, I like to discuss it with one or more other people.	1	2	3	4	5
2. If I'm facing a major decision, I like to get away from others to think it through.	5	4	3	2	1

	DS	D	N	A	AS
3. I get lonely working by myself.	1	2	3	4	5
4. Two heads are better than one.	1	2	3	4	5
5. A wide range of people should be consulted before making an executive decision.	1	2	3	4	5
6. To arrive at a creative solution to a problem, it is best to rely on a group.	1	2	3	4	5
7. From what I've seen so far, group decision-making is a waste of time.	5	4	3	2	1
8. Most great ideas stem from the solitary effort of great thinkers.	5	4	3	2	1
9. Important legal cases should be decided by a jury rather than by a judge.	1	2	3	4	5
10. Individuals rather than groups are better suited to solve technical problems.	5	4	3	2	1
Total score	—	—	—	—	—

Scoring and interpretation: Add the numbers you circled to obtain your total score.

46 to 50: You have strong positive attitudes toward group problem-solving and decision-making. You will, therefore, adapt well to the decision-making techniques widely used in organizations. Be careful, however, not to neglect your individual problem-solving skills.

30 to 45: You have neutral attitudes toward group problem-solving and decision-making. You may need to remind yourself that group problem-solving is well accepted in business, and that you need the group approach in many leadership situations.

10 to 29: You much prefer individual to group decision-making. Retain your pride in your ability to think independently, but do not overlook the contribution of group problem-solving and decision-making. You may need to develop more patience for group problem-solving and decision-making as you carry out most of your leadership assignments.

Are Six Heads Better Than One, or Is One Head Better Than Six?

Although this might be the era of empowerment and teamwork, there are still times when decisive, independent thinking by a leader is valuable. This is one reason why business firms are willing to pay astronomical compensation to a person who can point the firm in the right direction without taking a poll before every decision. Sometimes, however, the most effective leadership tactic is to heavily involve a wide range of people in making key decisions. As Jack Welch, the former CEO of GE, told

Fortune, "The only ideas that count are the A ideas. There is no second place. That means we have to get everybody in the organization involved. If you do that right, the best ideas will rise to the top."

Welch's penchant for collecting ideas before making a major decision does not detract from his decisiveness or independent thinking; he just has a good sense of when it is appropriate to collect input from others.

The real issue is not whether a leader should make authoritarian or consensus decisions. Of more importance for effective leadership is recognizing which style of decision is necessary for each situation. A few rules of thumb follow:

➤ If commitment to implementing the decision is important, it is helpful to consult with group members before making the decision. Even better than consulting with them is achieving consensus, or general agreement.

➤ When creativity is important for solving a major problem, it is best to involve a group of people from different specialties. The various points of view are likely to spark creative thinking. Just listening to the various viewpoints might spark your thinking for arriving at a useful decision. The corporate group at McDonald's claims that some of its best ideas for menu diversification come from franchise owners.

➤ In general, important decisions are better suited for group decision-making than minor decisions. It is sometimes difficult to gauge how important a decision might be to group members, as in the case of Emily's arranging the holiday party.

➤ When a strategic decision is needed and most group members do not understand the big picture, independent decision-making from the leader might be best. A good backup is to collect a few points of view in a consultative style without implying that you are searching for consensus.

➤ When an issue is so political that it is difficult to obtain an unbiased point of view from group members, it is probably best for the leader to make the decision independently. An example is deciding to hire an assistant manager from outside the company.

➤ When time is at a premium, such as in a crisis, unilateral decision-making is usually best. If it appears that input from others is needed, use participative decision-making—within a tight time limit such as a two-hour meeting.

Another Perspective

A consensus decision-making style means that the leader encourages group discussion about an issue and then makes a decision that reflects general agreement and is supported by group members. Supporting a decision can mean that even if certain groups members don't agree entirely with the decision, they will not block its implementation.

The general rule here is to carefully analyze the situation, and then choose the most appropriate decision-making style. If you really believe in group decision-making, you might enlist others to help you decide whether to make the decision mostly by yourself or with the help of the group.

Ahh, It Feels So Right to Contribute

If your goal is to encourage group decision-making, one of the key steps you can take is creating an atmosphere in which group members believe that their input is welcome. Creating the right atmosphere for group decision-making is similar to creating one that fosters creative thinking. The most influential step a manager can take to encourage group decision-making and creative problem-solving is developing a permissive atmosphere. A permissive atmosphere contributes to generating input from group members because it encourages people to think freely and take intellectual risks. At the same time, group members must feel that they won't be penalized for making honest mistakes.

Microsoft is a stellar example of an organization in which leaders encourage workers at all levels to contribute ideas to influence major decisions. A relatively low-ranking member of the organization told top management that it was behind the times by not developing Internet-related products. The suggestions led to quick strategic decisions and actions that made Microsoft a dominant player in Internet services.

Here is a sampling of actions and techniques that contribute to a permissive atmosphere that encourages widespread input on decisions, including creative suggestions:

➤ Consistently ask group members challenging questions such as, "How would you solve this problem?" or "What fresh ideas can you offer me?"

➤ Send e-mail messages periodically asking group members questions such as, "How do you think our group should handle this problem?" or "What should we do next?" Also make a declarative statement such as, "I need everybody's input on this one."

➤ Let group members know when you implement a suggestion from a group member.

➤ Give recognition to good ideas by mentioning them in e-mail messages and at staff meetings.

➤ Minimize the occasions when you penalize mistakes stemming from implementing

Watch Out!

As you encourage participation in decision-making, you may collect input you perceive to be worthless. Be careful to let the people down gently who give you these unusable ideas. Otherwise, they will clam up in the future. If you are too accepting of unworkable ideas, people will keep submitting half-processed suggestions. Point out in a positive tone why a particular idea might not be usable at this time.

alternative solutions to problems. Creative problem-solving is a numbers game in which the vast majority of ideas fail.

➤ Make periodic statements such as, "Based on our collective thinking, here's the recommendation I'll make to top management."

If It Worked for Edison, Einstein, and Salk, Why Not for Us?

When team members get together to solve a problem, they typically hold a discussion rather than rely on formal problem-solving techniques. Although this approach can be effective, the probability of solving the problem well (and, therefore, making the right decision) increases when the team follows systematic procedures. The following guidelines represent a time-tested way of solving problems and making decisions within a group. You might recognize these steps as having a lot in common with the scientific method.

Step 1: Identify the problem. Describe specifically what the problem is and how it manifests itself. If your true problem is not identified, you will never find a true solution. For example, a company might attempt to find creative ways to lower the cost of a product, and then discover that the product still sells poorly. The real problem is that the product is out of favor with consumers, such as a monster-size SUV.

Step 2: Clarify your problem. If group members do not perceive the problem the same way, they might offer divergent solutions. For example, one person might perceive the problem as mechanical in nature, whereas another person might think the problem is poor supervision.

Step 3: Analyze the cause. To close the gap between the real and the ideal, the group must understand the causes of the specific problem and find ways to overcome these causes. Remember the story about fixing the problem with the minivan windshield wipers? Until a bright engineer figured out that the cause was unwanted serrated edges on a crank shaft, the group could not solve the problem.

Step 4: Search for alternative solutions. Remember that multiple solutions can apply to most problems. The essence of creative problem-solving is exploring a large number of alternatives, such as the thinking that led to relieving AIDS symptoms by selecting the right combination of drugs (the drug cocktail).

Step 5: Choose one or more good alternatives. Identify the criteria that solutions must meet and then discuss the pros and cons of the proposed alternatives. Examples of criteria include cost limitations, speed of implementation, and acceptability to top management. In the spirit of brainstorming, no solution should be scorned.

Step 6: Plan for implementation. Decide what actions are necessary to execute the chosen solution to the problem. With the windshield wiper problem, either the supplier had to provide smoother crankshafts or the group had to find another supplier who could make crankshafts without serrated surfaces.

Step 7: Establish contracts and commitments. The contract is a statement of what group members agreed to and the deadlines for accomplishments. Many groups lose potential productivity because nobody takes responsibility for implementing the chosen solution. An important part of this step is developing action plans for who does what such as, "Josie will meet with the supplier this week to smooth out the problem about the rough edges." The people involved in the action plan are held accountable for the results.

Step 8: Follow through by evaluating results. After the action plan is implemented, reconvene to discuss the progress. Group members are held accountable for holding up their end of the action plan. You should give compliments as deserved, such as, "Josie, we like how smoothly you got the supplier to eliminate the rough edges."

If you encourage the team to use an orderly group decision-making process, your leadership status will be enhanced. Your group is likely to have more productive meetings if you adhere closely to these steps for effective decision-making.

Another Perspective

Some people argue that rigidly using the systematic problem-solving technique can inhibit spontaneity. (The same concern applies for the other methods presented in this chapter.) It can be constraining if the team leader keeps reminding people that they skipped a particular step or jumped ahead. However, it is still important to cover the basics such as exploring the root of the problem under consideration.

Mirror, Mirror on the Wall, Which Is the Fairest Solution of All?

The group leader who must make a decision about an important issue sometimes needs to know what alternatives are available and how people would react to them. In such cases, group input can be helpful. Brainstorming is not advisable because the problem is still in the exploration phases and requires more than a list of alternative solutions. Another problem with group brainstorming is that the process inhibits some people. More dominant members get to contribute most of the ideas.

A well-accepted problem-solving method called the *nominal group technique* (NGT) was developed to fit the situation. The group is called *nominal* (in name only) because people first present their ideas without interacting with each other as they would in a real group. However, group discussion does take place at a later stage in the process.

Key Word

The **nominal group technique (NGT)** is a group problem-solving method that calls people together in a structured meeting with limited interaction. Each participant has an equal opportunity for contributing ideas, and these ideas are later evaluated by the rest of the group.

A problem that is an appropriate candidate for the NGT is a decision about which suppliers or vendors should be eliminated. Many companies decrease their number of suppliers because they believe that working with a smaller number of suppliers can lead to higher-quality components. A decision of this type can lead to hurt feelings and lost friendships. Suppose that Pedro, the team leader, is empowered to make this decision about reducing the number of suppliers. The nominal group technique involves a six-step decision process:

1. Team members are assembled because they will all participate in the decision to reduce the number of companies that serve as suppliers to the team. All team members are told in advance of the meeting and the agenda.

2. The team leader presents a specific question. Pedro tells the group, "Top management says we must reduce our number of suppliers by two thirds. It's difficult to keep track of all these different suppliers and train them to meet our quality specs. Right now our team is doing business with 12 suppliers, and we should shrink the number to 4. Your assignment is to develop criteria for choosing which suppliers to eliminate. I also need to know how you feel about the decision you make on supplier reduction and how it might affect the operation of our team."

3. Individual team members write down their ideas independently without speaking to other members. Using notepads, the five team members write down their ideas about reducing the number of suppliers by two thirds.

4. Each team member, in turn, presents one idea to the group. The group does not discuss the ideas. An office assistant summarizes each idea by writing it on a flip chart, white board, or on a computer file sent to all participants. Here are the ideas submitted by the team members:

    Alternative A: We carefully study the prices offered by all 12 suppliers. The eight suppliers with the highest average prices for comparable goods get the boot. I like this idea because our company will save a bundle of money.

    Alternative B: Keep the four suppliers who have the best quality record. If a company has won a quality award, it makes the retained list. We'll include awards from their customers or outside standards such as ISO 9000. If more than four of the suppliers have won awards, we'll retain those with the most impressive awards.

    Alternative C: I say we reward good service. We keep the 4 suppliers among the 12 who have made the most prompt deliveries. We'll also take into account how the suppliers react to accepting returns of damaged or defective merchandise.

    Alternative D: Here's an opportunity to get in good with top management. Stop kidding each other. We know that the plant general manager, Jake, has his favorite suppliers. Some of them are his fishing and golfing buddies. The suppliers who are friends with Jake get our vote. In this way, Jake will think our team shows really good judgment.

Alternative E: Let's reward the suppliers who have served us best. We'll rate each supplier on a 1-to-10 scale on 3 dimensions: the quality of goods they provided us, price, and service in terms of prompt delivery and returns policy. We could assign the ratings in less than one hour.

5. After each team member presents his or her idea, the group clarifies and evaluates the suggestions. The length of the discussion for each of the ideas varies substantially. For example, the suggestion made to rate each supplier on three criteria precipitated a 30-minute discussion. The suggestion about retaining the plant manager's political connections lasted only five minutes.

6. The meeting ends with a silent, independent rating of the alternatives. The final group decision is the pooled outcome of the individual votes. The team members are instructed to rate each alternative on a 1-to-10 scale, with 10 the most favorable rating. The ratings that follows are the *pooled ratings* (the sum of the individual ratings) received for each alternative. The maximum score is 50 (10 points × 5 raters).

Alternative A: Price alone: 35

Alternative B: Quality-award record: 30

Alternative C: Good service: 39

Alternative D: Plant manager's favorites: 14

Alternative E: Combination of quality, price, and service: 44

Team leader Pedro agrees with the group's preference for choosing the four suppliers with the best combination of quality, price, and service. He schedules a meeting to decide which suppliers meet these standards. Pedro brings the team's recommendations to the plant manager, and they are accepted. Although the team is empowered to make the decision, it is still brought forth to management for final approval.

Ladies and Gentlemen, Start Your Pens, Pencils, and Felt-Tip Markers

Assume that as the leader of a decision-making group, you must prepare a written report of your findings for the next level of management. To complete this type of assignment, I recommend you use the following seven-step procedure for quickly producing superior-quality reports that reflect group consensus. I have used this method with success many times, and several other people I know report favorably on its effectiveness. The decision-making technique to be described is an easy application of using e-mail and an attached file.

Step 1: Contact the other members of the task force or committee, notifying them of what output management expects from the group and the date of the first meeting of the group. Send along the necessary documentation so the group members can carefully study the issue beforehand.

Step 2: During the first meeting, discuss thoroughly the alternatives facing the group and the supporting facts. Encourage widespread participation by maintaining a listening posture and being supportive of all ideas. Describe the decision-making process to be used (the one described here). Announce that unless the issues take much longer to explore than predicted, most of the heavy decision-making will be completed at the next meeting.

Advisor

In applying word-processing-assisted decision-making, as well as the other techniques described in this chapter, effective written and oral communication techniques are essential. No matter how well structured a technique, the people using it must communicate with each other in a clear and pleasant manner. Have you ever visited a Web site with great technical expertise yet so crudely written that you ignored the message? The same idea applies to decision-making techniques: They work best when supported by effective communication skills.

Step 3: At the second meeting, you act as both the group leader and record keeper. The advantages and disadvantages of each alternative are explored in thorough detail. Toward the conclusion of the meeting, you summarize what you have heard the group members say. Identifying who said what is unnecessary in this type of group decision-making.

Step 4: The most difficult—yet most intellectually stimulating—part of the job now occurs. Prepare a report on whatever the group decision covered (such as purchase of capital equipment or vendor selection) that incorporates the opinions of all the group members, including your own. In preparing the word-processed report, use triple spacing and wide margins. Next, distribute your report to group members by e-mail, instructing them to jot down on the report itself (included as an attached file) all their recommended changes. The task should take each group member about 15 minutes. Your team will relish the chance to edit somebody else's work.

Step 5: After you receive all the copies of your report, incorporate all the suggestions of the group members. Instead of integrating your report with five or six other reports, you have one basic document that incorporates the ideas of everyone. It is usually best to print the revised attachments from all the members, then incorporate the changes in your file. Now distribute this next-to-final document (again triple-spaced) to group members, and ask them to make any further refinements.

Advisor

When using word processing to assist group decision-making, you are sometimes faced with one or two opinions that deviate from the mainstream. You can include these as "minority opinions" at the end of the report, in the same way as the Supreme Court.

Step 6: Incorporate any additional changes suggested in the previous step. You can now use single spacing. At this point, virtually all the bloopers, glitches, and word-choice errors have been eliminated. Approximately 30 minutes is required to complete this step.

Step 7: Send the final report to top management and all the group members. Be sure to list the names of all the team members, preferably in alphabetical order.

This seven-step procedure makes you look sharp as a leader because the finished product integrates the thinking of the group. You encouraged input from everyone; you used participative leadership; and you exercised expert power.

The Least You Need to Know

➤ Group input is needed in decision-making primarily when commitment to the decision is necessary and the decision is a major one.

➤ Establish a climate that encourages group decision-making through such means as creating a permissive atmosphere that welcomes opinions.

➤ Apply the basic problem-solving model to group decision-making by identifying and clarifying the problem, analyzing the cause, choosing an alternative, implementing the alternative, and evaluating the results.

➤ Use the nominal group technique (NGT) by having team members evaluate and rank the alternative solutions suggested by each other.

➤ Use word processing to enhance group decision-making by the group leader giving group members an opportunity to edit a report prepared by him or her that reflects member input.

Chapter 19

Winning the Support of Group Members

In This Chapter

➤ Making group members feel important

➤ Projecting confidence in group members

➤ Treating workers as a family

➤ Promoting your group throughout the organization

➤ Soliciting opinions before taking action

➤ Letting bad ideas down gently

➤ Preparing thoughtful performance reviews

Information systems manager Marty was close to the high point of his career. He was under consideration for the position of chief information officer of another division of his company. Aside from doubling his pay, this new position would give Marty an extraordinary opportunity to develop his leadership and management skills.

One final hurdle remained. The president of the division where Marty would be working wanted to learn more about his effectiveness and contacted four people who reported to Marty. The internal reference checks included these comments from each person he interviewed:

➤ "Marty is a wonderful manager and leader. He's a great people-person who could certainly step up to the next level."

➤ "He's clearly the best manager I've worked for in my 20 years here. He gives you plenty of room to swim, but if you start to drown, he'll throw you a life preserver."

➤ "If Marty goes, my resumé will follow him. He's a manager who gets results and a real warm human being. I'd like to be on his team again."

➤ "I'm not so sure if Marty would be effective as a top executive. He cares too much about people. He's too honest. He's not enough of a political animal to work in the executive suite. Marty is needed here. Find somebody else."

With three glowing references and a negative comment that was actually a compliment, the selection process was complete. Marty was appointed as the CIO of the other division. The good-bye party was wonderful.

One of the many factors that propelled Marty into a dream position was the fact that his group members supported him. Following the advice given in the other 24 chapters of this book should help you win the support of group members. The strategies and tactics described in this chapter, however, represent a direct assault on the challenge of getting group members on your side. You need their support to get your job done—and on occasion to help you advance your career.

You Make Me Feel So Good

The chapter on motivation emphasized the importance of appealing to the recognition need of others to spur them on to high levels of productivity. Making group members feel important is also important for gaining their support for you as a leader. A basic step in making others feel important is to visualize that every person performing work for you is wearing a pin that says, "Please make me feel important." Your work as a leader is unfinished until you satisfy this need for recognition. Presented next is a sampling of ways you can make the people working for you feel appreciated and important.

Watch Out!

To avoid doing hokey things to make others feel important, size up the climate. Some group members might be too sophisticated to be impressed by an Employee Appreciation Day. Instead, get them a token gift such as a music CD accompanied by a note of appreciation.

Hold an Employee Appreciation Day

A simple ceremony to celebrate the contribution of staffers can make them feel important. Alice is the manager of the subscription billing department at a daily newspaper. She was aware that employee morale had dipped during one of the newspaper's busy promotions. The 20 employees reporting to Alice were working 6 days a week, 12 hours a day. To show appreciation and ease tensions, Alice decided to throw an all-day employee recognition party.

Alice funded the Employee Appreciation Day party with $400 from a miscellaneous expense account. On the Sunday evening preceding the Monday party, Alice decorated the office. She taped a hand-written thank-you note on the bottom of each person's chair and included an instant lottery ticket. Alice bought each employee a small gift related to his or her interests. Donuts, bagels, fruit juices, coffee, and tea awaited the employees when they reported to work Monday. Pizza and soft drinks were served for lunch.

The staffers took kindly to Employee Appreciation Day. Morale surged, everyone was in a better mood, and the department achieved above-average productivity that day. Alice's team was impressed with the time and effort she put into creating the appreciation day. They were doubly impressed with Alice's genuineness when they figured out that she bought the gifts with her own money.

I can hear some of you muttering to yourself, "What does this anecdote about Alice and the office party have to do with leadership? I thought leadership was about creating visions, forming strategic alliances, and establishing uplifting values." You are correct, but leadership is also about day-by-day good human relations.

Advisor

Making people feel important by complimenting a demographic characteristic is much less effective than drawing attention to work accomplishment. For example, you might want a group member to serve as a mentor because she is wise and experienced, not *old*. In Eastern cultures, however, respecting people just because they are old might be more effective. You might, therefore, say to a 63-year-old Korean worker, "We need you on this task force. Your mature age and accumulated wisdom give you a great perspective."

Respect Seniority

In recent years, unprecedented numbers of employees over age 45 are offered enticements to accept early retirement. Despite tough laws against age discrimination, many job seekers over age 50 believe that their age is a liability. In such a climate, showing appreciation for seniority is extra impressive. Showing respect for seniority in this context means that you appreciate the employee's long-term contribution. Consider these possibilities for respecting seniority:

➤ Assign long-term group members some responsibility for training newcomers to the unit.

➤ Ask more senior group members to serve as mentors for younger members.

➤ Frame questions to senior members of the group in a manner such as, "Based on your experience, how should this problem be handled?"

➤ Do not make assumptions about older workers based on stereotypes that are not universally applicable. For example, many senior workers enjoy the challenge of high technology and new learning in general.

➤ Avoid references to seniority and age that are unlikely to make people feel good, such as "You must be a fixture around here," or "I bet you are looking forward to your golden years."

Give Small Gifts and Send Greeting Cards Throughout the Year

How much appreciation did you feel the last time you received a season's greeting card or a major religious holiday gift from your boss? Probably not nearly as much as if you had received a card or small gift at an unpredictable time. Cards and gifts sent or handed to employees at times other than Christmas or Hanukkah are likely to be more appreciated because they seem less like a ritual and more thoughtful. Consider sending cards to employees and buying small gifts on President's Day, Martin Luther King Jr. Day, St. Patrick's Day, Kwanza, Labor Day, Easter, and Passover. To help you develop the right mental set, here are several more suggestions for being thoughtful throughout the year:

➤ To get more appreciation-mileage out of cards and small gifts, send them at unpredictable times related to job performance.

➤ Write a small poem or limerick celebrating the outstanding accomplishment of a group member.

➤ When a group member accomplishes something exceptional off the job, such as earning professional certification, make a public fuss about it in the office.

➤ Send a hand-written note of appreciation to a person's home when the person achieves a certain milestone such as 10 years of service or 5 years without a sick day. (Consultant Tom Peters says this is the most effective form of recognition available to managers.)

Your uniqueness will help you stand out as a leader, and your unexpected card or gift is more likely to be interpreted as expressing appreciation.

You Can Do It; I Know You Can

A subtle way to impress group members and, therefore, gain their support is to show through your actions and spontaneous comments that you believe in them. Assume, for example, that an assistant says to you, "I'll get all those figures to you by Friday."

If you say "That's good" with a skeptical expression, your assistant will not think you have much confidence in him or her. If your comment "That's good" is accompanied by a convincing facial expression, your assistant will be impressed that you believe in him or her.

Projecting confidence in team members wins them so much to your side that they are likely to live up to your expectations, the phenomenon known as the *Pygmalion effect.* Leaders use the Pygmalion effect when they motivate team members by looking and speaking as if they expected team members to succeed. Here are a few specific ways of applying the Pygmalion effect to gain the support of group members—and raise productivity:

➤ You are the e-tailing manager and sales targets are off by 20 percent. Instead of berating the Web design group for poor sales, you state: "I know we can do better. Find out some way to reach your sales targets, and let me know how you are progressing. Get us more eyeballs, and get more of them to click on our shopping cart." (You expressed faith in the group's professionalism. The group will choose the methods for improving sales.)

➤ As the advertising manager, you bring a sample of the competitive advertising to the office. You point to one of the advertising slogans and say, "Here is the pap the competition created. Show me your competitive response by next Wednesday." (You have motivated the team by implying that they can do better.)

➤ You are trying to run some new software, but you can't get it to do anything but show up on the screen. You invite the office assistant into your office and say to her, "I'm in over my head, and I can't imagine who else can bail me out." (The assurance you project that she is uniquely qualified to assist you technically boosts her ego and gets her in your corner. The lift you give her self-confidence will also help her figure out what went wrong.)

Key Word

The **Pygmalion effect** is when people perform according to expectations, particularly with respect to relationships between the leader and group member. According to Greek mythology, Pygmalion was a sculptor and the king of Cyprus. He carved an ivory statue of a maiden and fell in love with the statue. The statue was brought to life in response to his prayer (expectation).

Hi, Son; Hi, Daughter; Hi, Cousin Kim

Konosuke Matsushita, the founder of the giant company that sells products under the Panasonic brand name, is an example of a leader who believed that an effective leader treats the people of his or her business like family members. In his good-natured view of the world, Matsushita ignored the violence that erupts in so many families. Make the assumption here that this discussion refers to a functional family.

Many successful leaders who are business owners echo Matsushita's sentiment. Employees who are treated as if they are family members are generally supportive of management. Treating group members as family members implies that you have a deep-rooted concern for their welfare and avoid actions that work against their best interests. The implication is that you have an emotional bond to group members that approaches love. Here is a sampling of family-style actions a leader can take to treat people as if they are family:

➤ Sponsor an occasional family-style event for your unit such as a picnic or amusement park outing.

➤ Be an advocate for family-friendly programs such as dependent-care centers and flexible working hours.

➤ Make frequent use of warm, caring expressions in reference to the group such as, "I think you people are wonderful," and "You're like close personal friends to me."

Another Perspective

Not all executives and management advisors agree that the leader and group members should constitute a family–like group. When this occurs, the leader is crossing over too far from a work role to an intrusion in the emotional life of group members. To avoid role confusion, the leader should maintain courteous but professional relationships with people.

➤ Avoid layoffs whenever possible by taking such actions as aggressively searching for work for surplus employees. Family-type leaders have had surplus workers do maintenance, build product for inventory, or become an additional door-to-door sales force for the firm. Doing subcontract work for other companies is another feasible method for retaining surplus employees. An extreme measure along these lines is for a company leader to pump personal funds into the business to help meet payroll.

➤ Keep a mental or written file on the family situation and personal interests of as many group members as possible. Using this information, regularly enter into conversations with employees about their family and personal interests.

➤ Frequently repeat the mantra, "We are like a big happy family." Your statements might gradually move workers toward thinking that they are part of a family. They will, therefore, show greater respect for their leaders.

Let Me Tell You About This Wonderful Group of Guys and Gals

You will impress your group members if you function as an ardent spokesperson for the group throughout the organization. Collect glory for the group as well as for yourself, and you will improve the chances of developing loyal supporters. An easy approach to being a spokesperson is to develop a one-minute summary of the purposes and processes of your group. At every sensible opportunity, give your one-minute spiel to an outsider.

A more elaborate approach to being a spokesperson for your group is to develop a full-length presentation about your group's activities and goals. One leader who used this approach was Jason, a data services manager in a manufacturing company. He developed a presentation for his user groups to illustrate the steps necessary and the time required to develop new software programs for their needs. Jason identified typical problem areas for a user group doing an exceptional job and outlined how the data services department deals with the problems. Jason's presentations were sprinkled with comments about his "high performing" and "thoroughly professional" group.

When members of the data services team helped user groups, they typically met a good reception. The group was objective enough to realize that Jason had done considerable pre-selling of their capabilities. As a result, the group worked extra hard to live up to Jason's expectations.

Here are three additional suggestions for promoting your group throughout the organization to facilitate obtaining the support of the group:

➤ Let the group know how hard you are working on their behalf. People cannot appreciate a leader's actions of which they are unaware.

➤ Ask departments throughout the organization for the opportunity to make a 15-minute presentation about your group's activities. Many managers like to spice up staff meetings with a presentation by outsiders.

➤ From time to time, send a widely distributed e-mail message with a one- or two-paragraph mention of the group's major activities and accomplishments. However, don't clog cyberspace with puffery about your group.

In short, actively communicate what you are doing for your group and what your group is doing for the organization.

Watch Out!

Promoting your group throughout the organization is important, but be mindful of how much time the activity is taking. Too much time spent promoting the group could hurt your own productivity. Also, you do not want to develop a reputation as someone who spends too much time away from working with his or her own group.

What Do You Think I Should Do?

In many leadership situations, you face the choice of whether to take bold, decisive action by yourself or consult with group members. Chapter 18, "Helping Groups Make Decisions," provided great detail on this topic. Think through whether participative decision-making will lead to a good result. To gain the support of group members, it is best to consult with them before executing a major decision.

Consulting with group members does not necessarily mean that you are looking for consensus. Just informing group members of your plans about a decision you know is right will often get them on your side. Advance information makes them feel included in the loop regardless of whether their input was needed. The fact that you talk over plans with them places group members in the role of confidante. Here are a few examples of this approach:

➤ The president of a small company decides that the company would increase sales if it expanded overseas, and he is thinking of negotiating with distributors. He calls the management team together for a luncheon meeting and announces, "Our sales growth has been flat now for three years. I'm thinking seriously of entering foreign markets. What do you think?" (There's about a 99.9 percent chance that the group will show at least some agreement on this initiative. Even a skeptic would agree to explore the possibilities.)

➤ A department head says to the group, "I'm getting a little discouraged with the appearance of our office layout and furnishings. Do you think we should ask Tom (the vice president to whom the group reports) to fund refurbishing?" (How can you lose by asking people if they want cleaner, more comfortable surroundings?)

I Appreciate Your Suggestion; It's a Start

As mentioned in the previous chapter, one of the problems with encouraging group members to participate in decision-making is that you often wind up with unusable suggestions. If you flatly reject the suggestions you receive from group members, you are perceived as not really interested in empowerment. If you are tactful about turning down the worst ideas, however, at least you create the impression of being a good listener. You are then less likely to lose the support of the team members whose ideas are rejected. Here are a few sample diplomatic rejection notices of ideas submitted from group members:

➤ "You say that we could save considerable money by eliminating executive bonuses. The best I can do is bring that idea to the next management meeting."

➤ "You recommend that we could save a lot of energy costs during the cold months if employees were encouraged to keep on their coats and hats while working. I'll number and date your idea and keep it on file for review at our next cost-reduction meeting."

➤ "You say that we should get out of the auto-parts business because automobile parts last longer than ever today. When I am next invited to a marketing strategy meeting, I will mention your idea."

➤ "I appreciate your suggestion that I worry too much about the group reaching its goals. Maybe I should invest time in reviewing my attitudes about how well our group performs."

Here's the Once-a-Year Event You've Been Anticipating

An honorable and meritorious way of gaining the support of group members is to prepare and conduct thoughtful performance reviews. Conducting careful reviews might also increase your stature as a leader in the eyes of higher management because performance appraisals are important company documents. Promotions and raises are usually based on the results of performance appraisals. In addition, thoughtful performance appraisals help defend a company against charges of discrimination.

Suppose a worker believes that he was refused a promotion because he had been convicted of a crime and served time in prison many years ago. Assume also the man had received a series of well-documented performance appraisals indicating below-average performance. His charges of discrimination hold less merit. (Of course, the man might counter-charge that he received below-average performance appraisals because of his prison record.)

Performance appraisals appear much more thoughtful if you follow these suggestions:

➤ Say a few kind things about everybody whose performance you appraise. If you have nothing positive to say, it appears you did not carefully observe the person's work. If nothing else comes to mind, try this one: "She was able to solve most of the routine problems she faced without needing the assistance of others."

➤ Base your appraisals on critical incidents rather than subjective opinions. Instead of using a phrase such as "highly creative," provide a couple of examples of the group member's imaginative problem-solving.

➤ Instead of relying on memory, keep a careful record of employee accomplishments and failures. During performance appraisal, use these incidents as raw material for documenting your conclusions. An example is, "During a trade show, Doris gathered 25 qualified leads for further follow-up by a sales representative."

➤ Don't depend on hearsay. Base your performance appraisal on results that you and your manager have seen directly. Accept second-party opinions only if they can be carefully documented.

➤ Include constructive suggestions for further development during each appraisal session. The suggestions can include such factors as types of valuable experience, technical skills for further growth, and changes in work habits for improvement. You might also mention developing personal characteristics and behaviors such as listening skills and assertiveness. However, in these instances, follow the suggestions for giving feedback in Chapter 23, "Giving Feedback and Positive Reinforcement."

Advisor

A major challenge in giving thoughtful performance appraisals is that the majority of workers distrust them, are skeptical about them, or think they are pointless. You might be able to soften some of these negative attitudes if you patiently explain the many essential purposes of appraisals, such as salary administration and identifying good potential. Also, emphasize that the performance appraisal is an opportunity to showcase good performers.

Develop Some Rituals and Ceremonies

As already implied, a good way to get the group on your side is to develop a few pleasant rituals and ceremonies. The same approach is also good for developing teamwork. Ritual and ceremony afford opportunities for reinforcing values, revitalizing spirit, and bonding workers to one another and to you. Select rituals and ceremonies that are pleasant, but not too hokey or time-consuming. A ritual many people might find "hokey" is hold a candlelight ceremony when a group member is appointed as supervisor or team leader. Choose a ritual or ceremony to get the group on your side that you think will fit your group members and your corporate culture. Here are a few examples:

➤ Hold a team dinner whenever the group achieves a major milestone, such as making a winning bid on a major contract.

➤ Send the group on a brief retreat to further develop their mission and goals. A retreat held on a normal workday will create more positive feelings than one held on nonwork days, such as weekends for most corporate types.

➤ Follow the system used by Wal-Mart and many Korean and Japanese firms by having group physical exercises to start the day. Do it maybe once or twice a month to avoid annoying lots of workers who think physical exercise is a private matter. (Not all Wal-Mart employees start the day with exercise, either.)

The Least You Need to Know

➤ Group members can be made to feel important through such techniques as holding an employee appreciation day or respecting seniority.

➤ If you express confidence in group members, they are likely to live up to your expectations.

➤ Treating the group like a family will lead to a closely knit group that is loyal to you and the firm.

➤ Promote the contribution of your group throughout the organization so they will understand you are truly on their side.

➤ If you touch base with group members before taking action, the chances increase that you will receive their support.

➤ Let bad ideas down gently through such means as being tactful and saying that you will keep an idea on file that might not be useful now.

➤ Conduct thoughtful performance reviews through such techniques as pointing out at least one praiseworthy aspect of performance and keeping a file of critical incidents.

Chapter 20

Leading Others Through a Crisis

In This Chapter

➤ Becoming the take-charge person

➤ Adopting a crisis-management style

➤ Placing the crisis in a problem-solving mode

➤ Developing a turnaround strategy

➤ Keeping team members focused while the ship is sinking

➤ Taking advantage of the hidden opportunity

➤ Preparing in advance for the next crisis

A group of managers from different companies attended a leadership development program sponsored by a university. During one segment of the program, each of the participants was asked to describe a work experience that contributed substantially to his or her development as a leader and manager. Consider the key points of the testimony of several of the participants:

Person A: Two years ago, a new CEO decided that what our department did contributed no value to the company. We had about two weeks to figure out what we could do that would add value in the eyes of the CEO.

Person B: I was promoted to the director of corporate communications. Four days into my new position, I was hit with an absolutely fabricated charge of sexual harassment. I had to deal with all the innuendoes and snickering.

Person C: During new model introduction time, we experienced a vicious labor strike. It looked like we wouldn't be able to ship any product for a year. I was one of the key managers working through that mess.

Person D: We were the biggest distributors of home hardware supplies, toys, and garden supplies in our region. All of a sudden, our three largest accounts modernized their distribution system so they could order directly from manufacturers. In three months, our sales plummeted 50 percent. It was my job to bring the company back from near collapse. We had to develop a viable Internet strategy or become obsolete.

After hearing these anecdotes, the seminar leader told the group, "You just illustrated the main point of today's seminar. A great way to accelerate your development as a manager and a leader is to successfully handle a crisis." In this chapter, you will learn some of the most important methods and tactics for managing a crisis, thus strengthening your leadership effectiveness.

There Are Two Seconds Left on the Clock; Throw Me the Ball

At crunch time, strong leaders emerge. They rise to the occasion and are willing to take the primary responsibility for leading the team out of a *crisis*. Business crises include such phenomena as …

➤ The firm is facing bankruptcy.

➤ Rumors are spreading that a sampling of one of the company's food products was poisoned by a deranged employee.

➤ A *Consumer Report* article concludes that your best-selling vehicle rolls over too readily.

➤ Public disclosure reveals that a major corporate executive is indicted for a serious crime.

➤ Negative reports about the financial health of your company stop most dealers from ordering your product.

➤ A mass murder occurs on company premises.

➤ An earthquake hits company headquarters.

➤ There is a fatal food poisoning of two customers at one store in your chain of restaurants.

➤ Another company develops an Internet strategy that threatens to make your company's basic service obsolete.

➤ A class-action suit claims racial discrimination by your company.

➤ The multiple deaths of airline passengers are attributed to faulty maintenance procedures by your airline's management.

➤ The media report that one of your company's electronic consumer products might explode during normal operation.

➤ You have a major factory in a distant country. A group of rebels takes over the government by force and intends to nationalize all private industry.

Key Word

A **crisis** is a major, unpredictable event that carries with it potential results of enormous negative consequence. The crisis and *its* aftermath can wreck an organization. A crisis goes far beyond the realm of a day-to-day business problems.

A good crisis manager might rely heavily on the skills of others to manage the crisis, but there is no doubt who is in charge. An axiom of leadership theory is that when the group faces a crisis, a directive and forceful style of leadership works best.

If participative decision-making and team management are so popular, however, you might wonder why people are willing to defer to a strong and decisive leader during a crisis. Among the possibilities are the following:

➤ It's normal cultural conditioning and almost a biological instinct to defer to a wiser or older person in a crisis. Children run to parents for protection; young adults, when in pain, yet far from home, often scream to their parents for help; people defer to the authority of a physician when gravely ill.

➤ Most people are not confident that they could make the right decision when facing a problem that involves the survival of the organization. They willingly defer to somebody else.

➤ Putting one person in primary charge of a crisis helps clear up ambiguity. For many people, this is a favorable condition because ambiguity is a major source of stress.

➤ Many people have a deeply ingrained belief that a crisis can best be resolved by a strong leader (such as a battlefield general or a president). In times of great turmoil, they are, therefore, preconditioned to look toward one person to rescue them.

Given that people facing a crisis are predisposed to accept one person moving them to high ground, it is easier for you to emerge as the take-charge person. If you are the formal leader, such as the department head, it is even easier to slip into the crisis-manager role. Unless you display the necessary self-confidence, however, people will not accept you as the take-charge person. They are less likely to mobilize their efforts in the directions you propose.

Advisor

If you project self-confidence, group members are more likely to accept your leadership during a crisis. Even if you don't feel highly self-confident to manage the crisis, fake it. Use the verbal talk and nonverbal behavior of a self-confident person as described in Chapter 2, "Build Your Self-Confidence." Make sure that your posture projects self-assurance. Smile occasionally to show that you have not moved into the panic zone. Yet do not smile to the point of appearing frivolous about the crisis.

You Can Reach Me at the Command Center

One of the dictates of crisis management is that a particular series of actions and behaviors is best suited to dealing with a crisis. To avoid confusion with actual leadership styles, I call this the *crisis management mode*. It has the following components, several of which were identified by crisis management consultant John Ramee:

Key Word

A **crisis management mode** is a series of actions and behaviors suitable for a leader helping a group out of a crisis. A crisis management mode recognizes that the fate of the organization is in jeopardy and calls for a systematic approach to resolving the upheaval.

1. **Stay cool under pressure.** Closely linked to self-confidence is the necessity for the crisis manager to stay cool under pressure. Act like a duck: Look calm and relaxed on the surface, but paddle like all fury underneath to work the group out of the problem. Help others gain perspective by engaging in occasional small talk without appearing frivolous. Also, act British by calmly understating the problem in objective terms such as, "We have a bit of a problem. Our balance sheet shows mostly expenses right now with very little cash inflow." Act like the crew captain who announces over the loudspeaker when the airplane is practically in a free-fall:

"This is your captain; please stay seated with seat belts fastened. We're in a descending pattern at the moment."

2. **Avoid the quick fix that will hurt the organization in the long run.** Many turnaround managers plunge into fixing an organization in crisis by laying off large numbers of people and selling off assets. They justify their actions by pointing out that the firm will not have a long run if the crisis is not fixed in the short run. The ideal approach is to correct the underlying problem. An example is improving the acceptance of a product or service rather than reducing the size of the organization to match declining sales.

3. **Seek new information.** A crisis fosters rapid change and makes information obsolete quickly. Gathering ample new information tells you whether your current strategies are valid or new strategies must be formulated. Assume that television ads were quickly formulated and broadcast to counteract false rumors about product poisoning. In this case, check to see whether the ads are bringing consumers back to your product.

4. **Revise strategies.** A vigilant crisis manager is prepared to modify new strategies whenever new information indicates the need. A typical strategy for a company facing a profit crisis is to sell assets to raise cash. In one company facing this problem, the CEO decided to purchase a small company that makes software for collecting payments over the Internet because of its growth potential. The leader's gamble paid off; the sale of the Internet software infused new cash into the firm.

5. **Have one center of authority.** When an entire company is facing a crisis, it is best for one center of authority to take responsibility for dealing with it. In this way, it is clear which person has the most responsibility for leading the organization out of the crisis. In a large organization, the need for a center of authority is more pronounced because fragmented power centers could arise. It is also important for workers not directly involved in resolving the crisis to concentrate on the daily operation of the business.

6. **Act quickly and decisively.** An unfortunate aspect of crisis management is that the cure often seems as bad as the problem. This is particularly true when massive numbers of employees are laid off and valuable assets are

Another Perspective

The crisis management mode generally calls for rapid action and going with your intuition, yet time invested in careful planning at the outset of the crisis might pay large dividends. An extra day spent exploring alternative solutions to your crisis might help you emerge as a triumphant crisis manager.

261

sold. Procrastination only deepens the crisis. It is important to select the best strategies and act quickly and decisively.

7. **Trust your intuition.** Part of acting quickly and decisively in a crisis is taking chances with your hunches. Make assignments rapidly for dealing with parts of the crisis rather than conduct lengthy investigations about who might be best qualified. Jump into the fray with statements such as, "Margot, find out how much cash we have left," and "Larry, check with remarketing firms to see if there is any market for our warehouse full of unsold neon-colored bathrobes." (A remarketing firm finds an outlet for a product in another distribution channel or sells the product for another use. Maybe the neon-colored bathrobes can be sold cheap as car rags.)

It's Back to Basics

A general method of dealing with crises is to regard the crisis as yet another important work problem requiring resolution. This is less dramatic than adopting the crisis management mode, but the problem-solving approach does overlap with the crisis mode. Placing the crisis in a problem-solving mode involves these familiar steps:

1. **Clarify the problem.** What is the real problem created by this crisis? Most crises can force a company out of business either through losing customers or paying fines and damages. Another real problem is that the firm's reputation and credibility might be in serious danger.

2. **Search for creative alternatives.** What options are open? Many managers choose stonewalling the problem over dealing with it openly and dig a deeper hole for themselves. Effective leaders are more likely to admit a mistake than stonewall a problem. A maneuver that helped restore the market share of Jaguar automobiles was top management's admission that the car had experienced reliability problems. At the same time, the company leaders explained how they instituted procedures to eliminate those problems. Later, when Ford Motor Company purchased Jaguar Motors, Ford engineers continued the quest for quality improvement with admirable results. The essential leadership question when facing a crisis is "What escape routes do we have?"

3. **Make a choice.** If the crisis is to be resolved, you must make a tough decision at some point. Steve Jobs faced a crisis when his newly formed company, NeXT Computer, could not sell enough computers to be profitable. The profitable alternative he chose was to convert NeXT into a software developer.

4. **Develop an action plan and implement it.** What steps must you take to get out of the mess? An effective crisis manager should explore shortcuts and innovative or unorthodox ways of getting things accomplished. Several automotive companies eased their way out of a recall crisis by combining recall visits to the

dealer with specials on car servicing and new car promotions. "As long as you're here getting an ignition switch fixed on your 10-year-old car, how about looking at a new model?"

5. **Evaluate the outcome.** Did the crisis-management plan work, or is another alternative required? Geico Corporation, the insurance company, once came close to facing bankruptcy because it was paying out too much in claims to customers. The action plan Geico leadership chose was to be selective about who they insured and to coddle safe drivers with low prices and good service. The strategy worked remarkably well. Geico is now one of the most profitable insurance companies.

Key Word

Macro level refers to a broad perspective, or overall view, that does not include details or specific goals. For example, at a macro level, AT&T is in the telecommunications business. Its strategy at a macro level is to provide high-quality telecommunications products and services. The opposite of macro level is micro level, or a detailed view.

Follow Me to the High Ground

Choosing an option to get through a crisis can also be framed as developing a turnaround strategy. The strategy is your master plan for getting through the crisis. As with any strategy, the turnaround strategy can be stated simply at a *macro level*. If the company is facing a financial crisis, the strategy might be, "Raise cash and cut costs." It's the implementation details that are difficult. Inspirational leadership is required to get people to implement turnaround strategies because some of the implementation plans are ugly. Employees, suppliers, and even customers are often treated shabbily as the company gropes to survive. At the top of my shabby list is a company that insists on prompt payments from customers yet severely delays paying suppliers.

Key Word

A **turnaround manager** is a leader or manager whose major responsibility is to quickly restore equilibrium to an organization facing collapse. The turnaround manager typically takes drastic steps, such as laying off half the workforce, to help the organization survive.

The Turnaround Manager Approach

Turnaround managers are usually called in from the outside by boards of directors, often under pressure from bankers who are worried about the company's deteriorating financial position. A turnaround manager's core strategy is to slash costs, including excising layers of management to improve the firm's financial position. Once the firm's financial health improves, it is often sold at a favorable price, such as when Al Dunlap merged Scott Paper Company with Kimberly Clark after revitalizing Scott. (Whether you like Dunlap or not, he maneuvered a few successful turnarounds in his day.) The cost-cutting strategy includes deciding what part of a company is healthy and then acting decisively to sell anything that is unhealthy.

The dramatic ways in which turnaround managers slash costs include enforcing a temporary pay cut, getting rid of company cars, selling a company headquarters building and leasing it back—and allowing no more fresh flowers in the lobby.

Bouncing Back from a Fire or Flood

Another good way for you to understand turnaround strategy is to examine a plan for a small business bouncing back from a fire or flood. Small business consultant Kurt Gage offers a plan for such a rebound that I highly endorse. Its components are as follows:

1. Start your comeback quickly. Find out how much was lost and how you plan to replace it.

2. Communicate with all parties with a stake in the business. Company leaders should talk with customers, employees, banks, and creditors and inform them of the company's plans and new developments. If your telecommunication system is down, rent facilities from another company.

3. Talk with competitors. Companies unable to meet customer demand might sometimes turn to competitors to meet customer requirements. Possibly some of that business will return when the crisis is over. At least you enhance your reputation, provided that you consulted with your customers about the switch in suppliers.

4. Be prepared. It is a good idea to have business interruption insurance, which can help a company meet payroll and pay creditors and taxes.

Lucky You, You're Becoming an Experienced Crisis Worker

It doesn't take an inspiring, charismatic leader to fire half the workforce or reduce salaries. Talent is required, however, to keep group members focused on their regular jobs and carry out crisis-related tasks while the company is spinning out of control. The general message that must be communicated is that equilibrium will return and that the workers who helped restore the firm will be forever appreciated. Consider these suggestions, easier written than implemented:

➤ Announce any good news coming into the organization, such as, "Just got a big order today," "We're getting another hearing from top management with respect to funding for next year," "Our loss for this quarter is smaller than the previous quarter's," or "Our biggest supplier agreed to ship components to us today in exchange for company stock."

➤ Give emotional support frequently. Invest a few minutes in asking people how they are holding up under the storm. Encourage other managers to do the same. Let people ventilate a little about their working hard under so much pressure.

➤ Remind people periodically that contributing to the survival of the company is an excellent growth opportunity. (Even if you are using the command-center approach to crisis management, people outside the center are contributing to company survival.)

➤ Give people small, achievable crisis-recovery goals on a regular basis. Each small goal achieved can have almost a therapeutic feeling. An example is, "Today I located five more customers whose billing information we lost in the fire."

➤ Put the whole crisis in proper perspective with occasional statements such as, "Don't worry; this is only a business crisis. We haven't lost our family members, health, professional skills, or personal reputations."

Advisor

Working your way out of a crisis is yet another application of lateral thinking or creative problem-solving. When facing a crisis, a major task is to dig for alternative solutions to your problem. If you calm down and keep thinking, you may find some surprising alternatives. An amusing example is that a reasonable number of laid-off middle managers eventually solved their crises by working as counselors in the outplacement hired to help them. When facing a crisis, stick in your cortex the following question: "What escape routes are available?" The answer might jump out in front of you at an unpredictable time.

Turn Your Burned-Down Business into a Parking Lot

An important principle of crisis leadership is to look for hidden opportunities within the negative circumstances. Many crises bring with them an opportunity for personal and organizational growth. The rub is that you must be extra perceptive to find these opportunities. Learning how to handle a crisis is a great skill and confidence builder.

Leading yourself and others through a crisis is a wonderful career accomplishment. Many people who were laid off during a downsizing or fired for some other reason also found hidden gold. They developed job search capabilities and identified skills they had not articulated previously.

The general principle is to be alert to the fact that there might be a hidden opportunity in every crisis. Here are a few examples to help you develop the right mental set:

➤ A manager whose new product group is dismantled by the company might start a new business on his or her own to develop and market that product.

➤ Many of the leading entrepreneurs in the telecommunications field were fired by a larger firm, which prompted them to start their own business.

➤ After a severe tumble in a stock price, some companies buy large blocks of shares of their own stock. By purchasing their own stock, companies stabilize prices for the stock and take advantage of good values. When the stock market rebounds, the company can sell the repurchased stock at a sizable profit.

➤ A company whose product fails might be forced to find new ways of generating revenue, such as becoming a subcontractor. Wang Computer was once the dominant player in word-processing equipment. Years later when they faced bankruptcy, the company stopped making word processors and became Computer Associates, a highly successful software developer.

➤ A crisis might point the way toward redefining a firm's mission, such as Xerox Corporation getting out of the financial services business and focusing exclusively on documents and digital imaging.

➤ A jewelry store was forced out of business by two large competitors who moved into the neighborhood. The owner survived financially by becoming the manager of the jewelry department of a large department store. The hidden opportunity was that the former store owner got a job with salary and benefits.

Watch Out!

Before jumping into a new opportunity during or after a crisis, research what you are getting yourself into. A company might shift into a field where it cannot compete successfully. An individual might make a career switch that proves to be a poor choice. People laid off from corporate positions have bought franchises that resulted in working excessive hours and earning not much better than minimum wage.

Build a Hurricane Shelter Now

As management awareness of the inevitability of crises increases, more thought goes into contingency planning for crises. Here I describe what many firms are doing, or should be doing, to lessen the impact of future crises. Part of leading an organization through a crisis is preparing in advance. Several important crisis management (and perhaps prevention) tactics are described next.

Engage in Crisis Forecasting

Contingency planning begins with forecasting. Based on past experience, management should estimate the type of crisis that could occur. For instance, an automotive company might predict future recalls based on the percentage of previous recalls. Companies located in some regions might do the best they can to be ready for a hurricane or an earthquake.

Develop Crisis-Management Policies and Procedures

An advanced form of contingency planning for crises is developing appropriate crisis-management policies and procedures. For example, establishing a crisis center in advance might mean developing rules for dealing with the media and outlining which people are informed immediately of the crisis.

Establish a Corporate Crisis-Management Team

Another preparedness tactic is to set up a corporate crisis-management team composed of employees who are trained to take charge in a sudden disaster. Some companies conduct simulated crises with the corporate crisis team or members of top management. The crisis-management groups are sometimes referred to as corporate SWAT teams to give them additional flair.

Crisis-management teams enabled Wells Fargo and Chevron to resume near-normal business soon after the 1989 Oakland, California, earthquake. Extensive planning and practice drills enabled these firms to rapidly implement actions plans that included hotlines and emergency computer backups.

Watch Out!

An important part of crisis forecasting is looking for early warning signals of impending crises. For example, just a couple of complaints about age discrimination could mean that a class-action suit is a future possibility. The presence of one disgruntled maintenance technician in a nuclear power plant could spell potential trouble.

Build Cash Reserves

Here's a suggestion applicable to preventing the sting of corporate and personal crises. Another way of managing a crisis in advance is to build substantial cash reserves. Cash on hand helps an organization weather most crises.

Cash reserves can help overcome a crisis, whereas not having enough cash on hand can create a crisis. Many firms that borrowed heavily to acquire other companies find themselves without sufficient operating funds. Loan payments consumed profits.

One more responsibility of a leader who wants to help others cope better with a future crisis is being a good cash manager. Cash is still king and queen in the world of high finance.

Avoid the Titanic Mentality

An effective mental set for preventing crises is to avoid complacency. Do not think that because you are on top now, you are invincible. M. Michael Markowich uses the term *Titanic Mentality* to describe companies that stay the course without much consideration that things could change or go wrong. Such companies do not take active steps to anticipate and avoid problems.

Another way of framing the Titanic Mentality is to think of the characteristic as an unwillingness to depart from a comfortable way of doing things. A strong *comfort-zone orientation* prompts us to ignore signals from the environment that it might be time to change or modify our customary approach. The following quiz gives you an opportunity to think about the extent of your comfort-zone orientation.

The way to avoid the Titanic Mentality and stay within your comfort zone is to think the unthinkable and then take action. Imagine what could go wrong, or listen to the doomsday thinkers around you, and then develop a plan to prevent doomsday from happening. Thinking in terms of preventing a disaster is not easy because so much emphasis is placed on being charismatic and positive.

Think about the icebergs your company could possibly encounter. Conduct simulated drills, such as one in which a group of travel agents says, "Suppose we lose 75 percent of our customers because they now book travel on their own through the Internet?"

The best defense against the Titanic Mentality is to see what changes need to be made before outside forces push you toward annihilation. Your clearest thinking is likely to take place before you are in a crisis-driven panic.

How Strong Is Your Comfort-Zone Orientation?

Describe how well you agree with the following statements. Use the following scale: Disagree Strongly (DS); Disagree (D); Neutral (N); Agree (A); Agree Strongly (AS).

	DS	D	N	A	AS
1. I often skip the news because it contains too many negative stories.	5	4	3	2	1
2. I like a little turmoil in my work environment.	1	2	3	4	5
3. Routine is good for my mental health.	5	4	3	2	1
4. Product recalls are so infrequent, company employees should not bother worrying about them.	5	4	3	2	1

	DS	D	N	A	AS
5. I hate to be inconvenienced unless a family member is faced with a crisis.	5	4	3	2	1
6. Fire drills are important even if they mean clearing all the people out of the building.	1	2	3	4	5
7. It's best to confront a difficult issue right away, because if left to linger the problem will probably worsen.	1	2	3	4	5
8. It's not worth the energy to worry about problems outside your own unit of the organization.	5	4	3	2	1
9. If an emergency comes along, I tend to put it aside until I have a pause in my regular responsibilities.	5	4	3	2	1
10. I do what I can to avoid minor pain for myself.	5	4	3	2	1
Total score	—	—	—	—	—

Scoring and interpretation: Add the numbers you have circled to obtain your score.

46 to 50: You have a strong orientation toward a willingness to deal with problems outside of your comfortable routine. You, therefore, have the right attitude toward being responsive to problems that could indicate an impending crisis.

30 to 45: You show a reasonable balance between wanting to stick with a comfortable routine and being responsive to problems that could indicate an impending crisis. However, to become good at preventing crises, you might stay tuned more carefully to impending problems.

10 to 29: You show a distinct tendency to want to stick with comfortable tasks and avoid confronting potential crises in your path. It's good that you do not engage in alarmist thinking, but you should heighten your sensitivity to dealing the unexpected and the problematic.

The Least You Need to Know

➤ A directive and forceful leadership style works so well during a crisis because people tend to be dependent on authority when facing big trouble.

➤ The components of a crisis-management mode include staying cool under pressure, avoiding a quick fix, and having one center of authority.

➤ Place the crisis in the problem-solving mode through such steps as clarifying the problem, developing creative alternatives, and developing an action plan.

➤ Develop a turnaround strategy that serves as the master plan for getting through the crisis.

➤ Keep team members focused on the task at hand during the crisis through such means as announcing any thread of good news.

➤ Hidden opportunities can sometimes be found during a crisis such as finding new ways of generating revenues.

➤ Prepare in advance for a crisis through such methods as forming a crisis-management team and building up cash reserves.

➤ Avoid the Titanic Mentality of thinking that an overwhelming, hidden crisis could not happen to you.

Chapter 21

Turning Around Problem People

In This Chapter

➤ Dealing with manipulators

➤ Dealing with dissenters

➤ Handling the personality quirks of others

➤ Negotiating with difficult people

➤ Giving recognition and affection to needy people

➤ Avoiding too much emotional involvement with difficult people

---

Nina, the manager of business services for an office equipment company, just returned from a conference on employee compensation. During her next staff meeting, she explained to the group, "There's a new development in employee compensation that's sweeping the country. It looks to me like an excellent fit for our company. The technique is called broadbanding. Basically, it means that employees are paid for their skills, talents, and other contributions instead of the job.

"In this way, employees can transfer readily from one job to another without worrying about changing pay grades. Broadbanding is a wonderful contributor to the corporate goal of a more flexible workforce. I'm ready to make a pitch to top management to begin experimenting with broadbanding."

Four of the other five managers present responded positively to Nina's leadership and asked how they could learn more about broadbanding. Two of the managers volunteered to serve on an implementation task force. Then Lenny introduced a dissenting point of view.

"Hold on, Nina. We're an empowered group of professionals. You, as the top administrator, learn about a hot new human resources technique and then try to impose it on the organization without input from us. That doesn't sound empowering to me. What about buy-in?"

"Also, where are the hard data showing that broadbanding actually improves productivity and morale and reduces payroll costs? I want to see some evidence before I go along with your proposal."

Nina had a pretty good leadership experience. Four out of five direct reports were inspired by her ideas for experimenting with a compensation system that could help the organization become more flexible. Lenny was his usual difficult self—throwing cold water on her leadership initiative. Lenny might be competent, intelligent, and generally productive, but he's still a thorn in Nina's side.

In this chapter, you will learn techniques for dealing constructively with those problem people who often undermine your leadership. A problem person is someone who is difficult but not necessarily a poor performer. Many talented people are a pain to work with despite their high productivity.

A starting point in our study of the care of difficult people is to take the accompanying quiz about dealing with and helping them. It will serve as a rough guide to your intuition about dealing effectively with work associates whose personalities represent a formidable challenge.

Helping Difficult People

For each of the following scenarios choose the method of handling the situation you think would be the most effective. Make a choice, even though more than one method of handling the situation seems plausible.

1. A team member in the cubicle next to you is talking loudly on the telephone about the fabulous weekend she and a few friends enjoyed. You are attempting to deal with a challenging work problem. To deal with this situation, you ...

   a. Get up from your chair, stand close to her, and say loudly, "Shut up, you jerk. I'm trying to do my work."

   b. Slip her a handwritten note that says, "I'm happy that you had a great weekend, but I have problems concentrating on my work when you are talking so loudly. Thanks for your help."

   c. Get the human resources manager on the phone, and ask that she please do something about the problem.

   d. Wait until lunch and then say to her, "I'm happy that you had a great weekend, but I have problems concentrating on my work when you are talking so loudly. Thanks for your help."

2. One of your co-workers, Olaf, rarely carries his fair load of the work. He forever has a good reason for not having the time to do an assignment. This morning he has approached you to load some new software onto his personal computer. You deal with this situation by ...

   a. Carefully explaining that you will help him, providing he will take over a certain specified task for you.

   b. Telling him that you absolutely refuse to help a person as lazy as he is.

   c. Counsel him about fair play and reciprocity.

   d. Review with him a list of five times in which he has asked other people to help him out. You then ask if he thinks this is a good way to treat co-workers.

3. In your role as supervisor, you have noticed that Diane, one of the group members, spends far too much work time laughing and joking. You schedule a meeting with her. As the meeting opens, you ...

   a. Joke and laugh with her to establish rapport.

   b. Explain to Diane that you have called this meeting to discuss her too-frequent laughing and joking.

   c. Talk for a few moments about the good things Diane has done for the department, then confront the real issue.

   d. Explain to Diane that she is on the verge of losing her job if she doesn't act more maturely.

4. As a team leader, you have become increasingly annoyed with Jerry's ethnic, racist, and sexist jokes. One day during a team meeting, he tells a joke you believe is particularly offensive. To deal with the situation, you ...

   a. Meet privately with your manager to discuss Jerry's offensive behavior.

   b. Catch up with Jerry later when he is alone and tell him how uncomfortable his joke made you feel.

   c. Confront Jerry on the spot and say, "Hold on Jerry. I find your joke to be offensive."

   d. Tell the group an even more offensive joke to illustrate how Jerry's behavior can get out of hand.

5. You have been placed on a task force to look for ways to save the company money, including making recommendations for eliminating jobs. You interview a supervisor about the efficiency of her department. She suddenly becomes rude and defensive. In response you ...

   a. Politely point out how her behavior is coming across to you.

   b. Get your revenge by recommending that three jobs be eliminated from her department.

c. Explain that you have used up enough of her time for today and ask for another meeting later in the week.

d. Tell her that unless she becomes more cooperative this interview cannot continue.

Scoring and interpretation: Use the following key to obtain your score:

1. a. 1	2. a. 4	3. a. 1	4. a. 2	5. a. 4
b. 4	b. 1	b. 4	b. 4	b. 1
c. 2	c. 3	c. 3	c. 3	c. 2
d. 3	d. 2	d. 2	d. 1	d. 3

18 to 20: You have good intuition for helping difficult people.

10 to 17: You have average intuition for helping difficult people.

5 to 9: You need to improve your sensitivity for helping difficult people.

An Intelligent, Well-Informed Person Would Agree with Me

Those slippery folks called manipulators are in every workplace. The *manipulator* shades the truth to gain advantage. For example, an employee might imply that if he were given a promotion, his father's company might become a good customer of the company. A group member might fake tears and talk about child-rearing responsibilities when asked to work every other Saturday.

Key Word

A **manipulator** attempts to influence people and circumstances to gain advantage through dishonest and unethical means. Even when the manipulator is not outright dishonest, he or she often stretches the truth by such means as exaggerating the consequences of an action.

When manipulation goes unchecked, it can interfere with group functioning, thus adversely affecting the leader's performance. The manipulator sees that threats or implied threats are working, so the person continues to manipulate. The other group members lose respect for the manager who is being manipulated. Honest workers might get discouraged when they see that deception and dishonesty are effective. Following are several common manipulative tactics and countermaneuvers.

Bandwagon Technique

The group member informs you that all other company managers are doing something such as granting personal time off to visit a lawyer. If you do not go along with this request, you are, therefore, wrong. The way to handle the bandwagon thrust is to close the case and not be manipulated into defending your position. An effective response here is, "What you say might be true for other managers, but here, we don't allow personal time off for appointments with lawyers."

"Always" Technique

The manipulator might say to you, "I always get assigned to the least important projects." Here the manipulator attempts to gain control of the discussion by indirectly prompting you to respond to a general accusation. The antidote is to demand specifics. Begin by asking, "What do you mean 'always'?" and continue digging until you reach the person's true concern. By forcing the person to be quite specific, you remove all the ammunition. You might probe, for example, "How many times have you been assigned to an unimportant project?" The group member might only be able to point to one or two poor assignments.

Door-in-the-Face Technique

The door-in-the-face technique is a manipulative way of getting a proposal accepted that a person believes might not be accepted. The group member attempting to influence you makes a major request that will most likely be rejected, such as sponsorship for a five-day training program in Honolulu. Shortly thereafter comes a more modest request, which was the real goal in the first place: The individual wants to attend a two-day training program in Chicago on the same topic. The person wants to make you feel guilty when you turn down the first request. With guilt being such a strong motivator, you are more likely to submit to the second, smaller demand.

Advisor

A challenge in dealing with manipulators is that they can upset you emotionally. By being upset, you may lose your edge in dealing constructively with the manipulation. If you use the time-tested techniques just described, your anti–manipulation skills should improve. Because dealing with manipulators is so difficult, I recommend that you rehearse some of these techniques with a friend. Take turns being the manipulator and the manipulated! Doing so will heighten your insights.

A good way of countering the door-in-the-face technique is to point out the discrepancy between the two demands: "This sounds strange to me. First, you thought you needed a five-day training program in Honolulu. Then, you figured that a two-day program in Chicago would get the job done. Why didn't you present me with the two alternatives the first time?" Next time around, the person is unlikely to use the door-in-the-face technique.

Threats

The most brazen of manipulators sometimes uses threats to intimidate and gain control. A manipulator might see you as passive and, therefore, threaten to go over your head, quit, or disclose embarrassing information about you.

To deal with manipulative threats, stand firm and repeat your position as many times as necessary: "No matter how you threaten to retaliate, I will not change my evaluation of your performance." When the manipulator realizes that you will not succumb to threats, he or she will usually back off.

Biased Reporting

To achieve his or her way, the manipulative group member presents information that supports an issue while omitting opposing data. For example, the person brags about shipments to achieve a bigger budget but does not refer to the high rate of customer returns. To handle this type of manipulation, reserve judgment until you further investigate an unfamiliar situation.

Psychological Sabotage

Highly manipulative group members might attempt to control your actions by purposely making you look bad or delaying the completion of work projects. These methods of psychological sabotage include intentionally overlooking, losing, or forgetting things intended to impede your productivity. Another form of this type of subversion is ignoring an important problem, such as not bringing a consistent customer complaint to your attention. The swiftest antidote to psychological sabotage is to invoke discipline, such as a written reprimand or suspension.

I'm Committed to Making Life Miserable for You

Constructive criticism is welcome in any healthy organization. Nevertheless, some "pills" out there raise dissent just to breed conflict and make life miserable for the manager. When a manager's life is filled with misery and conflict, it is difficult to exercise effective leadership. A vociferous dissenter can embarrass you and erode your power. A critical employee who has the good of the organization in mind can be handled without much difficulty. Explain to the person that sometimes he or she appears too harsh and disgruntled and that it is better to express criticism privately instead of at a staff meeting.

In contrast, a worker who repeatedly creates animosity by deceiving, lying, and accusing probably wants to achieve personal gain rather than offer help. Confrontation about the unacceptable behavior is important. Explain that extreme dissent is unacceptable. Ideally, take the next step and invoke problem-solving. The problem-solving episode might reveal that the true underlying issue is that the group member wants to be rebellious. Clarification of a problem sometimes leads to a change in behavior. Also consider these additional approaches to dealing with a dissenter:

➤ In dealing with a mild dissenter, help the person realize that it is preferable to express strong disagreement within the confines of the organizational unit. Point out that the unit could be weakened if outsiders perceive substantial disagreement within the unit.

➤ Discuss with the dissenter the merits of constructive criticism in contrast to destructive criticism.

➤ Keep an approximate log of the ratio of negative to positive comments made by the dissenter when the two of you are conversing or meeting together. If the negative comments seem unduly high in relation to positive ones (a ratio of one third or higher), discuss your finding with the dissenter. People sometimes don't realize how negative they are and might change in response to such data.

Advisor

It's important for leaders to invest the time in dealing constructively with problem people and diminishing the problems they create. The reason is that if a problem person keeps resurfacing with annoying issues, your time can be seriously drained, thus lowering your productivity. Besides, if problem people take much of your time, when are you going to squeeze in being a visionary and transformational leader? A natural problem is that it is easy to procrastinate dealing with problem people. Unless you are confrontational by nature, it is unpleasant to deal head-on with difficult people. Yet delays in taking action only intensify the problem.

Okay, So You're Weird; I Still Want You on the Team

Both on and off the job, many people have *personality quirks,* or peculiarities, that make them difficult to deal with. The manager is usually in the best position to help these people control their quirks so that job performance does not suffer. As the leader of the group, it is important for you to show others that quirks can be dealt with successfully.

Your best defense as a leader is to show sympathy for group members with these quirks without submitting to all their demands. Be understanding if you do not find all their behavior acceptable. If you show sympathy, the group member with the quirk might shift to more tolerable behavior. Presented next are several frequently observed personality quirks.

Key Word

A **personality quirk** is a persistent peculiarity of behavior that annoys or irritates other people. Nobody is expected to be perfect, but a quirk gets under the skin of even generally tolerant people.

The Person with a Strong Need to Be Correct

Group members with this quirk set up situations so that people who disagree with them are made to look naive or foolish. (In this way, they are manipulators.) An example is, "As any well-informed person would agree, this is the way we should proceed on this project. If anybody disagrees, please speak up now." You can sympathize in this manner: "I recognize, Leslie, that you research everything before reaching an opinion and that you are usually right. Nevertheless, I want to point out my perspective on this problem."

The Attention-Seeker

Attention-seekers might speak louder than others, play the role of the office clown, or tell co-workers all their woes. The point is that they crave attention for positive or negative reasons. You can sympathize in this manner: "We all know, Chris, that you like to be in the spotlight. You do deserve our attention, but now it is Amy's turn to speak."

The Anti-Control Freak

Some workers resent control, direction, or advice from others. People with this quirk are so oversensitive to being controlled that they misinterpret hints as suggestions and orders as direct challenges to their intelligence and self-worth. You might express sympathy yet still get to a group member with this quirk by a statement such as, "Lee, I know you like to be your own person. I admire you for it, but I have a small suggestion that could strengthen the graphics you just put together."

The Cynic About Management

Some group members view everything management does as negative and question every action in an attempt to uncover the true reason behind it. The suspiciousness of these people creates in other workers doubts that are similar to the ones they exhibit. Morale could suffer as a consequence. You can sympathize with cynics and perhaps help them achieve insight into their behavior with a comment such as, "I appreciate your analytical attitude, Bobbie, but did you ever think that management sometimes does something kind or generous? Is upper management really always the villain?"

The Passive-Aggressive Personality

A passive-aggressive worker typically becomes sulky, irritable, or forgetful when asked to do something he or she dislikes. The person expresses hostility passively by not performing the expected tasks. Explain to the passive-aggressive group member that you realize the task at hand is not something he or she relishes. Nevertheless, the project is an important part of a team effort.

> **Another Perspective**
>
> Not everybody agrees that one should sympathize with a person's personality quirk. In a highly competitive workplace that emphasizes teamwork, people should work smoothly with others without requiring special handling.

Let's See If We Can Work Out a Beautiful Deal

Although as the manager and leader you typically have more formal authority than the difficult person, negotiating with the person is necessary. Part of the problem is that resorting to formal authority does not always get the job done. As in all negotiations, you might need to compromise, and you are looking for a win-win solution. However, negotiating with a difficult person also requires a few special tactics:

➤ Shock the person to make sure you are taken seriously. Until you receive the person's full attention, you make no progress. The way to get the other's attention is to set a boundary on how much you will tolerate.

➤ Insist on playing by the rules. Difficult people attempt to get you to accept unreasonable agreements in a negotiating session. For example, the difficult person might make exorbitant demands for consenting to transfer to another location. Instead of succumbing to the pressure, insist on fair rules for both the negotiating process and the final settlement. (Of course, in this case, you might even be willing to pay money out of pocket for the person to transfer.)

➤ Make the difficult person justify his or her position.

When the difficult group member takes extreme stands and makes unreasonable demands, ask that person to explain the logic behind his or her position. You might say, "To understand your demands, I need to understand how you arrived at those points.

Why do you request $10,000 to assist your spouse with a job search in the new location? Does that include travel? A new wardrobe?" When the person answers, demands that cannot be justified lose their credibility.

I Hear You, I See You, and I Think You're Adorable

Problem people, like misbehaving people, are sometimes crying out for attention. If you give them recognition and affection, their counterproductive behavior *sometimes* ceases. If their negative behavior is a product of a deeper-rooted problem, recognition and affection do not work.

You must take other actions. The most direct tactic is to give the problem person attention and affection. If the negative behavior stops, you found the proper antidote. To illustrate the technique, here are a few examples:

➤ During a staff meeting, Mike keeps making negative comments about the contributions of others and also makes frequent wisecracks. You stop the meeting and say, "Let's give Mike center stage for a few moments. He seems to have so much energy today. Mike, you take the floor."

➤ During a staff meeting, Kate launches into a long anecdote about a job experience that appears to be unrelated to the subject at hand. You notice that other people at the meeting start rolling their eyes. You tell Kate, "Allow me to interrupt this great story for one moment. It seems to be of indirect interest to what we are doing right now. Would you be kind enough to send us all an e-mail version of this story later? I know we would all enjoy reading it at our leisure."

➤ Sam is forever complaining about how bad management is and how many mistakes it is making. You are concerned that his negative attitude will be contagious, yet you cannot deny there is some truth in what he says. You appeal to Sam's need for attention by saying, "Sam, you have a lot of interesting ideas about what's wrong with the company. I want you, on your own time, to write a five-page document suggesting ways in which the company can be improved. We'll then discuss it and perhaps send it to higher management."

Am I Your Boss or Your Therapist?

The theme of this chapter is that an effective leader should deal constructively with problem people. Recognize, however, that problem people often have many emotional problems. If you don't keep some psychological distance from problem people, you might become too emotionally involved with them to maintain a professional relationship. One of the traps is that you become so entangled in the group member's problems that you are not able to administer discipline if needed.

The situation of getting emotionally involved with a problem worker is similar to being sexually involved with that person. As long as he or she is performing well on the job, the situation is tolerable. However, you suffer from serious role conflict if the person must be disciplined or laid off. Imagine saying to your partner (and group member) on Sunday night, "I have fallen totally in love with you. By the way, I have to meet with you tomorrow morning in the office to discuss your serious job performance deficiencies."

When you find that you are too embroiled with a problem person, back off a little. Try to move the relationship to a more professional level. One way to show concern for the person yet at the same time set limits to your involvement is to use the tough love approach. Tough love has its origins in parent-child relationships. It aims to enable people to take responsibility for their own needs. You might say to a problem person, for example, "I know you like to complain a lot, but I find it disruptive and it undermines my authority as a leader. It's your responsibility to learn how to complain less in the office. The rest of the office will no longer adapt to you. You have to adapt to acceptable standards of behavior."

Advisor

Tough love is a philosophy about dealing with people you care about that enables and encourages them to take responsibility for meeting their own needs and regulating their own behavior. The parent might say to the teenager, "You cannot stay in this house when you are drunk. Stay with friends or sleep in the park. It's your problem." The boss might say to the problem person, "Stop manipulating me and others on the team with lies and half-truths. If you don't stop within 45 days, I am going to recommend that you be placed on official discipline. No excuses will be accepted."

If you think the person is becoming emotionally distraught, recommend that he or she visit the Employee Assistance Program or similar referral service. Make a suggestion such as, "I notice you are having difficulty concentrating on your work recently. I want you to visit our EAP counselor to get her input."

Here are some signs that you might be too emotionally embroiled in the problems of a problem person:

➤ Before going to sleep and when you wake up, you think about the person's difficult behavior and wonder why you can't help him or her change.

➤ You have frequent after-hours discussions with the person about his or her work life and personal life.

➤ The person telephones you frequently at home.

➤ The person asks for your advice almost daily on a wide range of matters.

➤ When the person isn't around, you miss him or her despite all the person's complaints and antics.

➤ You find yourself defending the person's behavior, often pointing out that he or she is the victim of mistreatment by others.

➤ You spend so much time counseling with the problem person that you neglect other job responsibilities including spending enough time with other group members.

If many of the symptoms just described are present, it is a clear signal that you have become too emotionally involved with the person. Back off and encourage him or her to seek help elsewhere.

The Least You Need to Know

➤ Combat manipulators through such direct methods as pointing out discrepancies between reality and what they are saying or implying.

➤ Combat dissenters by making it clear that constructive criticism is welcome but that their behavior is unacceptable.

➤ Deal with the personality quirks of group members through such means as showing sympathy without submitting to all their demands.

➤ Negotiate with difficult people because you will need more than formal authority to work out a peaceful arrangement.

➤ Giving recognition and attention to needy people is important because they often create a disturbance to satisfy their frustrated needs for recognition and attention.

➤ Getting too embroiled in the psyche of difficult people is hazardous because you might lose your objectivity in dealing with them—and it is draining.

Part 5

Helping Others Develop Their Potential

A vice president of marketing was a guest lecturer at a business-strategy course given at Harvard Business School. The executive began by asking the students what questions they had and what topics they wanted to explore. Among the questions were the following:

> *"What was your greatest strategic decision?"*
>
> *"What is your company's strategic intent?"*
>
> *"How are you going to clobber the competition?"*
>
> *"What are your profit margins on goods sold to third-world countries?"*

After listening to a five-minute barrage of such questions, the executive responded, "I know this is Harvard Business School with all its emphasis on business competitiveness, but I'm a little disappointed. Not one question dealt with the most important and satisfying part of leader's job. Not a person in this room asked me about developing people."

Developing people is a major leadership and management activity. In this part of the book, you will receive in-depth information about such topics as being a nurturing boss, acting as a coach, and being a mentor. All these activities contribute to bottom-line success in the long run.

How to Become a Nurturing Leader

After 15 years of being a full-time homemaker, Louise considered herself fortunate to be back in the workforce as a customer service representative at a gas and electric company. After years of dealing with family conflicts, Louise thought she had the basic skills necessary to deal with customer complaints and inquiries. Jeannine, Louise's boss, thought so, too. In addition to explaining certain techniques and company regulations to Louise, Jeannine encouraged her frequently.

After six months, Louise had her first performance appraisal. Jeannine's comments were favorable but included a few suggestions for improvement such as accepting empowerment more readily. At the close of the interview, Louise said to Jeannine, "Now, I want a few minutes to evaluate you as my boss and leader. Is that okay?"

With a smile, Jeannine said, "Of course; why not? Feedback goes both ways in a modern company."

"You might be about 12 years younger than I am," said Louise. "But you have been like a big sister, supportive parent, and wise friend. You gave me a chance to get back into the workforce when my confidence was low. You helped me put into proper perspective the work days from hell I've encountered a few times. Because of this, I rate your performance an A."

Do you want to be a leader like Jeannine? In this chapter, you will learn some attitudes and techniques that will help you become a nurturing leader. First take the following quiz to measure your attitudes toward helping others.

Attitudes Toward Helping Others

Describe how well you agree with the following statements by using a three-point scale: Agree (A); Neutral (N); Disagree (D).

	A	N	D
1. If I see a coworker make a mistake, I do not inform him or her of the mistake.	1	2	3
2. It should be part of everybody's job to share skills and ideas with group members.	3	2	1
3. The manager should have exclusive responsibility for coaching people within the work unit.	1	2	3
4. I can think of many instances in my life when somebody thanked me for showing him or her how to do something.	3	2	1
5. I have very little patience with group members who do not give me their full cooperation.	1	2	3
6. To save time, I will do a task for a group member rather than invest the time showing him or her how to do it.	1	2	3
7. I would take the initiative to put an inexperienced group member under my wing.	3	2	1
8. As a child, I often took the time to show younger children how to do things.	3	2	1
9. Rather than ask each other for help, I think group members should wait until the manager is available.	1	2	3
10. It is best not to share key information with a group member, because that person could then perform as well as or better than me.	1	2	3
		TOTAL	

Scoring and interpretation: Use the following scoring key to obtain your score for each answer, and then calculate your total score.

25 to 30: Very positive attitudes toward helping, developing, and training others in the workplace. Such attitudes reflect a strong nurturing attitude and compassion for the growth needs of others.

16 to 24: Mixed positive and negative attitudes toward helping, developing, and training others in the workplace. You might need to develop more sensitivity to the growth needs of others to be considered a strong nurturing leader.

10 to 15: Negative attitudes toward helping, developing, and training others in the workplace. Guard against being so self-centered that it is held against you.

Nobody Leaves My Nest Without Being Able to Fly

Another constructive and exciting role for a leader is to nurture group members, helping them grow and develop. The group members who want to be nurtured (such as Louise the customer service rep) become your strong supporters. It is easy for you to spot the people who do not want to be nurtured. They back away mentally when you attempt to help them or get too close to them emotionally.

Nurturing is a fuzzy word, but it can be translated into specific practices such as …

➤ Showing a genuine concern for the welfare of group members. (This is the starting point and the foundation attitude.)

➤ Investing substantial time into listening to the work problems of group members.

➤ Investing an adequate amount of time in listening to the personal problems of group members.

➤ Demonstrating by your comments that you worry about the setbacks and disappointments of group members.

➤ Congratulating group members regularly when they demonstrate skill development.

➤ Using your power to help group members resolve bothersome problems.

➤ Being an effective coach by making useful suggestions for improvement and giving ample encouragement.

➤ Getting excited when a group member develops a complex skill with which you helped him or her.

➤ Looking at your success as a leader partially in terms of how many people you helped develop.

➤ Being available to mentor group members who seek your counsel and friendship.

Key Word

A **nurturing** leader actively promotes the growth of group members in terms of skills, knowledge, and emotional well-being.

Who Wants to Fly Like an Eagle?

To be a nurturing leader, you must first recognize that almost everybody has a need for self-fulfillment. A subtlety, however, is that people vary in the extent of this need. You can tell people have a strong growth need when they display some of the following behaviors and attitudes:

➤ Asking frequent questions about why the company is pursuing a particular strategy

➤ Asking frequently for more responsibility

➤ Developing new skills regularly

➤ Engaging in self-improvement activities such as taking courses and self-study

➤ Talking about their future in terms of broadening their skills and acquiring new knowledge

➤ Frequently asking other people questions about their job

➤ Making frequent suggestions for improving methods and procedures in your unit

➤ Rarely responding "That's nothing new" when told about a new development

➤ Eagerly taking on assignments that require developing new skills

Key Word

Supportive communication *is a communication style that delivers the message accurately and supports or enhances the relationship between two parties. A supportive communicator consistently attempts to make people feel good about themselves rather than cut them down with insults and hostile humor. Do you remember how television's Mr. Rogers said so frequently to children, "Aren't you glad you're you?" He was an outstanding supportive communicator.*

To satisfy growth needs, you might engage in interactions with group members such as sharing new skills with them, clipping relevant articles, or telling them about an important new Web site you discover. You might also talk with group members about their future because promotions and varied assignments are effective ways of satisfying growth needs.

A more specific approach to appealing to growth needs is to afford an individual the opportunity to do more of any of the behaviors included in the preceding list. For example, ask the group member his or her ideas for improving work methods and procedures in your unit.

I Think What You Say Is Wonderful

Communicating powerfully and dramatically facilitates influencing and inspiring people. A more mellow type of communication is needed to help people grow and develop. A leader who uses *supportive communication* nurtures group members and brings out their best. Supportive communication has seven principles or characteristics:

1. Supportive communication is problem-oriented, not person-oriented. Most people are more receptive to a discussion of what can be done to change a work method instead of what can be done to change them personally. Many people might readily agree that more alternative solutions are needed for a problem. Fewer people are willing to accept the message, "You need to be more creative."

2. Supportive communication is based on congruent verbal and nonverbal communication. As described in Chapter 5, "Communicate Like a Leader," this means your words, body language, and facial expressions are all consistent with one another and that you don't send those confusing *mixed messages*.

Key Word

A **mixed message** comes about when you say one thing, but your tone and body language say something else. For example, if you say "I really trust you," but you have your arms folded and a scowl on your face, that definitely sends a mixed message.

3. Supportive communication validates rather than invalidates people. Validating communication makes a person feel good because it accepts the presence, uniqueness, and importance of the other person. Whether the other person's ideas are totally accepted, he or she is acknowledged. For example, if during a meeting a person makes a recommendation that doesn't fit the agenda, you might reply, "What you recommend has merit. It doesn't quite fit today's agenda, so I'm asking you to make your recommendation at a future meeting."

4. Supportive communication is specific, not general. Most people benefit more from specific rather than general feedback. To illustrate, the statement, "We have terrible customer service" is too general to be useful. A more useful statement is "Our customer satisfaction ratings are down 25 percent from previous years." The second statement is more specific and provides an improvement target. This aspect of feedback is introduced again in the following chapter.

Watch Out!

When functioning as a supportive communicator, be careful not to overdo it to the point that you appear sappy. For example, if during a staff meeting a group member hurls an invective your way, do not respond, "Thank you for your candor. We can all grow from honest feedback."

5. Supportive communication is linked logically to previous messages, thus enhancing communication. When communication has logical links between what is said, it is easier for group members to follow the leader's thoughts. A subtle form of disjunctive communication is a long pause because listeners lose the speaker's train of thought.

6. Supportive communication is owned, not disowned. Effective communicators take responsibility for what they say, and don't attribute the authority behind their ideas to another person. The effective leader might say, "I want everybody to work 10 extra hours per week during this crunch period." The less-effective leader might say, "The company wants everybody to work 10 extra hours per week during the company crunch period."

7. Supportive communication requires listening as well as sending messages. The relationship between two parties cannot be enhanced unless both listen to each other. In addition, a key strategy for helping people grow and develop is to allow them to be heard.

I Need You to Work All Weekend, and How Is That Infection on Your Basset Hound's Paw?

The heavy emphasis on downsizing and reengineering has decelerated. Nevertheless, a major concern is that corporate leadership has little regard for the welfare of individual workers. The concern exists despite many corporate programs designed to make work life more tolerable for employees. Among such programs are company-sponsored dependent care, work-at-home programs, and flexible work schedules.

You can capitalize on employee concerns about corporate insensitivity by being purposely humanistic. At the same time, you will be a nurturing leader because you are giving people a chance to grow and develop through your humanism. Growth is also enhanced because you encourage the satisfaction of a wide range of needs.

"Being humanistic" is a catch-all term that can refer to almost any appeal to the emotions and feelings of other people. Presented next is a long list of humanistic attitudes and actions in relation to group members. Pick and choose among them to help you function as a humanistic and nurturing leader:

➤ Show an interest in the nonwork facets of the lives of group members without neglecting concern about good performance. Express an interest in the total individual and his or her multiple roles in life. Ask questions such as, "How did you and your son enjoy the Cub Scout dinner?" or "How is the self-study program on Russian going, Comrade?"

➤ Buy a baby gift for a new parent's child.

➤ Initiate a special dress-down day that encourages group members to dress in the type of casual clothing they ordinarily wear while doing household chores or running.

➤ Ask group members what they might do if they won a big lottery prize. (The answer to this question typically points to a person's ideal lifestyle.)

➤ Conduct a meeting to discuss all the programs the company offers that could make life easier for employees. Ask group members if they are taking advantage of programs such as flexible benefits, the Employee Assistance Program (EAP), and the tuition refund program.

➤ Grant an employee an afternoon off from work to invest in any activity that will make life easier.

➤ Ask group members how well their jobs are fitting into their career plans and what hopes they have for future jobs.

➤ Conduct a luncheon discussion about the major sources of stress on the job and what can be done about them.

➤ Write personal notes at mid-year to high-contributing workers expressing appreciation for their help in keeping the organization in operation. Also mention how they make life easier for you.

➤ Give group members proper credit for any ideas you use, thus enhancing their self-esteem. A major employee complaint is that managers use their ideas without giving appropriate credit.

➤ Invest at least a couple of hours per month listening to the personal problems and complaints of employees. Let them ventilate about their confusion and anger, but avoid becoming their counselor. If a group member's problem appears to be overwhelming, suggest that he or she visit the Employee Assistance Program or seek outside help.

➤ Pay a compliment at least once a month to members of the team. An easy, natural one is "Thanks for the nice job you did for me the other day." To avoid any potential charges of the threatening environment type of sexual harassment, make bland, unisex compliments about appearance. Stick to "Nice outfit" or "That suits you."

Advisor

The driving force behind being humanistic is the attitude that you want people to satisfy a wide range of needs on the job and to grow and develop. It is also a question of helping people feel better about themselves, brick by brick, and lead a better life.

You Can Grow If You Copy Me

Your skill in leading by example can indirectly help you become a nurturing leader. By serving as a role model, you can help another person develop. The person deliberately, or without realizing it directly, picks up positive ideas from you on how to function well in a work environment. Some behaviors and values that make you a positive role model include the following:

➤ A strong work ethic

➤ Job expertise

➤ Personal warmth

➤ Being good-natured and keeping your temper under control

➤ Good speaking and writing ability

➤ Outstanding facility with information technology

➤ Strong business ethics

➤ Treating people fairly

➤ A positive attitude toward the organization's strategy and mission

Being a good role model, therefore, means displaying a variety of positive human and work attributes. In short, effective, competent, warm individuals are good role models.

Another Perspective

A nurturing leader makes many contributions to people, organizations, and society. However, some independent-minded people resist being nurtured. In these cases, the best approach is to be a good role model for that person. Save your energy for nurturing others who want your help.

Key Word

As defined by Peter Frost and Sandra Robinson writing in the *Harvard Business Review*, a **toxic handler** is a person who shoulders the sadness, frustration, bitterness, anger, and despair of group members so they can work productively.

You Poor Baby, Let Me Lick Your Wounds

Another facet of being a nurturing, emotionally supportive leader involves being a *toxic handler,* or a healing manager. This type of leader/manager helps people deal with some of the most crippling emotional problems that arise in the workplace. Among these problems might be a nasty boss (but not you), layoffs, and rapid change. The ready willingness to be a sympathetic and empathic listener is a major part of being a toxic handler.

Dealing with a nasty boss requires some explanation. In this case, if you were a healing manager—or toxic handler—your job would be to help your co-workers cope with a boss who creates stress for everyone. You would become the listener and the buffer between co-workers and the nasty boss. A good example of this phenomenon was reported in the *Harvard Business Review:* A new CEO was brought into a public utility, and project manager Michael became one of his direct reports. According to Michael, the CEO walked all over people, making fun of and intimidating them. He criticized work needlessly and changed his plans almost every day. One of the other project managers was hospitalized with ulcers and took early retirement. People throughout the organization felt frightened and betrayed.

Michael stepped between his colleagues and the new CEO. He listened to their problems. During meetings Michael would defend his colleagues after they were verbally attacked by the new CEO. Yet, Michael always pointed out the CEO's *positive* qualities whenever he was asked about him.

As a toxin-dissipating leader you might also help a hurting employee find solutions to a vexing problem. Suppose, for example, that a high-performing temporary worker in your department has been trying for two years to become part of the permanent workforce. He is embittered because he works so hard and performs so well, yet still does not have all the rights and privileges of a full-time, permanent employee. You listen intently to his problem, then suggest a course of action. You recommend that he assemble a dossier of his accomplishments, including his resumé. With this information, the two of you can make a formal presentation to higher management about his candidacy for a permanent position. Even if your proposed solution does not work right away, you have given the employee a sensible action plan for overcoming his bitterness.

Watch Out!

Being a toxic handler for too long, however, has its price. Because you are adding the role of a part-time workplace therapist to your other responsibilities, your own workload may become unreasonable. Also, since you are dealing with so much emotional pain, you might burn out, like so many other people-helpers.

The Least You Need to Know

➤ A nurturing leader has a genuine concern for the welfare of group members and helps them grow and develop.

➤ Identify the growth needs of group members by such signs as the person asking frequently for more responsibility, and asking others about their jobs.

➤ Be a supportive communicator by communicating in such a way that enhances the relationship between you and the group member. For example, you might go out of your way to make somebody feel good.

➤ Be a humanistic leader by making an appeal to the emotions and feelings of other people.

➤ Being a good role model helps you to be a nurturing leader.

➤ Be a healer when you can, but watch out that you don't end up as the organizational therapist.

Chapter 23

Giving Feedback and Positive Reinforcement

In This Chapter

➤ Places to find feedback information

➤ Rules for effective feedback

➤ Rules for positive reinforcement

➤ Getting mileage out of praise and recognition

George, a purchasing supervisor, was reviewing his e-mail messages when he came upon one with an ominous tone from Alex, his manager. It said, "George, I must see you today to discuss your job status." One hour later George showed up in his manager's office.

"What's up, Alex?" asked George. "You said you want to discuss my job status."

"I might as well be blunt," responded Alex. "I'm demoting you to purchasing agent as of the first of the month. I've had complaints of sexist behavior and sexual harassment against you."

"What in the world are you talking about?" said George. "I never put down women. I have never hit on even one of my employees. I'm a respectable married man with four children. This is outrageous."

"Calm down, George; nobody said you weren't respectable. It's just that I've had a number of complaints that you use terms demeaning to women. One of the secretaries said you call her 'Honey.' Someone else said you call female sales representatives 'girls.' Our human resources manager claims that sexist language of this type is a form of sexual harassment. It's, therefore, necessary to demote you. Our company won't tolerate sexist behavior by supervisors or anybody else."

With an angry tone in his voice and a shocked expression, George said, "Nobody ever told me I was being sexist. I was just being friendly. Why didn't you tell me this a long time ago? I could have changed the terms I use in reference to women."

"I didn't want to mention the problem until I had plenty of evidence," said Alex. "Besides that, I didn't want to hurt your feelings."

"You didn't want to hurt my feelings?" said George. "How do you think I'm feeling now that you've demoted me and charged me with sexual harassment?"

George is guilty of being out of step with the times. Using sexist language is inappropriate for a supervisory leader. Alex is guilty of a major error as a manager and leader. He did not give timely feedback that could have steered a team member in the right direction.

In this chapter, I describe part of the nuts and bolts of a managerial leader's job—how to give both positive and negative feedback to group members. I also give step-by-step advice for using positive reinforcement, including praise and recognition. A review of these fundamentals will help in your quest to become a complete leader.

How About a Little Data?

Giving *feedback* to employees about their job performance and behavior is one of a leader's basic tasks. Feedback is necessary for motivating and coaching employees, conducting performance appraisals, administering discipline, and being an effective mentor. Feedback also helps employees grow, develop, and correct their mistakes. Despite the many positive uses of feedback, it requires no cash outlay, but it does require an expenditure of time and mental energy.

Key Word

This definition—developed by Charles Seashore and Edith Seashore—helps direct your thinking toward the importance of feedback: **Feedback** is information about past behavior, delivered in the present, which might influence future behavior.

Before you can capitalize on the potential value of feedback, it helps to be aware of the sources of information that are available. Some of these sources are obvious; some are not. Here is a checklist of places to look for feedback data to help the members of your team or work group:

❏ Collect objective indices of performance including sales records, productivity information, scrap rates, money saved, and performance against goals.

❏ As you stroll through the work area, make mental notes of what group members are doing right and doing wrong. Keep a record for each employee. An example is, "May 15: Jessica dropped what she was doing to assist Jack in calculating a foreign currency exchange. Great teamwork!"

❏ Pay careful attention to written and spoken comments from customers about group members' performance and behavior. An example is "December 3: New customer sent letter to CEO saying that Jake spent one hour tracking down a $10 part for her printer. Said she would call us first for her next piece of office equipment."

❏ Scan customer satisfaction ratings that relate to the group member's areas of responsibility. For example, consult the customer satisfaction ratings compiled by a hotel for which the group member is the manager in charge.

❏ Listen for gossip and secondhand information about staffers. Before using this information for feedback, however, look for consistency from at least two sources. An undocumented negative comment is usually not good fodder for feedback. It can upset a person to face an unfair accusation. The only harm done by repeating undocumented positive feedback is that the recipient might develop a false sense of confidence in an area that needs improvement.

Another Perspective

Some management advisors believe that feedback should focus almost entirely on how well a group member achieves work results. Following this idea, you do not give a person feedback on such factors as a negative or positive attitude or teamwork. The counter-argument is that intangible factors such as attitudes contribute to achieving results in the long run.

How to Make Feedback a Joyous Experience (Well, Almost)

Giving feedback is one of the major tasks of face-to-face leadership. Given properly, both positive and negative feedback can help others grow and develop and can also be a motivating force. Giving feedback does not come easily to managers and leaders. As a consequence, offering effective feedback requires following a few basic suggestions and then practicing them. If you can get feedback on your feedback, you will develop even more quickly. However, one-way mirrors and video cameras can create problems of their own. Some people believe that taking a video of somebody in action prevents them from behaving naturally. Others believe that one-way mirrors are unethical because the parties usually do not know they are being observed.

Give Specific Feedback

To help a group member achieve higher performance, the leader pinpoints what specific behavior, attitude, or skill requires improvement. A good coach might say, "I read the production expansion proposal you submitted. It's okay, but it falls short of your usual level of creativity. Each product you mentioned is already carried by competitors."

Specific feedback is preferable to generalities, such as saying "Your report is not up to par" without giving further explanation. After providing the group member specifics, general feedback can be effective, such as saying, "The examples I've given you point to the fact that you are not performing as well this quarter as last." Generalizations of a positive nature are usually well accepted when supported by specific feedback. An example is, "The examples I've given you point to the fact that you've become a superior performer."

Another Perspective

The feedback process once again emphasizes the importance of two-way communication for effective leadership. By conducting a dialogue with the individual receiving the feedback, you can better understand the person's behavior. Two-way communication is particularly important in multicultural groups because one person might not correctly interpret the behavior of a person from another culture.

Put the Ball in the Group Member's Court

After presenting your feedback to the group member, ask for his or her input to clarify what the person's behavior means. Ask the person why his or her performance is down (or up) for the quarter. The person whose performance is down might say, "True enough, my performance is down in our team for this quarter. But my total contribution to the corporation is up. You might recall that I was assigned part-time to two other projects. I'm spread too thin to do a great job in any one place."

On the positive side, the group member might say, "Yes, my performance is up. It's partly because our team is working so smoothly this quarter. Working with winners helps make me a winner."

Getting the group member's explanation of what went right or wrong contributes to your stature as a leader. The reason is that an effective leader strives to help people understand themselves better in ways such as analyzing the causes for their behavior.

Deliver Feedback Close in Time to the Event

Positive or negative, feedback is most effective when it is delivered close in time to when the behavior was observed. An e-mail message can be an effective medium for delivering positive feedback shortly after a meritorious incident occurred. For example, if a group member got up a few hours early to accommodate a customer's time zone, send the person a congratulatory e-mail message that afternoon. You should not use e-mail, however, for negative feedback. Negative messages somehow seem more severe in writing than in speaking. It is also bad for a person's mental health not to be able to respond immediately and face-to-face to the person who delivers the negative feedback.

Immediate feedback is preferable to saving up incidents for the annual, or semi-annual, performance appraisal. One reason is that people learn better when they can link feedback to an incident fresh in their mind. Also, most people dislike being hit at performance appraisal time with a laundry list of things they did wrong during the review period. No laundry list of positive behaviors is too long!

Focus on Behavior Rather Than Personality

An axiom of giving negative feedback is that the manager should focus on the negative behavior rather than make interpretations of the group member's personality or character. Assume that a person reporting to you has been hypercritical of other team members during the past several team meetings. To focus on behavior, you say, "I've noticed that during the last few team meetings, you strongly attacked many other people's ideas. This tends to make them clam up. As a result, the meetings are less productive than they could be." Your feedback might help the person look upon your criticism as mostly a work problem that can be improved.

Watch Out!

Feedback about unsatisfactory or substandard behavior should be delivered close to the time observed. If you wait until you accumulate a laundry list of wrong-doings and then deliver the list all at once, the recipient will feel abused. As a result, he or she might become resentful and defensive. Many people find it traumatic to be hit with a number of complaints at once.

An example of focusing on personality over the same issue is "I'm concerned that you have an attitude problem. During the last several meetings, you've been a hypercritical pest. You've been an annoyance to me and the other teammates." Instead of reflecting on how to change a work problem, the group member will become defensive and resentful. He or she was nailed with a heavy diagnosis. You might be right, but the defensiveness will block any immediate efforts toward change. Remember, as a leader, one of your goals is to bring about positive change.

Many industrial psychologists believe that positive feedback should also focus more on behavior than personality. A high producer should, therefore, be told that during the period in question, he or she exceeded expectations by 15 percent. This is preferable to saying, "You're a real winner and a person with a great work ethic." Part of the reasoning is that some people feel self-conscious when labeled and might also wonder if they can live up to your future expectations. My opinion is that you should not worry too much about praising the character of an effective group member. Egos being what they are, most people relish praise about their personality and character.

For example, a colleague of mine asked for my feedback about his chances for promotion. He said he wanted my opinion because he thought I was candid and honest. I gladly accepted the compliment without asking my colleague to cite specific examples of my honesty and candor. (Maybe I was concerned that he wouldn't be able to find supporting evidence for his assertion.) Be that as it may, it is a plus if you can give an example to support a positive statement about someone else's character.

Advisor

Becoming good at giving positive feedback requires practice, particularly because many people lack skill in complimenting others. Use straightforward compliments that do not include a hostile joke along with the positive feedback such as saying to a staff member, "You did a good job dealing with the angry customer considering that you are an engineer." Positive feedback statements about the customer incident would include, "Nice job resolving the customer problem. We could have lost a big account" or "I was impressed with how you resolved the customer problem so quickly."

Firsthand Feedback Is Better Than Secondhand

At the outset of the chapter, I mentioned a variety of sources of feedback, including firsthand, secondhand, and perhaps thirdhand. Direct, or firsthand, feedback is the best because it is more credible and arouses less suspicion when the feedback is negative. Notice the difference:

> **Firsthand feedback:** "Remember when we entertained our client from San Francisco the other night? I think it was a bad idea for you to have that third drink. Your speech became slurred, and you made too many personal comments about the client's appearance."

> **Secondhand feedback:** "Word got back to me that you drink too much when entertaining clients at dinner. I hear that your speech gets slurred and that you make too many personal comments about the appearance of clients."

The group member is likely to become more defensive when hearing secondhand feedback. In addition, he or she will wonder who is doing the tattling.

Honest Feedback Is the Best

A leader who wants a group member to feel good must resist the temptation to give positive but unmerited feedback. Rather than collect genuine data for the feedback, the leader fabricates a compliment. The group member is likely to perceive such feedback as patronizing. In one situation, a young attorney learned from the office manager that she ranked last in the firm in terms of hours billed to clients. The next day, the attorney's supervisor told her, "Ellen, keep up the good work. You are coming along great in making productive use of your time." Ellen thought to herself that her boss either didn't want to spend time helping her or just wanted to avoid conflict. In either case, the supervising attorney lost some of his credibility as a leader.

Advisor

When dealing with a sensitive issue, such as illegal or immoral behavior, secondhand or thirdhand feedback is better than none at all. Attempt to corroborate the feedback, but if you can't, do what you can with the information you have. Begin gently with a statement such as, "I've heard some disturbing news about your actions. I want to talk to you directly about the feedback I have received. It's too important to ignore."

Fabricating negative feedback to justify criticism is more devastating than giving unmerited positive feedback. In other words, the manager invents negative comments about the group member's work to support his or her opinion. Quite often, this coloring of the truth takes the form of "They say" or "Rumor has it." One manager developed a credibility problem when he told a group member, "I heard that the people in our Toronto office said your presentation needs better graphics." (The manager had been on the group member's case about making better graphics.) The group member replied, "That's strange. Because of fog at the Toronto airport, my meeting was postponed. I'm going there next week."

How to Water Human Plants

Many managers take a dim view of *positive reinforcement,* commenting, "Why do you have to reward people for doing what they are paid to do?" Effective leaders are more likely to understand that giving positive reinforcement to workers is necessary because about 95 percent of people perform better when they receive rewards in addition to pay. (Please send me a letter or e-mail telling me how much you enjoyed this book.) Even people who find work self-rewarding (or intrinsically motivating) still crave external recognition. Visual artists and photographers love to receive ribbons for their work.

I have noticed that researchers who condemn positive reinforcement as gimmicky and manipulative enjoy receiving compliments about their work! Also, they like to receive big fees for giving talks that condemn external rewards.

Positive reinforcement as a systematic method of rewarding and encouraging people has been in the workplace for about 45 years. Specifically, the first programs of behavior modification in industry were implemented at Emory Air Freight in the early 1960s. The following eight rules will help you apply positive reinforcement successfully:

Rule 1: Choose an appropriate reward. An appropriate reward is effective in motivating a given group member or group and feasible from the company standpoint. If one reward does not work, try another. Feasible rewards include money, recognition, challenging new assignments, and status symbols such as a private work area. A handwritten thank-you note is an unusually effective and low-cost reward; so is a smile for a job well done. These days, being removed from a temporary to a permanent job can also be a potent reward.

Rule 2: State clearly the behavior or actions that will lead to a reward. What constitutes good performance, or goals, must be agreed upon by the manager-leader and group members. Clarification could take this form: "What I need are inventory reports without missing data. When you achieve this, you will be credited with good performance."

Key Word

Positive reinforcement is increasing the probability that behavior will be repeated by rewarding people for making the desired response. Note carefully that just handing a person a compliment or award is not positive reinforcement. The compliment or award must be tied to doing something right, such as meeting quota.

Rule 3: Supply ample feedback. Positive reinforcement cannot work without frequent feedback to individuals and groups. Everything you have learned about giving feedback can be applied to becoming a leader who applies positive reinforcement successfully.

Rule 4: Do not give everyone the same size reward. Average performance is encouraged when all forms of accomplishment receive the same reward. Don't give everybody in the department the same watch with the company name embossed on the face. Suppose that one group member makes substantial progress in providing input for a strategic plan. He or she should receive more recognition (or a different reward) than a group member who makes only a minor contribution. How would you feel if you were the top performer in your group yet received the same reward as the poorest performer?

Rule 5: Schedule rewards every once in a while. You should not give rewards for good performance on every occasion. Intermittent rewards keep desired behavior going longer and also slow down the pace of good behavior fading away when it is not rewarded. If a person is rewarded for every instance of good performance, he or she is likely to keep up the level of performance until the reward comes and then slack off.

Another problem is that a reward that is given continuously might lose its impact. For example, a leader who keeps saying "Great job," "Attaboy," or "Attagal" begins to sound like a myna bird.

A practical value of giving an occasional reward is that it saves time. Most leaders probably do not have enough time to hand out rewards for every good deed accomplished by team members.

Rule 6: Rewards should follow the desired behavior closely in time. For maximum effectiveness, people should be rewarded shortly after doing something right. (Punishment shortly after doing something wrong works well, too.) This rule is identical to the one about giving feedback soon after observing an action worthy of feedback. Many effective leaders get in touch with people quickly to congratulate them on an outstanding accomplishment.

Rule 7: Change the reward periodically. Rewards do not retain their effectiveness indefinitely. As mentioned previously, this is particularly true of a repetitive statement such as "Nice job" or "Congratulations." Plaques for outstanding performance also lose their motivational appeal after a group receives many of them. An effective leadership technique is to formulate a list of feasible rewards and use different ones from time to time.

Rule 8: Make the reward visible to the recipient and others. The person who receives the reward should be aware that it has been received. (This is another one of these "Duhhh" factors for your consideration.) For example, a person might receive a small bonus for good performance, but if this reward is virtually hidden in his or her paycheck, it will go unnoticed and have a negligible impact on future behavior. Ideally, rewards should be made visible to other employees as well as the recipient. Rewards that are made public increase the status of the recipient and also let other employees know what kind of behavior gets rewarded.

You might also have the group rate each one of these feasible rewards on a 1-to-10 scale. Using this technique, one manager learned that the group members gave a 10 rating to a $20 cash award. They gave a 5 rating to a company dinner (with spouse or other guest), which cost about $35 per person. Also of note, the group gave a rating of 8 to a company-sponsored night out with co-workers. Let the marriage and relationship counselors interpret this one.

Watch Out!

The most frequent misapplication of positive reinforcement is to assume that the same reward is effective for many people. This assumption violates the rule of giving a reward that is appropriate for the target person. Take into account individual differences; an awards banquet might be a reward for some workers but a punishment for others who perceive it as another chore in an already crowded schedule.

It's Great to Feel Appreciated

The most basic way of motivating people is also frequently the most effective. Workers at all levels, from custodial workers to top executives, share the same psychological need of wanting to be recognized. It probably does not take much convincing that entry-level workers want recognition. You might be more skeptical about the hunger for recognition among top executives, the very people whose high-level leadership positions bring them oodles of attention. As an experiment, check out the Web sites for a few well-known executives. The "infomercials" on these sights are usually one-sided reports indicating all the wonderful accomplishments and charitable deeds of the executive in question.

Advisor

How important is recognition and appreciation in the eyes of employees? Seventy-five years of satisfaction and morale surveys have shown that the number-one worker concern is not receiving enough recognition and appreciation for a job well done. Over and over again, one hears the sentiment, "The only time you hear from management is when we do something wrong." Although this employee perception may exaggerate reality, it reinforces the idea that most people crave recognition and appreciation.

All the suggestions and cautions for using positive reinforcement apply to appreciating and recognizing group members. In addition, to capitalize on this low-cost or no-cost motivator, pick and choose from among these suggestions:

➤ Hold an occasional worker appreciation day with a modest celebration close to the end of the workday.

➤ Send out individual e-mail messages to group members, such as "Job well done. Just the information I needed to fix my software problem."

➤ During a luncheon or staff meeting, read a David Letterman–style list of "The top 10 best things our group accomplished this month."

➤ Explain to staffers, "The company appreciates and recognizes your outstanding accomplishments of last month. Here is what we are going to do in return."

➤ Explain to the office assistant, "Without your exceptional effort, this project would never have been accomplished on time."

If you are responsible for setting up a recognition program for your company, or if you are contributing to its design, three macro points should be kept in mind.

➤ Make sure that reward and recognition programs are linked to organizational goals. For example, if part of company strategy is to develop a more culturally diverse workforce at all levels, an employee should be recognized for recruiting a Latino computer scientist.

➤ It is useful to get input from employees about the types of rewards and recognition they value most. The rating system previously described is helpful. One company found that it was spending a lot of money giving away grandfather clocks only to find that employees preferred gift certificates to movies as a form of reward and recognition.

➤ It is important to evaluate the effectiveness of any reward and recognition program. First, the company should establish baseline measures of performance, administer the rewards and recognition program, and then measure performance again. This is idealistic, but it is an important consideration for any company that cares about return on investment (ROI).

Keep in mind that the best established principle of human behavior is that rewarded behavior tends to be repeated. If you want somebody to repeat a good deed, give him or her positive reinforcement for the deed.

The Least You Need to Know

➤ Look for information to use as feedback in such sources as productivity information, performance against goals, and casual observations of what workers are doing.

➤ Give feedback effectively by using specific feedback, obtaining the other person's reaction to the feedback, giving timely feedback, and focusing on behavior rather than personality.

➤ Follow the rules for giving positive reinforcement including choosing an appropriate reward, supplying ample feedback, not giving everyone the same size reward, and changing the reward periodically.

➤ Praise and recognition are excellent motivators and can be given in many ways, including holding a worker appreciation day and sending individualized e-mail messages of praise.

Chapter 24

Your Role as Coach and Facilitator

In This Chapter

➤ Developing a philosophy of coaching and facilitating

➤ Checking discrepancies between desired and actual performance

➤ Engaging in active listening and explaining valid reasons for solving problems

➤ Giving constructive advice and emotional support

➤ Gaining a commitment to change

➤ Receiving help from an executive coach

Two friends from college, Rich and Karen, were having a conversation about how well they were progressing in their careers as purchasing specialists. Rich explained that he was learning something new almost every day in his supervisory position. "It makes going to work fun. I'm getting paid to learn."

Karen said that she also felt she was progressing but that her job had become some-what repetitive. "I'm learning some new techniques," she commented, "but I don't seem to be learning as much as you, Rich. I wonder what we are doing differently."

Rich replied, "What is your approach to learning?"

Karen said, "I attend a few seminars and training programs on topics related to pur-chasing. I read business publications and books about management and leadership. I check out a few Web sites about management. I'm also a self-help nut. I try to apply a lot of the ideas I study to the job. All of this has been helping."

Looking intently at Karen, Rich said: "Everything you told me makes sense. I do those things, too. You can't call yourself a professional today unless you gobble up information. But it sounds like you are missing the icing on the cake. That one little plus that can help you keep climbing the learning curve."

"You haven't said anything about your manager being a good coach. My manager is a wonderful coach. He gives me little tips here and there that help me pull all my learning together."

Rich's observations support an important truth about leadership. Coaching is a major approach to training and influencing group members. To be a good face-to-face leader (as opposed to being a visionary and strategic leader), you have to be a good coach. Coaching is also important because it fits the modern role of a manager and leader—one who facilitates goal accomplishment by team members.

In this chapter, you will learn specific concepts and ideas you can use to improve your ability to coach and facilitate. Regard this information as a logical continuation of instructions for being a nurturing boss and providing feedback and positive reinforcement.

Coaching Isn't Just My Job, It's My Philosophy

Coaching, or helping others directly to improve their performance, has been around for a long time. Recently, however, it has emerged as a philosophy of leadership and a way of looking at the relationship between the leader and the group member.

Key Word

Coaching helps workers grow and improve their job performance by providing suggestions and encouragement. Coaching can be applied to helping substandard performers meet standards, as well as helping average and above-average performers elevate their performance.

The quality of the relationship between the coach and the person being coached distinguishes coaching from other forms of leader-member interactions. The person being coached trusts the leader's judgment and experience and listens to advice and suggestions. Similarly, the coach believes in the capacity of the group member to learn and to profit from his or her advice. The coach is a trusted manager, and the person being coached is a trusted group member.

These statements serve as a backdrop to putting coaching on a philosophical plane. With the right attitudes and values, it's easier to develop coaching and facilitating skills. An important purpose of coaching is achieving enthusiasm and high performance in a team setting; a coach is, therefore, a motivator and a cheerleader. I now shift the attention to some specific attitudes and values that support being a coach and facilitator.

A coach and facilitator …

➤ Respects the knowledge, skills, and abilities the group members bring to the effort.

➤ Believes that workers should be as free as possible from controls that restrict their freedom to exercise initiative and innovation. (However, an effective coach is not so naive as to believe an organization can be successful without any controls.)

➤ Understands that helping others develop is one of the most meritorious forms of human interaction.

Coaching is more than a set of techniques for improving performance. It is a complex and helpful way of helping others realize their potential:

➤ Coaching is a partnership for achieving results in which both the manager and the group member play a vital part.

➤ Coaching relies more on motivation and interpersonal influence than on getting others to comply through formal authority and a chain of command.

➤ Effective coaching and facilitation is based on giving instructions to others along with listening to them and observing their behavior.

➤ Coaching, like mentoring, is not a mechanical process that can be carried out well between any leader-group member pair. Instead, it requires good chemistry between the two people.

Coaching can facilitate breakthroughs in performance because it helps people achieve insights into problems that could be blocking their progress. A sales manager, for example, helped one of her sales representatives increase her sales 30 percent with the observation, "From what I've seen, you do everything right except that you neglect to actually ask for the order."

Here's the Ideal, Here's the Real, and Here's Your Gap

Coaching is only necessary and feasible when the manager-leader or the group members perceive a need for improvement. In the traditional view of coaching, this need for improvement deals with performance problems such as low productivity, absenteeism and tardiness, and poor safety practices. In the broader view, coaching also includes helping satisfactory and high-level performers reach new heights of achievement. In either case, coaching cannot take place without an agreed-upon definition of what constitutes standard or average performance.

What constitutes standard performance can be found in a goal statement, a job description, or rules of thumb long-used by a firm. For example, many legal firms and consulting firms use the 65 percent billed-time standard. This means that full-time professionals not engaged in administrative work should bill at least 65 percent of their workweek to clients.

Whether you are coaching to fix a serious problem or to boost performance, the next step in coaching is to observe the discrepancy between desired and actual performance. You might notice, for example, that a group member follows through on only two thirds of the small projects he says he will complete. You might investigate why so many projects are not completed and then coach him about learning to follow through. You might coach him on improving his ability to estimate how much work he can handle.

Advisor

Effective coaching usually consists of more than meeting once with a group member and pointing out the discrepancy between the ideal and the actual. You might need to discuss why the problem exists, help the person develop new skills, and attend several follow-up meetings to discuss progress. An important part of coaching is to ask a series of questions to uncover the root of the problem. Effective questions include, "Then what happened?" or "What else did you try?" or "At what point were you the closest to solving the problem?" Even an inspirational leader might need to work hard with the individual to bring about necessary improvements.

Your initial coaching session about the discrepancy between the real and the desired state of affairs can take two approaches. It can be a formal, sit-down session or an impromptu meeting in the group member's work area. Get to the heart of the issue quickly but tactfully without disguising the purpose of the discussion. Beginning the session with a compliment might not be effective. The problem is that the person being coached develops the mental set that no problem of consequence exists. Here are several effective opening statements to use as a guide:

➤ "I see you developing a pattern that is causing work assignment problems for me. Several times during the last six months, you agreed to take on a project, but you didn't follow through. One example is that you said you would investigate the feasibility of adding an audio component to our Web site. That was two months ago. What happened?"

➤ "I asked you to meet with me because I'm concerned about how often your reports are late. I hope we can work out this problem together."

➤ "I'm concerned about your sales being flat for so many months. I want us to fig-ure out together how you can get off this plateau. You're doing fine, but I know you can do better."

Observe that these questions are not accusatory and noninflammatory and, therefore, minimize the chances of the person becoming defensive and retaliatory.

I'm Going to Set the Bar Just Two Inches Higher Now

The fact that you are coaching somebody means that in your opinion, the person needs to achieve a higher level of performance. If the improvement goals are too high, such as tripling productivity in 30 days, the group member is likely to fail and become frustrated. If improvement goals are set too low, the group member's per-formance might not improve fast enough. As implied in Chapter 12, "You Can Be-come a Motivational Force," a realistic improvement goal pushes a person but does not set him or her up for failure.

You, as the leader and facilitator, can help the group member set realistic improve-ment goals by encouraging a discussion of each one. Setting realistic goals does not mean you are giving up on performance standards that are important to the compa-ny. It just means that the worker cannot reach the performance level you want in one jump.

The changes in behavior necessary to achieve an improvement goal are often easy to bring about, providing the person wants to change. For example, the person might say, "Great idea. I will always ask for the sale toward the end of the sales call." At other times, you and the group member must develop an *action plan* for making the changes. Sometimes the action plan involves skill training. A person whose client reports contain no exciting graphics might attend a seminar on com-puter graphics at the company's expense. Maybe the sales rep who doesn't seem able to ask for the sale could benefit from assertiveness training.

The general point is that you as the leader and fa-cilitator should stand ready to include action plans in your coaching. An action plan is a description of the steps that should be taken to achieve an ob-jective or bring performance back to an acceptable standard. If you do not suggest an action plan, you can be accused of being a "hit-and-run coach."

Key Word

Sometimes the **action plan** sim-ply involves the person exercising self-discipline to initiate the nec-essary changes.

The Facts Show That I'm Giving You Great Advice

Your stature as a leader will sometimes be sufficient to convince the person you're coaching that improvement is necessary. In many situations, however, justifying your request with a solid business reason is more convincing. Not all workers are aware of the organizational consequences of their below-standard performance—nor might an acceptable performer be aware of how a slight performance gain can make a big impact on the organization. Several examples of valid business reasons to justify the need for performance improvement follow:

Watch Out!

When you justify your coaching recommendations with factual information, make sure the facts are true. False information might be discovered, and you will be perceived as a manipulator. As a consequence, your leadership credibility will erode quickly.

➤ "Our costs per adding new magazine subscribers have jumped 25 percent in the last year. This is why we need higher productivity from each telemarketer."

➤ "If most employees were consistently tardy, the productivity drain on the company would be enormous. If every employee lost three hours of productivity per year because of tardiness, the company would have a productivity drain of 150,000 hours of work per year."

➤ "If you could develop just one more breakthrough idea per year, our product-design group would be world-class."

➤ "If you as our senior staff member can increase quality just one notch, you would be a great role model for the junior staff members."

➤ "If you could shave costs on supplies by $50,000 per year, that is the bottom-line equivalent of selling another $500,000 worth of product per year."

Key Word

Active listening is listening for full meaning without making premature judgments or interpretations. A person must concentrate extra hard to be an active listener because people often use subtle and indirect language to communicate their thoughts. In addition, nonverbal signs of communication often flash by quickly.

I Hear and See What You're Saying

Active listening is an essential ingredient in any coaching session. An active listener tries to grasp both the facts of what is said and the feelings behind the words. Observing the group member's nonverbal communication is another part of active listening. The leader must also be patient and not be poised to present a rebuttal to any differences of opinion between him or her and the group member.

Practicing a few basic techniques will help you become an active listener:

➤ Part of being a good listener is encouraging the person being coached to talk about his or her performance. Asking open-ended questions, rather than questions that require only a one-word response, facilitates a flow of conversation. An example of an *open-ended question* is, "How are you coming along on the safety study of latex gloves?"

➤ A good coach is adept at reflecting feelings. The leader's reflection of feelings communicates that he or she understands the problem. Feeling understood, the group member might be better motivated to improve.

➤ A good coach also reflects content or meaning. An effective way of reflecting meaning is to rephrase and summarize concisely what the group member is saying.

A poorly performing group member might say, "The reason I've fallen so far behind is that our company has turned into a bureaucratic nightmare. I have to fill out forms all day long." You might reflect, "You're falling so far behind because you have so many forms that require attention." The group member might then respond, "That's exactly what I mean. I'm glad you understand my problem."

Key Word

An **open-ended question** is one that requires an answer with explanation rather than yes or no, agree or disagree, or for or against. A key benefit of an open-ended question is that it usually facilitates the dialogue necessary for problem-solving.

➤ After you listen to a group member for a while, give your interpretation of what he or she has said. You can use this interpretation to give the person insight into the nature of the problem.

Hey, Let's Kick Barriers

Two closely related techniques for facilitating good performance are giving advice and removing barriers. Too much advice-giving interferes with two-way communication, yet some advice can lead to improved performance. Recognize also that giving expert advice is an important leadership role. Consider yourself a consultant to the group member who seeks an outside, well-informed opinion.

Assist the person you're coaching to answer the question, "What can I do about this problem?" Advice in the form of a question or suppositional statement is often effective. One example is, "Could the root of your problem be insufficient planning?" A direct statement such as "The root of your problem is obviously insufficient planning" often makes people resentful and defensive. By responding to a question, the person being coached is likely to feel more involved in making improvements.

Many managers believe they can best help group members by being barrier busters. This is a constructive perspective because many problems of poor work performance are caused by factors beyond a worker's control. By showing a willingness to intervene in problems of this kind, the leader displays a helpful and constructive attitude and gives emotional support. A sampling of the type of factors beyond a worker's control that could benefit from intervention by the manager include the following:

Another Perspective

Some psychologically oriented counselors believe that advice-giving is usually counterproductive. Instead of making his or her own discoveries, the group member becomes dependent upon the leader-manager. (I don't buy this argument, but I want you to be aware of an interesting perspective.)

➤ Insufficient support staff to manage a peak workload.

➤ Not having enough equipment for the work that needs to be done, which leads to employees waiting to use equipment and lowered productivity.

➤ The presence of a hostile, uncooperative co-worker who drags down group productivity.

➤ Lack of cooperation from members of another department.

➤ A lengthy approval process required to borrow human or material resources from another department.

➤ Extensive documentation required to execute a procedure that deviates from standard.

➤ An insufficient budget to carry out an important assignment.

I Want to Make You Feel Good

By being helpful and constructive and busting barriers, you provide much-needed emotional support to the person who needs help in improving job performance. A coaching session should not be an interrogation. An effective way of providing emotional support is to use positive rather than negative motivators. For example, as a team leader you might say to a team member, "Your job performance is above average right now. If you learn how to measure cash flow accurately, you will be eligible for an outstanding performance review."

On the same topic, a negative motivator that provides no emotional support might be, "If you don't learn how to measure cash flow accurately, you're going to get zapped on your performance review."

Emotional support linked to coaching can take many other forms, including the following:

➤ Encourage the person by saying, "A person with your talent can easily make these changes."

➤ Follow up a coaching session by stopping at the group member's work area and saying, "How are you holding up under the pressure of making those changes we discussed?"

➤ Walk up to the person you've been coaching and say, "Do you need any help from me today?"

➤ Spontaneously comment to the person during an ordinary work interaction, "You seem on top of things today" or "You look chipper."

Emotionally supportive statements are a wonderful leadership tool. They usually put workers in a good mental state to work productively.

You Are Going to Change, Aren't You?

Gaining a commitment to change is yet another important part of coaching. Unless the leader receives a commitment from the group member to follow through with the proposed solution to a problem, the member might not improve performance.

An experienced manager/coach develops an intuitive feel for when workers are serious about improving their performance. One clue that commitment to change is lacking is if a group member is overly enthusiastic about the need for change. Another clue is agreeing to change without a display of emotion.

Advisor

Changing attitudes and behavior is an important part of leadership, but it's a slow process. A 3-minute coaching session is unlikely to change an attitude or behavior pattern that has been developing for 10 years. Yet by being understanding and supportive, you will be able to at least see some small changes in the right direction, such as getting a worker to be more responsive to customer needs.

Suppose that as part of a process redesign, the procurement team agrees to stop interacting directly with sales representatives, including being entertained at lunch.

Instead, the team agrees to do almost all purchasing through the Internet. This includes dealing with companies directly and going through buyer exchanges. The idea behind the change is to save buyers time and boost productivity.

One of the buyers continues to spend a lot of time in and outside the office interacting with his favorite sales representatives. You coach the buyer about the problem. At the end of the session, he says, "Okay, sure," with a disinterested expression. You should probably monitor his performance closely because he doesn't seem committed to the change.

What About a Coach for the Coach?

An explosive trend in coaching is being attributed to managers and professional-level workers who are hiring coaches of their own. Or, sometimes the organization pays for the coach as a form of leadership development. Either way, this means that the leader who is coaching others often gets his or her own personal coach—much like a personal trainer for athletics. *Executive coaches* (or *business coaches*) provide such a wide variety of services that they have been characterized by *Washington Post* Career Track columnist Amy Joyce as a combination of "counselor, adviser, mentor, cheerleader, and best friend."

Key Word

An **executive coach** (or **business coach**) is an outside specialist who gives advice on personal improvement and suggests changes in behavior.

Typically, the coach spends about one hour per week with the client. Many coaches rely on the telephone and e-mail to conduct much of their coaching. For example, the leader might send an e-mail message to the coach asking for advice about how to handle an upcoming meeting. The coach would then respond within 24 hours.

In the past, business psychologists were typically hired as outside coaches to help managers become more effective leaders. Today, people from a wide variety of backgrounds become business coaches. An effective business coach might help you become a more effective leader in some of the following ways:

➤ Counseling you about weaknesses that could interfere with your effectiveness, such as being too hostile or impatient

➤ Helping you understand and process feedback from 360-degree surveys

➤ Serving as a sounding board when you face a complex decision about strategy, operations, or human resources issues

➤ Making specific suggestions about self-promotion and image enhancement, including suggestions about appearance and mannerisms

➤ Helping you achieve a better balance between work and family life, thereby giving you more focused energy for the leadership role

➤ Helping you uncover personal assets and strengths you may not have been aware of, such as creativity and imagination

➤ Serving as a trusted confidante to discuss issues you might feel uncomfortable talking about with others—for example, feelings of insecurity about your position

➤ Pointing out a blind spot in your decision-making, such as neglecting part of the human consequences of a decision

➤ Giving your advice about career management, such as developing a career path

Notice that the coach works as an advisor about behavior, but does not explicitly help the leader with functional details of the job, such as how to develop a new product strategy, or design an organization.

Watch Out!

Executive coaching has some potential drawbacks to the leader. A major problem is that a coach may give advice that backfires. A coach told a manager in an information technology firm that she should become more decisive and less dependent on consensus. The advice backfired because the culture of the firm emphasized consensus decision-making.

The Least You Need to Know

➤ Look for discrepancies between desired and actual performance because these discrepancies give you the raw material for coaching.

➤ Establish realistic improvement goals by helping the worker set goals that will stretch his or her capability but that are not most likely to result in failure and frustration.

➤ Be an active listener by grasping both the facts of what is said and the feelings behind the words.

➤ Give constructive advice and bust barriers to round out your coaching effectiveness. A "barrier buster" helps a worker remove impediments to good performance that are beyond his or her control.

➤ Give emotional support in relation to coaching through such means as encouraging the individual and making positive comments about the person's demeanor.

➤ Gain a commitment to change by asking the person coached what he or she is going to do differently.

➤ Hiring your own executive coach might give your career a boost.

How to Mentor

Priscilla Chatworth looked buoyant and confident as she stood at the lectern and talked into the microphone. Priscilla was feeling great. Her management teammates had arranged a party to celebrate her leaving the company to accept a position as a CEO. Priscilla's business associates were disappointed to see such a wonderful friend and productive contributor leave the company. However, most people attending the banquet realized that she was leaving under honorable circumstances to embark upon an extraordinary opportunity.

"I have a lot to be thankful for," said Priscilla. "I have a wonderful husband and two fabulous children, and we are relocating together as a family. My career has turned out better than I could have dreamed.

"My time with the company has been so productive and so happy. I've formed so many great friendships that it's difficult for me to leave, yet I'm very excited about the formidable challenges facing me."

"I remember so clearly joining this company as a management trainee 21 years ago. I appreciate how much responsibility I was given early in my career. So many managers, co-workers, and employees reporting to me have contributed much to my development. However, one person stands out as having made the biggest impact on my career."

"Without this person, I would never have learned so much so fast. He helped me navigate many of the hurdles I faced in my career. He showed me the ropes; he gave me the confidence to keep going when times were rough. He was my first manager and a person I will never forget. That man is Bill Nevins, my mentor. Bill, will you please join me at this table for a few moments?"

Bill moved promptly to the lectern. After exchanging hugs with Priscilla, Bill said, "I appreciate your kind words, Priscilla. Bringing you into this firm and watching you develop into a powerhouse manager and leader is one of my biggest contributions to our company. You make me very proud."

Bill Nevins had an important point to make. A major contribution a leader can make to an organization is being a mentor to the right protégé (or mentoree). In this chapter, you will learn how to be a good mentor through such means as understanding the functions mentors perform and some guidelines for effective mentoring.

Key Word

A **mentor** is an individual with advanced experience and knowledge who is committed to giving support and career advice to a less experienced person. Much of the career advice centers around upward mobility. A mentor is a helper and confidante, as opposed to a rival or a detached manager. A **protégé** often does report to his or her manager in a hierarchy.

I Hear the Word Every Day, but What Does It Really Mean?

In Homer's tale, *The Odyssey,* Mentor was a wise and trusted friend as well as a counselor and adviser to Odysseus. Odysseus's confidence in Mentor was so great that Odysseus entrusted him with the full care and education of his son. The term *mentor* has become a buzzword in the workplace. It literally means a wise and trustworthy sage and advisor. The less experienced person whom the mentor assists is the *protégé* (from the French word for "protected").

A mentor usually outranks the protégé and is usually older. Be aware, however, that one co-worker can be a mentor to another. As long as you are more experienced and wiser than a co-worker in some important aspect of the job, you can be a mentor. Whatever your rank is relative to the other person, being a mentor is an act of leadership. The mentor inspires and helps another person grow.

Mentors may or may not be employed in the same organization or be in the protégé's chain of command. The internal mentor is easiest to understand, such as Bill Nevins being a mentor to Priscilla Chatworth. External mentors, however, are also important because so many career people today are concerned with career mobility across organizations. An example of external mentoring is being a mentor to an alumnus of your college who works for another company.

What Have You Done for Me Lately?

To be a mentor, a person engages in a wide range of helping behaviors that go beyond a simple definition of the term.

An awareness of these multiple activities will help you pick and choose among them to become a first-rate mentor. As you study the various mentoring activities, recognize that one mentor is not expected to carry out all of them. You might be extremely helpful to a protégé, for example, just by teaching him or her the ropes.

The activities of mentors can be divided into two primary functions. First, mentors provide help in career development. Second, mentors take emotional and social roles by offering friendship and emotional support. Although these two major mentoring activities might overlap a bit, they are still useful distinctions in terms of understanding what a mentor does.

Another Perspective

Most successful people have at least one mentor in their career, even when they do not label the influential person as a mentor. Larry Ellison of Oracle Corp. has been an important mentor for Ray Lane, his president and chief operating officer. Although the two men have different styles (Ellison is more flamboyant), the two leaders complement each other well. Both men are relentless competitors.

Career Development and Mentoring

A big part of a mentor's role is to assist the protégé with career advancement. A survey of large companies found that 96 percent of executives credited mentoring as an important developmental method. Seventy-five percent of the group said mentoring played a key role in their success.

Mentoring, as conducted by senior managers and co-workers, has become recognized as an important vehicle for the advancement of minorities in the workplace. As reported by Gannett News Service, a survey of successful minority executives indicated that 48 percent of the respondents said they had a role model who guided them toward early career goals. The role model/mentors were primarily the same ethnic, racial, or cultural origin. A specific finding was that minorities with supportive managers and co-workers received more raises and progressed more rapidly in their careers than those without such support.

A sponsor of the survey said, "Minority executives believe that mentors are very helpful in advocating for upward mobility and teaching them how to navigate through the corporation."

The mentor's advice is likely to be taken seriously because he or she is a trusted friend. Next is a list of specific ways in which mentors help others advance their careers:

➤ **Sponsorship.** A mentor usually nominates somebody else for promotions and desirable positions. Sponsorship is very important in a company that bases many promotions on recommendations from managers throughout the organization. Without a sponsor, it is difficult to get promoted. A major factor driving office politics is the desire to find a sponsor. The more powerful you are, the more likely less experienced people in the organization will seek you as a sponsor.

➤ **Challenging assignments.** A major growth vehicle is to receive challenging assignments. A mentor, therefore, helps the protégé advance his or her career by making assignments that lead to growth in job skills. Learning these skills also contributes to the growth of self-confidence. One way of giving challenging assignments is through delegation of part of the mentor's job.

➤ **Encouragement of problem-solving.** Mentors help their protégés solve problems by themselves and make their own discoveries. A comment frequently made to mentors is "I'm glad you made me think through the problem by myself. You jogged my mind."

➤ **Assistance in technical problem solving.** A mentor can play a major role in the protégé's career development by helping him or her solve technical problems and learn new technologies. If the mentor knows more about a new technology than the protégé, he or she can shorten the person's learning time. Mentoring, for example, has always been a standard part of learning job-relevant skills in medicine. A more experienced ophthalmologist, for example, might show the protégé how to use laser surgery to adjust near-sightedness. Many developments in information technology are likely to be taught by a co-worker serving as a mentor, because a manager often has less current technology knowledge than a group member. A mentor giving assistance in problem-solving often begins with heavy involvement and then stands back when the protégé acquires more knowledge.

➤ **Advice in career planning.** A natural role for the mentor is to give advice about career planning for growth both in the company and outside. A mentor, for example, might encourage the protégé to accept any opportunity to serve on a cross-functional team because it is a broadening experience. Going one step further, the mentor might then act as a sponsor and nominate the mentoree for such a team.

➤ **Coaching.** A mentor gives on-the-spot advice to the protégé to help him or her improve skills. Coaching is such an important part of being a mentor that it is difficult for a leader to be an effective mentor unless he or she is also a good coach.

➤ **Learning the ropes.** A general-purpose function of the mentor is to help the protégé learn the ropes, which translates into explaining the values and do's and don'ts of the organization. Mentors give such advice as "Emphasize how much money the firm will save by implementing your program. It's important because the company has a history of emphasizing cost savings." Another representative piece of inside advice is, "Never hint that another company made you a job offer. Top management highly values loyalty, and your stock will go down if it appears you are shopping around."

As implied by the preceding list, mentoring is a complex activity that involves a variety of helping behaviors. To develop mentoring skills, you need to offer help to several people for at least six months.

Advisor

Pay careful attention to the leader/mentor's role in encouraging protégés to solve problems by themselves. It saves the leader time to virtually solve difficult problems for protégés, but people grow more rapidly when they are encouraged to solve their own problems. The mentor can still give good hints to get the problem-solving process going. A great gift a leader can give a group member is to help that person develop the confidence and skills necessary to solve problems independently.

Emotional Support and Mentoring

Have you ever noticed how attached some career people are to their mentors? One explanation is that a mentor-protégé relationship, like any good friendship, is emotional. In the conventional type of mentoring relationship, the mentor and protégé choose each other spontaneously. In some organizations, the mentor and mentoree are assigned to each other, based on a company analysis of their compatibility. In these arranged pairings, the emotional bond might be weaker.

Watch Out!

It is important for the protégé to support the mentor's ideas, but he or she should not go overboard. The person who continually heaps lavish praise on the mentor, or on his or her ideas, may quickly be perceived as a sycophant who lacks sincerity. Praise for the mentor will then be discounted.

The emotional-support aspects of mentoring build further on the initial positive chemistry between the mentor and protégé. Presented next is a rundown of the emotional-support facets of mentoring that help form bonds. Yet, like any friendship, a mentor-protégé relationship can dwindle or have a falling out.

➤ **Friendship.** A mentor is, above all, a trusted friend, and the friendship extends two ways. *Trusted* means that the mentor will not pass on confidential information or stab the protégé in the back. Also, a trusted friend does not knowingly give bad career advice.

➤ **Role modeling.** An important part of being a mentor is to give the protégé a pattern of values and behaviors to emulate. The mentor thus leads by example to teach the mentoree. (Role modeling might also be considered a career-development activity because the protégé might observe some good ideas for getting ahead.)

➤ **Acceptance.** A mentor can be helpful just by giving support and encouragement. In turn, the protégé is supposed to support the mentor by offering compliments and defending the mentor's ideas. The protégé can thus become an ally in the organization. In a team meeting, the protégé might make a statement such as "I think John's (the mentor) ideas will work wonders. We should give them a try."

➤ **Counseling.** A mentor listens to the protégé's problems and offers advice. In many mentor-mentoree pairings, the mentor becomes a trusted confidante to which the mentoree feels free to express a wide variety of work and personal opinions. The mentor is trusted not to report any negative comments made by the protégé. Mentors, like coaches, should be skilled at active listening.

➤ **Protection.** A mentor might shield a junior person from potentially harmful situations or from the boss. For example, the mentor might tell her protégé, "In your meeting today with the boss, make sure you are well prepared and have all your facts in hand. He is in an ugly mood and will attack any weakness."

➤ **Referral agent.** An indirect way of giving emotional support to a protégé is to show him or her where to find help with a variety of problems. The mentor sometimes refers the protégé to resources inside and outside the company to help with a particular problem. For example, the protégé might want to know how to obtain a company grant for adopting a child.

➤ **Stress reducer.** Add to the list of useful mentoring activities the ability to reduce stress for protégés. Research about job stress indicates that the most effective stress-reducing activity for a manager is to be emotionally supportive, including being a good listener. Of course, you as the leader could conduct yoga sessions in your office! Being a stress-reducing mentor is a by-product of other effective mentoring activities.

Advisor

Mutual trust between the mentor and the protégé is essential for the relationship to blossom. For example, it is difficult to accept emotional support from a mentor you do not trust. Similarly, the mentor expects the protégé not to pass along any information that would discredit him or her.

You Are My Hero, My Heroine, My Everything

What does it take to be an effective mentor? The broad answer can be found in the preceding 24 chapters. An effective leader makes an effective mentor. It is easiest to learn from a person who is inspiring, intelligent, self-confident, and nurturing, among other good characteristics.

Despite this disclaimer, the following list suggests the characteristics to emphasize and develop to enhance your effectiveness as a mentor:

➤ **Risk-taker.** Strong mentors are adventurers and risk-takers, thereby encouraging such behavior in their protégés. A major criticism of many young people employed by large business firms is that they are low risk-takers who prefer analysis to action. An adventuresome, risk-taking mentor can be a big help in encouraging risk-taking.

Another Perspective

It is difficult to specify the characteristics of an effective mentor because the needs of protégés differ widely. Some people, for example, are most comfortable with a dynamic, brash, and charismatic mentor (like Larry Ellison of Oracle). Others feel more comfortable and learn better from a more subdued, counselor-type mentor.

➤ **Trustworthy.** Being trustworthy is a fundamental requirement for effective mentoring, as explained earlier in the description of mentoring activities. Unless a leader has a reputation for trustworthiness, few people will seek him or her out as a potential mentor.

➤ **Knowledgeable.** An effective mentor has a high level of technical expertise or business knowledge. This characteristic is easy to accept if you regard a protégé as an apprentice and the mentor as the master. Most people expect to acquire arcane knowledge from their mentors. As a commercial real estate broker said about her mentor, "He taught me secrets about closing deals you won't find revealed by anybody else in the business."

➤ **Influential.** Being an influential, well-connected person multiplies your impact as a mentor. For example, you need power and influence to be a successful sponsor. A major magnet for attracting talented protégés is your clout in moving them into good positions.

➤ **Committed.** Effective mentors not only believe that mentoring is an effective vehicle for human learning, but they are also willing to invest the time in such activities. A self-centered, glory-seeking leader might not want to sit still for mentoring.

➤ **Emotionally stable.** Effective mentors are emotionally secure enough not to be threatened by the presence of talented protégés. Such mentors can glow in the success of their protégé's accomplishments without feeling overshadowed. The situation is much like a sports coach not being concerned that a team member gets more publicity than he or she does.

Not Just Any Old Protégé Will Do

Just as there are certain characteristics that contribute to effective mentoring, certain characteristics enhance being a worthwhile protégé. From your perspective as a leader, you might want to select protégés who will make you proud through their accomplishments. (On the other hand, you could take the benevolent attitude that you want to help those most in need of help.) Many of the same characteristics that make people good leaders make them good protégés because many protégés are potential leaders. Here are a few specific characteristics and behaviors to look for when seeking out a protégé or agreeing to be someone's mentor:

➤ Trustworthiness is at the top of the list. One mentor I know tests the trustworthiness of potential protégés with a diabolical trick. Upon a first meeting, he tells the potential protégé a preposterous story he has never told anyone else. If the story later circulates as a rumor, the manager knows the protégé cannot be trusted. For example, he once told a potential protégé: "I'm thinking of retiring soon so I can devote full time to running an alligator ranch in South America."

Two days later, a supervisor said to the manager, "Hey, good luck with your alligator ranch." Case closed; potential protégé dropped.

➤ Effective protégés are independent enough to take responsibility for their own fate yet not so independent that they will not accept advice from the mentor. The underlying personality characteristic here is a willingness to accept authority. A complete rebel makes a poor protégé because the person will reject advice and thus not promulgate the mentor's ideas.

➤ Effective protégés are hungry for knowledge and eager to try new ideas. Given that a mentor is a teacher, it's nice to have people try your ideas and report back to you how well they work. For example, an executive who believes strongly in employee empowerment wants his or her protégé to empower employees and report back the results.

➤ Effective protégés are talented winners with a strong desire to become successful leaders. When your protégé eventually becomes your boss, he or she will give you a lot of the credit and take good care of you. Maybe you can get to that alligator farm in South America sooner than you thought. Choosing winners as protégés also helps you because these people will be in a position to implement your ideas.

You, Too, Can Be a World-Class Mentor

The actions one should take to become an outstanding mentor stem naturally from an understanding of what mentors do, as already presented. To tie all this information together, I present next a series of guidelines for effective mentoring. Several of them stem from the research of Gary Yukl, reported in his text, *Leadership in Organizations*.

1. Show concern for the development of group members. Each group member should be encouraged to establish career goals that stretch his or her potential. Also, encourage self-development. Welcome all requests for advice and help.

2. Establish a *psychological contract* with your potential protégés. A psychological contract describes orally the kind of assistance you stand ready to give as a mentor and the kind of reciprocity you expect from the potential protégé. One clause of the contract might say, "I will give you the benefit of my wisdom in

Key Word

An unwritten agreement, or **psychological contract,** describes what management expects from a group member and vice versa. Such a contract is particularly important in a mentoring relationship because mentoring is more unique than a traditional superior-subordinate relationship.

helping you get ahead. I will expect you to try some of my ideas and not to undermine me in such ways as criticizing me publicly."

3. Provide ample and helpful advice. Traditional career advice focuses on climbing the organizational ladder. During the last decade, more protégés were advised to also think about learning new skills and developing within their jobs. Such advice has strong appeal to young professionals who recognize that in-depth skills are a real asset in being able to move from one organization to another. (The buzzword is "portable skills.")

4. Encourage enrollment in relevant training programs and studying that lead to skill development. An effective mentor encourages the continuing professional growth of team members and offers organizational support for such development of knowledge and skills.

5. Provide on-the-job opportunities for skill development. The mentoring activity of providing challenging assignments contributes directly to skill development. A major software producer wanted to acquire a 10-person outfit that develops multimedia software. The manager of corporate acquisitions gave a 25-year-old financial analyst primary responsibility for estimating the value of the small company. The financial analyst later said that she learned more doing that assignment than she did in her preceding two years on the job.

Watch Out!

One of the biggest pitfalls of the mentoring system is that mentors are accused of playing favorites with mentorees. Look out for your protégé's best interests, but do not go overboard in giving him or her such plum assignments and glowing praise that you provoke cries of favoritism.

6. Give the protégé enough rope to struggle with assignments. One of the best ways to learn from experience is to find solutions to challenging problems without too much intervention by the manager. An effective leader-mentor knows that allowing people to sweat a little is a real skill builder.

7. Promote the protégé's reputation. A major contribution by the mentor is informing others of how well the protégé performed on key assignments. The mentor can also enhance the protégé's reputation by sponsoring the person for visible assignments, such as task forces reporting to top executives.

In preparation for becoming a mentor, it is helpful to think of the type of person you would prefer as a protégé. The accompanying exercise is designed to help you think through this issue.

Selecting a Protégé

To be a successful mentor it is necessary to select protégés who would respond well to your advice and coaching. Since the mentoring-protégé relationship is personal, much like any friendship, one must choose protégés carefully. In about 50 words (in the space provided), describe the type of person you would like for a protégé. Include intellectual, personality, and demographic (group factors such as age, sex, or race) factors in your description. Indicate why you think the characteristics you chose are important. (And please don't just paint a self-portrait.)

My Ideal Protégé

_____

_____

_____

_____

_____

The Least You Need to Know

➤ The term "mentor" refers technically to a wise and trustworthy sage and advisor.

➤ Mentors engage in many activities, including helping with career advancement, sponsoring others for promotion, giving challenging assignments, encouraging problem-solving, and providing emotional support.

➤ The characteristics of an effective mentor include risk-taking, trustworthiness, business knowledge, being well connected, and being emotionally secure.

➤ The characteristics of an effective protégé include trustworthiness, taking responsibility for his or her own fate, and a desire to be a winner.

➤ Effective mentors engage in such activities as showing concern for the development of group members, giving good advice, allowing others to struggle a little, and promoting the protégé's reputation.

Additional Resources for Learning How to Lead Effectively

Web Sites

The following list is a sampling of Web sites that deal directly with leadership. The list purposely does not attempt to duplicate the journal references that anyone can access from databases commonly available in libraries. Instead, these Web sites can be found through typical search engines such as Yahoo!, Webcrawler, Google, and Northern-Light. Web sites appear and disappear quickly, so there is no guarantee that a particular site will be operational when you attempt to access it. However, this author has at least glanced through all of the following Web sites.

The Best CEOs
www.worth.com/articles/z9905co1.html

Building Self-Confidence Should Be Strategic Priority
www.changedynamic.com/articles/building.htm

The Business Coach—Coaching Q&A
www.the-business-coach.com/200.htm

Cultural Diversity: What Managers Need to Know
www.Katzassoc.com/cultural.html

Dare to Lead
www.dynamicleadership.com/main.html

Digital Leadership
www.strategy-business.com/strategy/00105

Emotional Intelligence in Business
www.eq.org/articles/ralston.html

Everyone Leads
www.canlead.com/everyone.htm

How to Be Politics Proof
www.ravenwerks.com/teamwork/howtobe.htm

How Does a Manager Become a Leader?
www.enleadership.com/articles/.html

Journeyman Leadership
www.coxgroup.com/articles/leader.html

Leadership and the Iceberg, Cornerstone Consulting Associates
www.ourfuture.com/wkart01.htm

Leadership and the Face of Change
www. lead_edge.com

Leadership in an Entrepreneurial Company
www.fed.org/leading_companies/nov96/lead.htm

Leaders Need Feelings
www.changedynamic.com.html

Leadership Versus Management: Do You Know the Difference?
www.leadership-trust.org/leadership.htm

Learning to Lead: A Creativity Leadership Seminar
www.cio.com/reprints/120799lead.html

Motivational Management: Developing Leadership Skills
adv-leadership-grp.com/articles/motivate.htm

Posturing for Success: Part 2
www.careermag.com/articles_index/299.html

Qualities of an Effective Leader
www.fpa.org/programs/tipbod6.html

Teamwork Starts at the Top
www.careermag.com/articles_index/547.html

Theory and Implications Regarding the Utilization of Strategic Humor by Leaders
www.fhsu.edu/htmlpages/faculty/COCC/lead03.htm

Tightrope Walkers: The Balancing Act of Youth Leadership
leadernet.org/articles.html

What's Wrong with Bob's Optimizing Team Diversity
www.millerhoward.com/articles/diversity.html

Why Team Building Programs Really Work
www.thinksmart.com/articles/teamprograms.html

www.themanager.com
Good general source for current articles about leadership.

Videos

Motivating Others (FYI Video, AMA)

Bringing Out the Leader in You (FYI Video, AMA)

Coaching Top Performance (FYI Video, AMA)

Keeping Teams Together (FYI Video, AMA)

Making Your Point Without Saying a Word (AMA)

Everyone's Teamwork Role (Communications Briefings)

Listening: The Key to Productivity (Communications Briefings)

Practical Coaching Skills for Managers (ETC/CareerTrack)

Conquering Team Conflict (ETC/CareerTrack)

High Impact Leadership: How to Be More Than a Manager (ETC/CareerTrack)

Be Prepared to Lead: Applied Leadership Skills for Business Managers (Toastmasters International)

The Manager as Coach (NIMCO)

Keeping Teams Together (NIMCO)

Styles of Leadership: At the Helm (Insight Media)

Information for Ordering Videos

AMA
1601 Broadway
New York, NY 10019-7520
Phone: 1-800-262-9699
Fax: 518-891-0368
E-mail: cust_serv@amanet.org

Communications Briefings, Dept VG.
1101 King Street, Suite 110 Alexandria, VA 22314
Phone: 1-800-888-2086
Fax: 703-684-2136

ETC/CareerTrack
MS20-13.3085 Center Green Drive
Boulder, CO 80301-5408
Phone: 1-800-334-1018
Fax: 1-800-622-6211
Web site: www.careertrack.com

Insight Media
2162 Broadway
New York, NY 10024
Phone: 212-721-6316
Fax: 212-799-5309

NIMCO
P.O. Box 9
102 Highway 81 North
Calhoun, KY 42327-0009
Phone: 1-800-962-6662
Fax: 502-273-5844

Toastmasters International
Kantola Productions
55 Sunnyside Avenue
Mill Valley, CA 94941-1924
Phone: 1-800-989-8273
Fax: 415-381-9801

Books

Barton, Laurence. *Crisis in Organizations: Managing and Communicating in the Heat of Chaos*. Cincinnati, OH: South-Western College Publishing, 1992.

Buckingham, Marcus, and Curt Coffman. *First, Break All the Rules: What the World's Greatest Managers Do Differently*. New York: Simon & Schuster, 1999.

Cashman, Kevin. *Leadership from the Inside Out.* Provo, Utah: Excellence Publishing, 1998.

Crandall, Rick, ed. *Thriving on Change in Organizations*. Corte Madera, CA: Select Press, 1997.

Fairhurst, Gail T., and Robert A. Sarr. *The Art of Framing: Managing the Language of Leadership*. San Francisco: Jossey-Bass Publishers, 1996.

Hesselbein, Frances, Marshall Goldsmith, and Richard Beckhard, eds. *The Leader of the Future: New Visions, Strategies, and Practices for the Next Era*. San Francisco: Jossey-Bass Publishers, 1996.

Kotter, John P. *John P. Kotter on What Leaders Really Do.* Boston, MA: Harvard Business School Publishing, 1999.

——. *Leading Change.* Boston: Harvard Business School Press, 1996.

McLean, J.W., and William Weitzel. *Leadership: Magic, Myth, or Method?* New York: AMACOM, 1992.

Parker, Glenn M. *Team Players and Teamwork.* San Francisco: Jossey-Bass Publishers, 1990.

Silberman, Mel, with Freda Hansburg. *PeopleSmart: Developing Your Interpersonal Intelligence.* Williston, VT: Berrett-Koehler, 2000.

Smith, Gregory P. *The New Leader: Bringing Creativity and Innovation to the Workplace.* Delray Beach, FL: St. Lucie Press, 1997.

Ulrich, Dave, Jack Zenger, and Norm Smallwood. *Results-Based Leadership.* Boston, MA: Harvard Business School Publishing, 1999.

Zand, Dale E. *The Leadership Triad: Knowledge, Trust, and Power.* New York: Oxford University Press, 1997.

Articles

Bennis, Warren, and James O'Toole. "Don't Hire the Wrong CEO." *Harvard Business Review,* May–June 2000, pp. 170–176.

Brown, Tom. "Politics and Managerial Leadership." *Management Review,* November 1996, pp. 10–15.

Caudron, Shari. "The Looming Leadership Crisis." *Workforce,* September 1999, pp. 72–79.

Collins, James C., and Jerry I. Porras. "Building Your Company's Vision." *Harvard Business Review*, September–October 1995, pp. 65–79.

Davis, Tim R. V. "Open-Book Management: Its Promises and Pitfalls." *Organizational Dynamics,* Winter 1997, pp. 7–20.

Greengard, Samuel. "25 Visionaries Who Shaped Today's Workplace." *Workforce,* January 1997, pp. 50–59.

Grossman, Robert J. "Heirs Unapparent: Leaders Wanted for the New Century." *HR Magazine,* February 1999, pp. 36–44.

Hamel, Gary. "Strategy as Revolution." *Harvard Business Review,* July–August 1996, pp. 69–83.

Hill, Linda, and Suzy Wetlaufer. "Leadership When There Is No One to Ask: An Interview with ENI's Franco Bernabè." *Harvard Business Review,* July–August 1998, pp. 80–94.

335

Maccoby, Michael. "Narcissistic Leaders: The Incredible Pros, the Inevitable Cons." *Harvard Business Review,* January–February 2000, pp. 68–77.

Nelson, Bob. "Does One Reward Fit All?" *Workforce,* February 1997, pp. 67–70.

Reingold, Jennifer. "Big Headhunter Is Watching You." *Business Week,* March 1, 1999, pp. 54–56.

Sittenfeld, Curtis. "The Most Creative Man in Silicon Valley." *Fast Company,* June 2000, pp. 274–292.

Smith, Scott S. "You Got Personality." *Entrepreneur,* September 1999, pp. 135–138.

Spitzer, Dean R. "Power Rewards: Rewards That Really Motivate." *Management Review,* May 1996, pp. 45–50.

Stewart, Thomas A. "Have You Got What It Takes?" *Fortune,* October 11, 1999, pp. 318–322.

Waldroop, James, and Timothy Butler. "Eight Failings That Bedevil the Best." *Fortune,* November 23, 1998, p. 293.

——. "The Executive as Coach." *Harvard Business Review,* November–December 1996, pp. 111–120.

Glossary

access to resources A situation in which workers are able to get the money, personnel, equipment, and supplies they need to get their work accomplished.

action orientation A personal characteristic of wanting to get things accomplished and decisions implemented.

action plan A description of the steps needed to be taken to achieve an objective or bring performance back to an acceptable standard.

active listening Listening for full meaning without making premature judgments or interpretations.

centrality The extent to which a unit's activities are linked into the mainstream of the rest of the organization.

charisma Personal charm and magnetism that are used to lead others. Also, a special quality of leaders whose purposes, powers, and extraordinary determination differentiate them from others.

coaching A method of helping workers grow and improve their job performance by providing suggestions and encouragement.

coalition A specific arrangement of parties working together to combine their power.

coercive power Power based on fear.

cognitive restructuring A method of softening conflict by mentally converting negative aspects into positive ones.

conflict The opposition of forces that gives rise to some tension. It occurs when two or more parties perceive mutually exclusive goals, values, or events.

congruence The consistency between the verbal and nonverbal parts of your message.

consensus decision-making style   A situation in which the leader encourages group discussion about an issue and then makes a decision that reflects general agreement and that will be supported by group members.

co-optation   A situation in which a potential adversary is brought into the fold. A co-optation thus prevents an erosion of your power as a leader.

crisis   A major, unpredictable event that carries with it potential results of enormous negative consequence.

crisis management mode   A series of actions and behaviors suited to a leader helping a group out of a crisis.

cross-functional team   A small group of employees from different functional units who work together on specific problems and projects such as product development.

cultural sensitivity   An awareness of and a willingness to investigate the reasons why people from another culture act as they do.

delegation   The assignment of formal authority and responsibility for accomplishing a specific task to another person.

disarming the opposition   A technique of conflict resolution in which one person disarms another by agreeing with his or her criticism.

effective leader   One whose actions facilitate group member's attainment of productivity, quality, and satisfaction.

empowerment   The passing of decision-making authority and responsibility from managers to group members.

enriched job   A job that is motivational and satisfying because it contains variety, responsibility, and managerial decision-making.

expectancy theory of motivation   A theory of motivation based on the premise that the amount of effort people expend depends on the reward they expect to receive in return.

feedback   Information about past behavior, delivered in the present, which may influence future behavior.

free-rein leader   The person in charge who turns over virtually all authority and control to the group.

goal   An event, circumstance, object, or condition a person strives to attain. It reflects the person's desire or intention to regulate his or her actions.

groupthink   A deterioration of mental efficiency, reality testing, and moral judgment in the interest of group cohesiveness.

influence   The ability to affect the behaviors of others in a particular direction.

influence target   The person that you (the influence agent) are attempting to influence to your way of thinking.

inspirational appeal   Influencing another person to act in a particular way by triggering a strong emotional response in him or her.

integrity   An unswerving adherence to moral and ethical principles. A person with high integrity is seen as honorable.

intuition   An experience-based way of knowing or reasoning in which weighing or balancing of the evidence are done automatically.

leadership   The process of persuading, inspiring, motivating, and influencing others and spearheading useful changes. Without influence, leadership cannot take place.

leadership polarity   The disparity in views of leaders; revered or vastly unpopular, but not neutral.

leadership style   The typical pattern of behavior engaged in by the leader when dealing with group members.

leading by example   Influencing others by acting as a positive role model.

linguistic style   A person's characteristic speaking pattern. It involves such aspects of speech as amount of directness, pacing and pausing, word choice, and the use of communication devices such as jokes, figures of speech, anecdotes, questions, and apologies.

management by anecdote   The technique of inspiring and instructing group members by telling fascinating stories.

manipulation   An indirect, subtle, and covert method of influencing others that may or may not involve some deception.

manipulator   A person who attempts to influence people and circumstances to gain advantage through dishonest and unethical means.

mentor   An individual with advanced experience and knowledge who is committed to giving support and career advice to a less experienced person.

micromanagement   The close monitoring of most aspects of group member activities by the manager or leader.

mirroring   Copying the behavior of another person in order to establish rapport with him or her.

mission   A definition of the general field in which a firm or organizational unit will operate. Also the unique purpose that sets a business or organizational unit apart from others of its type.

mixed message   A communication that has a built-in inconsistency or discrepancy such as saying to the sales staff, "Complete honesty is our policy but remember to charge whatever the traffic will bear." Another form of mixed message is when you say one thing but your tone and body language say something else.

multicultural leader   A leader with the skills and attitudes to relate effectively and motivate people of different races, sexes, ages, social attitudes, and lifestyles.

need   An inner striving or urge to do something, such as an urge to accomplish something worthwhile. A need can be regarded as a biological or psychological requirement.

nominal group technique   A group problem-solving method that calls people together in a structured meeting with limited interaction.

nonverbal communication   The transmission of messages through means other than words. It includes body language, as well as such diverse behavior as appearance, tone of voice, and the surroundings in which you deliver a message.

nouning   The practice of converting a large number of nouns into verbs, even when these new verbs cannot be found in any dictionary. For example, "anecdote your speech."

nurturing leader   A leader who actively promotes the growth of group members in terms of skills, knowledge, and emotional well-being.

open-ended question   A question that requires an explanatory answer rather than just selecting among two choices such as "yes" or "no," "agree" or "disagree," or "for" or "against."

organizational culture   A system of shared values and beliefs that actively influences the behavior of workers throughout the organization; also the norms of an organization.

organizational politics   Informal approaches to gaining power through means other than merit or luck.

participative leader   A leader who shares decision-making with group members.

personal ethical code   A definition of what you consider to be right and wrong, good and bad, ethical and unethical in the conduct of your job and career.

personality quirk   A persistent peculiarity of behavior that annoys or irritates other people.

political support   A situation in which others support your ideas because they feel a personal allegiance to you, and thus become champions of our ideas.

positive reinforcement   Increasing the probability that behavior will be repeated by rewarding people for making the desired response.

power   The ability or potential to influence decision and control resources.

psychological contract   An unwritten agreement that describes what management expects from a group member, and vice versa.

Pygmalion effect   The phenomenon in which people perform according to expectations of them, particularly with respect to relationships between a leader and group members.

role   In this context, the part an individual plays in a work group.

self-efficacy   The belief in one's capability to perform a task. It is akin to being self-confident with respect to a given task.

servant leader   A leader who serves constituents by working on their behalf to help them achieve their, not the leader's own, goals.

social support (in a group)   A situation in which group members voluntarily encourage and make life pleasant for each other.

strategic thinking   The ability to think in terms of how one's actions help the organization adapt to the outside world. It also involves understanding the long-range implications of one's thinking.

supportive communication   A communication style that delivers the message accurately and supports or enhances the relationship between the two parties.

synergy   A combination of people's efforts whereby the output is greater than the sum of the parts.

systems thinking   Understanding how any changes taken at one place in the firm create changes in the rest of the firm as well, now and into the future.

360-degree feedback   A formal evaluation of superiors based on input from people who work for and with them, sometimes including customers and suppliers.

team leader   A manager who coordinates the work of a small group of people, while acting as a facilitator and catalyst.

tough love   A philosophy of dealing with people you care about that enables and encourages them to take responsibility for meeting their own needs and regulating their own behavior.

tough question   An inquiry insisting that another person carefully examine why he or she is or is not carrying out a particular activity. At the same time, the question prompts the person to improve the status quo.

trait approach (or great person theory)   The observation that leadership effectiveness depends on certain personal attributes such as self-confidence.

transformational leader   A leader who helps organizations and people make positive changes in the way they conduct their activities.

turnaround manager   A leader or manager whose major responsibility is to quickly restore equilibrium in an organization facing collapse.

value   The importance a person attaches to something that serves as a guide to action.

virtual corporation   A temporary alliance of independent firms joining forces to share skills, costs, and access to each other's markets.

vision   An idealized scenario of what the future of an organization or an organizational unit can be. Also an exotic goal that points people toward a rosy future.

WIIFM   A universal motivational principle indicating that people are motivated to achieve goals to the extent that their self-interests will be satisfied. Another way of stating this principle is that self-interest is the great motivator.

win-win conflict resolution   A method of resolving conflict that searches for solutions to the conflict that result in both sides walking away with an important need met. Also referred to as "inventing options for mutual gain."

work ethic   A firm belief in the dignity of work.

Index

F

G

N

O